COVER ART
Chinese embroidered purse ca. 1930
Photo by Paul Macapia
Collection of Wing Luke Asian Museum
Seattle, WA
Cover Design by
Debbie Berrow

The "forbidden stitch" is the seedlike stitch seen in the blue and gold color fields that make up the butterfly design. One among many symbols found in the traditional Chinese embroidery, the butterfly connotes the "written word."

This project was funded in part by grants from the National Endowment for the Arts, the Oregon Arts Commission, the McKenzie River Gathering Foundation, and the following: MATRONS: Charlotte W. Billings, Camille Cox, Carol Gordon, Patricia L. Hefner, Joan Hoffman, Sheila James, Nancy Lenstrom, Dr. Shirley Lim, Rita Newhouse, Anne Scheetz, Shirley Sikes, Eleanor Wilner, The Adrienne Lee Memorial Trust. DONORS: Sujata P. Bhatt, Annabel Boissevain, Debra Bruce, Susan G. Butruille, Ann M. Davis, Pat Enders, Beverly Forsyth, In Memoria Rosemary Gillies, Miriam Gourley, Geraldine Henchy, Phyllis E. Lefohn, Kathy D. Liberatore, Kevyn Lutton, Lin Max-Gaskie, Beverly McFarland, M. Sue McGowan, Cheryl McLean, Mary Ellen Rowe, Danna W. Schaeffer, Saundra Timberlake, JoAnne J. Trow, Jane White, Joyce Winsor.

Suggested Library of Congress Cataloging in Publication Data main entry under title: The Forbidden stitch: an asian american women's anthology. bibliography: p. Includes index. 1. American literature—Asian-American authors. 2. American literature—Women authors. 3. American literature—20th century. 4. Asian American women—Literary collections. I. Lim, Shirley. II. Tsutakawa, Mayumi.
PS153.A84F66   1988   810'.8'09287   88-8117
ISBN 0-934971-10-2
ISBN 0-934971-04-8 (pbk.)

(Also published as Vol. 11 #2&3 of *Calyx, A Journal of Art and Literature by Women*, ISSN 0147-1627)
Published by *CALYX BOOKS*, PO BOX B, Corvallis, OR 97339.
Printed in the United States of America.

TALAT ABBASI,SIU WAI ANDERSON,ANJANA APPACHANA,TO-
MIE ARAI,MEI-MEI BERSSE[NB]UGGE,SUJATA BHATT,JANICE
BISHOP,VIRGINIA R. CERE[NIO],[DIANA] CHANG,MARILYN CHIN,
CHITRA DIVAKARUNI,[PHYLLIS EDE]LSON,MEI MEI EVANS,
LYNNE YAMAGU[CHI FLETCHER,JESSICA] HAGEDORN,SHALIN
HAI-JEW, MARG[O R. HARDER,SHARON HAS]HIMOTO,LORI KA-
YO HATTA,ROSE [FURUYA HAWKINS,JUDY HI]RAMOTO,BETTY
KANO,ALISON [KIM,MYUNG MI KIM,TINA KO]YAMA,BETTY
LA DUKE,CARO[LYN LAU,SUSAN K.C. LEE,GE]NNY LIM,SHIR-
LEY GEOK-LIN L[IM,AMY LING,VALERIE MA]TSUMOTO,CAROL
MATSUYOSHI,YO[NG SOON MIN,MASA]KO MIYATA,KYOTO
MORI,ARLENE NAGANA[WA,TAHIRA NA]QVI, FAE MYENNE NG,
MAYUMI ODA,MYUNG [KIM OH,MI]NE OKUBO,SONG-JOOK
PARK,KIT QUAN,MYRNA P[EÑA R]EYES,JESSICA SAIKI,HYUN-
JAE YEE SALLEE,STEPHANIE [SU]GIOKA,JEAN YAMASAKI TOY-
AMA,YOSHIKO UCHIDA,MARIANNE VILLANUEVA,PATTI WAR-
ASHINA,JULIA WATSON,NELLIE WONG,ROBERTA M. WONG,
MERL[E WOO,MITSUYE YAMADA,WAKAKO YAMAU]CHI,LE YO-

AN ASIAN AMERICAN WOMEN'S ANTHOLOGY

KOYAMA, ELAINE S. YONEOKA,TALAT ABBASI,SIU WAI ANDER
SON,ANJANA APPACHANA,TOMIE ARAI,MEI-MEI BERSSEN-
BRUGGE,SUJATA BHATT,JANICE BISHOP,VIRGINIA R. CERENIO,
DIANA CHANG,MARILYN CHIN,CHITRA DIVAKARUNI,PHYLLIS
EDELSON,MEI MEI EVANS,LYNNE YAMAGUCHI FLETCHER,JES
SICA HAGEDORN,SHALIN HAI-JEW, MARGO R. HARDER,SHARON
HASHIMOTO,LORI KAYO HAI IA,ROSE FURUYA HAWKINS,JUDY
HIRAMOTO,BETTY KANO,ALISON KIM,MYUNG MI KIM,TINA
KOYAMA,BETTY LA DUKE,CAROLYN LAU,SUSAN K.C. LEE,
GENNY LIM,SHIRLEY GEOK-LIN LIM,AMY LING,VALERIE MA
TSUMOTO,CAROL MATSUYOSHI,YONG SOON MIN,MASAKO
MIYATA,KYOTO MORI,ARLENE NAGANAWA,TAHIRA NAQVI,
FAE MYENNE NG, MAYUMI ODA,MYUNG KIM OH,MINE OKU
BO,SONG-JOOK PARK,KIT QUAN,MYRNA PEÑA REYES,JESSICA

Edited by

Shirley Geok-lin Lim
Mayumi Tsutakawa
Margarita Donnelly (Managing Editor)

CALYX BOOKS
CORVALLIS, OR

Acknowledgements

Grateful acknowledgement is made to the following for permission to reprint copyrighted material: Sujata Bhatt, "Go to Ahmedabad" and "Muliebrity" originally published in *Brunizem* (Carcanet Press, 1988), © 1988 Sujata Bhatt ; Mei-mei Berssenbrugge, "Chronicle" originally published in *Summits Move with the Tide* (Greenfield Review Press, 1982), © 1982 Mei-mei Berssenbrugge; Mei-mei Berssenbrugge, "Duration of Water" originally published in *Conjunctions*, 1985, © 1985 Mei-mei Berssenbrugge; Marilyn Chin, "We are Americans Now, We Live in the Tundra" originally published in *Dwarf Bamboo* (Greenfield Review Press, 1987), © 1987 Marilyn Chin; Shirley Geok-lin Lim, review of *Picture Bride* by Cathy Song originally published in *MELUS*, 10:3, Fall 1983, © 1983 Shirley Geok-lin Lim; Shirley Geok-lin Lim, "Pantoun for Chinese Women" originally published in *No Man's Grove* (National University of Singapore, 1985), © 1985 Shirley Geok-lin Lim; Fae Myenne Ng, "Last Night" originally published in *City Lights Review*, No. 1, 1987, © 1987 Fae Myenne Ng; Mayumi Oda, "Samansabadra" originally published in *Goddesses*, (Volcano Press, © copyright 1988); Miné Okubo drawings excerpted from *Citizen 13660* (University of Washington Press, © copyright 1983); Song-jook Park, translated by Hyun-jae Sallee, "On Such a Day" originally published in *Wyoming, The Hub of the Wheel*, issue #5, December 1987, © copyright 1987 Hyun-jae Sallee; Yoshiko Uchida, "Tears of Autumn" reprinted by permission of Simon & Schuster, Inc. from *Picture Bride* (Simon and Schuster, 1987), © 1987 Yoshiko Uchida; Merle Woo, "untitled" originally published in *Practising Angels* (Seismograph Publications, 1986), © 1986 Merle Woo; Mitsuye Yamada, "The Club" originally published in *Desert Run, Poems and Stories* (Kitchen Table Press, 1988), © 1988 Mitsuye Yamada.

THE FORBIDDEN STITCH
AN ASIAN AMERICAN WOMEN'S ANTHOLOGY

CONTENTS

Editors' Introductions

Shirley Geok-lin Lim	10	
Mayumi Tsutakawa	13	
Margarita Donnelly	15	

POETRY

Marilyn Chin	17	*We Are Americans Now, We Live in the Tundra*
Myung Mi Kim	18	*Into Such Assembly*
	20	*A Rose of Sharon*
Rose Furuya Hawkins	21	Excerpts from *Proud Upon an Alien Shore*
Sujata Bhatt	25	*Go To Ahmedabad*
	28	*Muliebrity*
Chitra Divakaruni	29	*At Muktinath*
Virginia R. Cerenio	77	*Family Photos: Black and White: 1960*
Marian Yee	78	*The Handbook of Sex of the Plain Girl*
	80	*Wintermelons*
Kyoko Mori	82	*Heat in October*
Mitsuye Yamada	84	*The Club*
Nellie Wong	86	*For An Asian Woman Who Says My Poetry Gives Her a Stomachache*
Stephanie Sugioka	88	*Legacy*
Shalin Hai-Jew	91	*Father's Belt*
Lynne Yamaguchi Fletcher	119	*After Delivering Your Lunch*
	120	*Higashiyama Crematorium, November 16, 1983*
	122	*The Way April Leads to Autumn*
Diana Chang	123	*On Being in the Midwest*
	124	*On The Fly*
Carolyn Lau	126	*Zhoukoudian Bride's Harvest*
Tina Koyama	128	*Currents*
	129	*Downtown Seattle in the Fog*

Song-jook Park	130	*On Such A Day*
Translated by		
Hyun-jae Yee Sallee		
Merle Woo	131	*untitled*
	132	*Whenever You're Cornered, the Only Way Out Is to Fight*
Myrna Peña Reyes	142	*San Juan*
	143	*Toads Mate and Father Cleans the Pool*
Jessica Hagedorn	144	*The Song of Bullets*
Mei-mei Berssenbrugge	147	*Duration of Water*
	148	*Chronicle*
Genny Lim	196	*Children Are Color-blind*
Sharon Hashimoto	198	*Standing in the Doorway, I Watch the Young Child Sleep*
	199	*Eleven A.M. On My Day Off, My Sister Phones Desperate for a Babysitter*
Arlene Naganawa	200	*Learning to Swim*
Jean Yamasaki Toyama	201	*Red*
Susan K.C. Lee	202	*Letter from Turtle Beach*
Alison Kim	203	*Sewing Woman*
Shirley Geok-lin Lim	204	*Pantoun for Chinese Women*
	206	*Visiting Malacca*

PROSE

Kyoko Mori	31	*Yellow Mittens and Early Violets*
Yoshiko Uchida	39	*Tears of Autumn*
Valerie Matsumoto	45	*Two Deserts*
Siu Wai Anderson	54	*Autumn Gardening*
Susan K.C. Lee	92	*A Letter for Dar*
Marianne Villanueva	99	*Siko*
Shirley Geok-lin Lim	109	*Native Daughter*
Mei Mei Evans	150	*Gussuk*
Fae Myenne Ng	165	*Last Night*
Diana Chang	171	*The Oriental Contingent*
Betty LaDuke	189	*Miné Okubo: An American Experience*
Tahira Naqvi	207	*Paths Upon Water*
Talat Abbasi	218	*Sari Petticoats*
Anjana Appachana	221	*To Rise Above*
	228	*My Only Gods*

ART

Lori Kayo Hatta	62	Obachan *Hatta, Kailua-Kona Fields*
	63	Obachan *Hatta, Kaimalino Housing*
	64	Obachan *Matano, Honolulu*
Tomie Arai	65	*Self Portrait*
	66	*Portrait of a Japanese Girl*
	67	*Rice Eaters*
	68	*Garden*
	69	*Chinese Family*
Yong Soon Min	70	*Back of the Bus, 1953*
	71	*American Friend*
	72	*Echoes of Gold Mountain*
	73	*Whirl War*
Roberta May Wong	74	*All Orientals Look Alike*
	75	*All Orientals Look Alike (detail)*
	76	*The Last Supper*
Patti Warashina	134	*Manning the Shroud*
	135	*A Procession*
Judy Hiramoto	136	*Cactus Heart*
	137	*Fool's Play*
	138	*Desert*
	139	*Piano Solo*
Carol Matsuyoshi	140	*Fish Jumping*
Elaine S. Yoneoka	141	*Ring of Forgotten Knowledge*
Mayumi Oda	178	*Mamala the Surf Rider*
	179	*Samansabadra*
Myung Kim Oh	180	*Kite*
	181	Baek-do
Alison Kim	182	*untitled*
Betty Nobue Kano	183	*To Winnie Mandela*
Masako Miyata	184	*Carry Me Back to Old Virginny*
	185	*Tatooed Geta With Two States*
Miné Okubo	186	*Girl With Vase of Flowers*
	187	*Cat with Flags*
	188	*Drawings from Citizen 13660*

REVIEWS

Shirley Geok-lin Lim 235 *Picture Bride*
Cathy Song

238 *Asian-American Literature: An Introduction to the Writings & Their Social Context*
Elaine H. Kim

239 *Obasan*
Joy Kogawa

Jessica Saiki 241 *Dangerous Music*
Jessica Hagedorn

Janice Bishop 241 *What Matisse Is After*
Diana Chang

Marian Yee 243 *In The City of Contradictions*
Fay Chiang
Dreams in Harrison Railroad Park
Nellie Wong
Camp Notes and Other Poems
Mitsuye Yamada

Margo P. Harder 247 *Thousand Pieces of Gold*
Ruthanne Lum McCunn

Marianne Villanueva 248 *Wings of Stone*
Linda Ty-Casper

Amy Ling 250 *Beyond Manzanar: Views of Asian American Womanhood*
Jeanne Wakatsuki Houston

Kit Quan 251 *With Silk Wings: Asian American Women at Work*
Elaine H. Kim with Janice Otani

Julia Watson 253 *This Bridge Called My Back: Writings by Radical Women of Color*
Edited by Cherríe Moraga, Gloria Anzaldua

Phyllis Edelson 255 *Crossing the Peninsula and Other Poems,*
No Man's Grove,
Another Country and
Other Stories
Shirley Lim

Shalin Hai-Jew   259   *Summits Move With the Tide,*
                       The Heat Bird
                       Mei-mei Berssenbrugge
                 260   *Cruelty,*
                       Killing Floor,
                       Sin
                       Ai
                 262   *Dwarf Bamboo*
                       Marilyn Chin
Michelle Yokoyama   263   *Angel Island Prisoner 1922*
                       Helen Chetin

CONTRIBUTOR NOTES AND INDEX

264

BIBLIOGRAPHY

272

INTRODUCTIONS

A DAZZLING QUILT

SHIRLEY GEOK-LIN LIM

When I accepted the offer to help edit this anthology of Asian American women's writing, I knew I was in for some exciting experiences. As a first-generation "Asian American woman," for one thing, I knew there was no such thing as an "Asian American woman." Within this homogenizing labelling of an exotica, I knew there were entire racial/national/cultural/sexual-preferenced groups, many of whom find each other as alien as mainstream America apparently finds us.

If the women's movement has discovered "difference" to be a liberating rather than oppressive principle, through which new visions, new understandings, and new orders of society can be generated, the experience of being an "Asian American woman" is an exemplar of living in difference. Despite the still-flourishing stereotype of the "Asian American woman" as more submissive, more domestic, and therefore, in a dominantly patriarchal society, more sexually available than her other American sisters, Asian American women exhibit a bewildering display of differences. We do not share a common history, a common original culture or language, not even a common physique or color. We are descended from Hindus of Uttar Pradesh, Chinese from Hong Kong, Japanese from Honshu, Ilocanos from the Philippines, Vietnamese from Saigon (now Ho Chi Minh City), Koreans, Malaysians, Pakistanis. Spanning hundreds of tribes, language groups, a variety of immigration histories (from first-generation Chinese Americans, arriving from Taiwan or Hong Kong or the Mainland, who have different stories to tell, to the *Sansei,* third-generation Japanese Americans whose American roots go back to the early nineteenth century), we "Asian American women" are not single but plural. If we form a thread, the thread is a multi-colored, many-layered, complexly knotted stitch.

This anthology takes its name from an embroidery knot which, while it resulted in a luxurious beauty, was so difficult to sew that it led to blindness in many of the Chinese artisans assigned to embroider the robes and altar hangings so beloved in feudal China. Maxine Hong Kingston tells the ancient story in her own way:

> *Long ago in China, knot-makers tied strings into buttons and frogs, and rope into bell-pulls. There was one knot so complicated that it blinded the knot-maker. Finally*

an emperor outlawed this cruel knot, and the nobles could not order it anymore.
If I had lived in China, I would have been an outlaw knot-maker.
                                            The Woman Warrior (Knopf, 1976)

The writing in this anthology has for too long been forbidden to Asian American women. The homogenizing marker has worked to make us invisible not only to the western observer but to ourselves. In these pages we can no longer deny the differences that lie between the Pakistani American woman and the Filipina, between the Hawaiian Japanese who is fourth-generation American and the first-generation Hong Kong American in Chinatown who is still looking behind. The voices are so plural as to cast doubt on the unity of the anthology. Sanskrit, Tagalog, Mandarin, Korean, Bahasa Malaysia, Hindi, Japanese: a very counterpoint of Asian Pacific tongues is heard in the background to this plainsong of trans-Atlantic English. (Because of the variety of linguistic groups, no attempt has been made to make the spelling of English or of any other language uniform among the stories. Uniformity was looked for only within the individual pieces. Thus, for example, in some pieces, Mandarin words are spelled in Pinyin, and not so in others.) One aim of this anthology is to awaken the reader to the vitality of cultural difference itself, its visible markers in the lives (and spelling!) of these women. If the stitch is multi-colored and complexly knotted, still it holds together a dazzling quilt.

Asians first came to the United States in the 1840's. Thousands of Chinese, Japanese and Korean immigrant men crossed the Pacific to work in the plantations, railroads, mines and fields of Hawaii and the West Coast, work which white Americans would not do. By 1924, racist reactions to Asian immigrants (in a nation which prided itself on equality and compassionate immigration policies) resulted in exclusion laws which effectively kept the proportion of Asian Americans to an invisible minimum. Asian women found it difficult to follow their sons and husbands to the new land. Generations of Filipino, Chinese and Japanese men struggled to begin a new life without the support of the women.

Poor, working-class Asian American women denied entry, or caught in an economic black hole, cooped up in factories, broken by unremitting labor, had neither leisure nor the skills to make their voices heard. Understandably, the literature produced by first-generation Asian American women writers reflects relatively privileged backgrounds. They were women of high social status, well-educated, and acceptable to a white reading public. The autobiographical works of women such as Adet and Anor Lin, Etsu Sugimoto and Anna Chennault (Chinese widow of General Chennault who commanded the celebrated Flying

Tigers Division which fought the Japanese in China during World War II) show their desire to present their Asian worlds and selves in the best possible light. Another generation of women, American daughters of Asian parents, express a different set of thematics; writers such as Jade Snow Wong and Monica Sone, embracing the American present, inform us of the painful familial and psychological divisions that Asian ethnicity can give rise to in a deeply homogenizing society.

Younger Asian American women writers have inherited the scene. While they are not pioneers in the sense that these older writers were, they are striking new notes and registers in their exploration of subjectivity as gendered and identified against the backdrop of white "otherness." "We are not exotic," these women appear to claim. "This is our life. It makes sense to us. It is for you, the other, to understand us." This anthology is, therefore, very much a pioneering effort. As it goes to press, it is the first anthology of Asian American women's writing to appear in the United States. Until now, we have been linked with our men, our sisters of color, our other identities. This anthology celebrates our plural singularity.

The anthology resulted from an open call for submissions. As such, it does not claim to be representative or comprehensive in its selections. Many remarkable and well-known "Asian American" writers do not appear in these pages. Still, many others with single volume publications, or manuscripts in progress, or hidden pages written in stolen hours, wrote to *Calyx* with submissions and good wishes for the project. There was no dearth of fresh, exciting writing; and the younger writers appear to be willing to strike themes which had remained taboo for their older sisters: sexual abuse, self-destructiveness, a harsher critique of the mother-culture, madness; in short, those cruelties visited on women, especially women of color, in an anomie-producing nation. In bringing these multiple selves together, the editors of *Calyx* are undertaking a larger project of community-healing and community-teaching. I wish to thank them all for including me in this work. They did the work; I had the pleasure of participating.

SHIRLEY GEOK-LIN LIM

Discovering new voices and planning their escape from the fate of anonymity: this was my dual goal in editing *The Forbidden Stitch.*

Women in traditional China, even those of the higher classes who escaped daily toil in the fields, were assigned to, and judged by, the fine embroidery patterns they created. Indeed, the finest stitchery was not worn by women, but reserved for the emperor's costume. The expert costume creator stood anonymously by, not even allowed to gaze on her breathtaking handwork as the emperor passed.

The forbidden stitch itself, similar to the French knot, was so tiny it was said to cause blindness. But what was an anonymous artisan's blindness to an emperor?

This anthology brings an opportunity for the anonymous word craftperson, the lonely writer, to strike out with her personal thoughts and expressions. The book represents a fine diversity of Asian American writers, women who may claim their native soil in Oakland or Tucson or Manila or New Delhi. These writers and artists, many of them young or publishing for the first time, are breaking down a barrier to make a statement. Wherever they live, in an Asian ghetto or as the only Asian family in a suburban subdivision or Midwest college town, they are dealing with the majority culture daily. They are, in many cases, living with husbands or children who don't know/don't care about/for the Asian culture the woman may tenaciously cling to.

For some women, a poem or short story is the method they have found for expressing sexual longing or romance—or of sexual harassment, of sorrowing after a mother who committed suicide, of documenting craziness among neighbors.

Some have chosen to include decidedly political content in their work—of life in the war zones of the Philippines, of the fate of atomic bomb victims or of organizing women against rape.

There is no single definition of Asian/Pacific American literature, no uniformly homogenized theme as may have been the case ten or fifteen years ago. In selecting and editing the pieces for this anthology, I sought to go beyond the detention camps, beyond the "my mother was a pioneer and how she suffered" writing. I was looking for contemporary ideas and new works by individual artists, not sameness of observation or circumstance. Contemporary

Asian American culture is not dictated from a central committee, or by husbands and brothers in charge. It is not duplicating traditional patterns, handed down over generations. It is the creative voice generated by the spirit and expression of personal situations tempered with factors both political and social.

Perhaps the most refreshing aspect of the collective pattern here is the addition of some clear new voices of women born in South and Southeast Asian countries: for instance, the woman who had to make a traditional Indian dinner for her husband's friends although she was exhausted from work, or the elderly mother who dared not remove her *shalwar*, gingerly admitting she would like to dip her toes into the ocean despite her disgust at bikini-clad American women. Cross-cultural stories also were wonderfully insightful, such as that of the Chinese American nurse serving an Alaskan native community.

As I read manuscripts, I thought of the writers and their individual lives. I wondered how do these women face jobs, children, homes, meals, homework, bosses and sagging bodies and still do their art? How they can buy the time to create is my biggest wonder. As editor, I cherished and anguished over all the submissions and wished I could meet and recognize the dozens of women who submitted works which are valid and insightful personal statements. We also are grateful to the many visual artists who submitted slides for consideration.

It may strike some readers that we have included far too many writers with too few pieces each. But I found it difficult to turn away pieces from these Asian women writers who had made the concerted effort to be a part of this special collection.

At the same time, we had to bypass some manuscripts reflecting experimental forms, some by very young writers and some which did not carry a recognizable Asian voice. To the women who submitted these pieces, I say thank you for wanting to break the anonymity barrier, the social politeness barrier which no doubt all of us Asian women have grown up with. I encourage all to continue to work on their written art and to submit their work to publishers.

No one should think of this book as the single definitive text on the lives and thoughts of Asian American women. This is not a book with a shelf life of forever, as with many textbooks resembling packaged foods shot with preservatives. This anthology gladly serves as an invitation for another editor, another publisher to call for the next batch of manuscripts by exciting Asian women writers living and thinking and making art today.

I thank *Calyx*, an organization of dedicated sisters who have made this anthology of contemporary Asian American women a reality. The forbidden stitch is no longer with us—it is replaced with the art work which is both beautifully crafted and no longer anonymous.

MAYUMI TSUTAKAWA

DIFFICULT BIRTHING   *MARGARITA DONNELLY*

The call for manuscripts and art for this anthology went out in 1985. The production was planned for 1986. Little did we know at the time the difficulties and delays we would encounter in bringing this anthology to life. It has been a long gestation with a difficult and painful birth, but the child is beautiful and we know she has been worth the struggle.

When the editorial collective decided to do this anthology, we did not know then that there were no Asian American women's anthologies in existence in the U.S.A. We were surprised to discover this anthology was a first and still is as it goes to press—an important indicator of the level of invisibility Asian American women experience in this society.

In our naivete we initially chose "Asian American Women's Anthology" as an acceptable and descriptive title for the anthology. During production and the ensuing editorial discussions we discovered that title does not accurately describe the diverse cultural groups included in this anthology. Since the book had already been assigned the title we didn't want to change it and have the book lost in production by the book business, so the original title was kept as the subtitle.

Many women have worked on this anthology. We wish to thank the student interns from Oberlin College (OH): Teresa Vazquez who put out the call and made the original contacts, and Sara Davis who laboriously coordinated the bibliography under the supervision of volunteer librarian Lynn Christopher. We also want to thank *Calyx* volunteers Karen Theiling, Mary Ann Hardy, Sara Swanberg Spiegel, Carol Pennock, Suzie Lisser, Lisa Domitrovich, Catherine Holdorf, Cheryl McLean, Linda Smith, Barbara Lewis, and Beverly McFarland who helped with copy editing, proofreading, and the computer technology involved in the complex bibliography. We are especially grateful for the bibliographic work by Librarian Susan Searing from the University of Wisconsin, Professor Gail Tremblay at The Evergreen State College (WA), Alison Kim for

15

her Asian Lesbian Bibliography, and for bibliographic citations compiled by Dr. Amy Ling, Shirley Geok-lin Lim, Lynn Christensen, Linda Shult, and Christina Wagner.

We are most grateful to Shirley Geok-lin Lim and Mayumi Tsutakawa for being the guest editors and for their suggestions and advice during the long selection and production process. We are particularly grateful that both Shirley and Mayumi were open to working with our collective editorial process and allowed our editorial staff the experience of participating closely in the production of this anthology. We also want to thank the many women artists and writers who responded to our initial call and helped through solicitation of submissions from writers and artists they knew. It has been a rich and rewarding experience to have been able to participate at the birth of this "new" voice in American literature.

I would also like to thank two college friends from the 1960's, Tokiko Ide Noricks and Mary Tom. Their friendship opened my eyes to the experiences of first-generation Asian American women. Unwaringly our friendship planted a seed that resulted in this anthology so many years later.

MARGARITA DONNELLY
For the Calyx Editorial Collective

WE ARE AMERICANS NOW, WE LIVE IN THE TUNDRA

Today in hazy San Francisco, I face seaward
Toward China, a giant begonia—

Pink, fragrant, bitten
By verdigris and insects. I sing her

A blues song; even a Chinese girl gets the blues,
Her reticence is black and blue.

Let's sing about the extinct
Bengal tigers, about giant Pandas—

"Ling Ling loves Xing Xing . . . yet,
We will not mate. We are

Not impotent, we are important.
We blame the environment, we blame the zoo!"

What shall we plant for the future?
Bamboo, sasagrass, coconut palms? No!

Legumes, wheat, maize, old swines
To milk the new.

We are Americans now, we live in the tundra
Of the logical, a sea of cities, a wood of cars.

Farewell my ancestors:
Hirsute Taoists, failed scholars, farewell

My wetnurse who feared and loathed the Catholics,
Who called out:

> Now that the half-men have occupied Canton
> Hide your daughters, lock your doors!

MARILYN CHIN

INTO SUCH ASSEMBLY

1.

Can you read and write English? Yes __. No __.
Write down the following sentences in English as I dictate them.
    There is a dog in the road.
    It is raining.
Do you renounce allegiance to any other country but this?
Now tell me, who is the president of the United States?
You will all stand now. Raise your right hands.

Cable car rides over swan-flecked ponds
Red lacquer chests in our slateblue house
Chrysanthemums trailing bloom after bloom
Ivory, russet, pale yellow petals crushed
Between fingers, that green smell, if jade would smell
So-Sah's thatched roofs shading miso hung to dry—
Sweet potatoes grow on the rock-choked side of the mountain
The other, the pine wet green side of the mountain
Hides a lush clearing where we picnic and sing:
    Sung-Bul-Sah, geep eun bahm ae

Neither, neither

Who is mother tongue, who is father country?

2.

Do they have trees in Korea? Do the children eat out of garbage cans?

We had a Dalmation
We rode the train on weekends from Seoul to So-Sah where we grew grapes

We ate on the patio surrounded by dahlias

Over there, ass is cheap—those girls live to make you happy

Over there, we had a slateblue house with a flat roof where
I made many snowmen, over there

No, "th", "th", put your tongue against the roof of your mouth,
lean slightly against the back of the top teeth, then bring your

bottom teeth up to barely touch your tongue and breathe out, and you should feel the tongue vibrating, "th", "th", look in the mirror, that's better

And with distance traveled, as part of it

How often when it rains here does it rain there?

One gives over to a language and then

What is given, given over?

3.

This rain eats into most anything

> And when we had been scattered over the face of the earth
> We could not speak to one another

The creek rises, the rain-fed current rises

> Color given up, sap given up
> Weeds branches groves what they make as one

This rain gouging already gouged valleys
And they fill, fill, flow over

> What gives way losing gulch, mesa, peak, state, nation

Land, ocean dissolving
The continent and the peninsula, the peninsula and continent
Of one piece sweeping

One table laden with one crumb
Every mouthful off a spoon whole

Each drop strewn into such assembly

MYUNG MI KIM

A ROSE OF SHARON

Is it because my hair is golden brown that even when I wear it
in pigtails like them they still snicker and push me away from
the twirling rope?

By the time I finish my newspaper cone of fried sweet potatoes
you will be standing on the corner wearing spit-shined shoes. By
the time I choose the shape I want and watch the old man pour the
brown melted sugar into the hot mold, when I'm about to lick the bronze
candy rabbit on a stick you will wave to me getting off a crowded bus.

I will know it is you because you will be tall and you will be
handsome. You will know it is me because my eyes are round and big
like a doll's that other girls buy.

Do you have a dog? When's your birthday?

After mom leaves, grandmother fixes my supper. Was he kind? Tell me
one little thing he said. I don't remember, she says. Where did
he come from? I don't know, she says, gnashing on tidbits of pickled
roots, a fish head. What color hair? Just an American, a Big Nose—
eat that soup.

I could tell you how many apples the fruit vendor has piled on his
cart, how the holes in front of the house fill, thick with mud. I'll
tell you what they are saying today.

They say two Big Noses threw her out a window. They say her hands
were tied, and she had no clothes on. It is well after noon. She
would have washed her hair by now and lain down. I would be fanning
the dust, heat, or stray fly away from her, watching her sleep.

MYUNG MI KIM

Rose of Sharon is the Korean national flower.

Excerpts From
PROUD UPON AN ALIEN SHORE   *ROSE FURUYA HAWKINS*

I. Issei Men: The First Generation

Japan, 1921

All that autumn of austerity
We wandered over withered fields
Like lost butterflies,
Feeding on half-bowls of rice,
Stealing warmth
From pale cups
of tea.

As leaves warped and fell
We talked of a golden land
And late into the night
We huddled over letters
From west across the Pacific.
We sipped our tea and dreamed
Until the paper turned to shreds,
The ink smearing, then fading
Under the moon's cold shadow.

What was this unknown force
That stirred our hearts?
What fire? What song?
What new adventure?

Far into the season
We burned with fever
Whistling in our tea
With noisy slurps.

Finally, before the silent snow
We stole away at dawn,
Silent samurai, heavy with hope,
Watching, waiting, until the rising sun
Swallowed up our God, our emperor,
And our most honorable parents.

America! America!
After forty-seven days at sea
We glimpsed the fertile ground
So dark against a yellow sky.
And leaving the ship on sea legs
We stood tall—*Issei* men,
Proud upon an alien shore.

VI. *Nisei* Daughter: The Second Generation

When people ask
About my mother
I look away and say,
"Oh, she's been gone
A long time now.
I hardly knew her
Anyway."

But I know she was
A renegade. Why else
Was she standing on some foreign shore,
Uncomfortable in high-heeled shoes
And black dress with bust darts,
Her cherry blossom kimono
Left far behind?

How else did she consent
To trade her rice paper walls
For corrugated tin
And to love, honor, and obey
This crude stranger, *Ito-San*
Who sipped Coca-Cola
Through a straw?

Yes, my mother was a renegade.
She braved the future
By swallowing her pride,

Her delicate fingers
Shaping paper swans
After a long day
Of picking cotton
In the Imperial Valley.

She sewed dresses
For my doll
Long after her feet
Were too tired to work the treadle
Of her prized Singer.
She taught me words:
Mi-mi, ha-na, ku-chi,
Pointing to my ear
My nose, my mouth.
She fed me full
Of fat rice balls
And pickled radishes,
Afraid I might ask
For bologna sandwiches.

Mama, forgive me.
I guess I knew you well.
I was your miracle child,
Your second generation
Nisei daughter,
Born to you
When you were already too old,
Already too torn
By barbed wire fences
And mixed loyalty.

Oh, where have you gone
Little moon-faced child,
Who once chased fireflies
For paper lanterns
In old Japan?

VII. *Sansei:* The Third Generation

Early this morning
I woke up heart-heavy,
Dreaming of my grandfather.
I pictured him, the immigrant,
Standing tall upon the alien shore
With hope enough
For all who dared
And dreams enough
To feed a nation.

I remember him standing
In his victory garden
Body so small,
Hair so white,
Bent against
The bright wisteria.
The blossoms were
Scattering, scattering
Like so many monarchs,
Free, at last, in the wind.

ROSE FURUYA HAWKINS

GO TO AHMEDABAD   *SUJATA BHATT*

Go walk the streets of Baroda,
go to Ahmedabad,
go breathe the dust
until you choke and get sick
with a fever no doctor's heard of.
Don't ask me
for I will tell you nothing
about hunger and suffering.

As a girl I learned
never to turn anyone away
from our door. Ma told me
give fresh water, good food,
nothing you wouldn't eat.
Hunger is when your mother
tells you years later
in America the doctor says
she is malnourished,
her bones are weak
because there was never enough
food for the children,
hers and the women who came
to our door with theirs.
The children must always be fed.
Hunger is when your mother is sick
in America because she wanted you
to eat well. Hunger is
when you walk
down the streets of Ahmedabad
and instead of handing out
coins to everyone
you give them tomatoes, cucumbers,
and go home with your mouth
tasting of burnt eucalyptus leaves
because you've lost
your appetite.
And yet, I say nothing
about hunger, nothing.

I have friends everywhere.
This time we met after ten years.
Someone died.
Someone got married.
Someone just had a baby.
And I hold the baby
because he's crying,
because there's a strange rash
all over his chest.
And my friend says
do you have a child? Why not?
When will you get married?
And the bus arrives
crowded with people hanging
out the doors and windows.
And her baby cries
in my arms, cries
so an old man wakes up and yells
at me: how could I let
my child get so sick?
Luckily, just then
someone tells a good joke.

I have friends everywhere.
This time we met after ten years.
And suffering is
when I walk around Ahmedabad
for this is the place
I always loved
this is the place
I always hated
for this is the place
I can never be at home in
this is the place
I will always be at home in.
Suffering is
When I'm in Ahmedabad
after ten years
and I learn for the first time

I will never choose
to live here. Suffering is
living in America
and not being able
to write a damn thing
about it. Suffering is
not for me to tell you about.

Go walk the streets of Baroda,
go to Ahmedabad
and step around the cow dung
but don't forget
to look at the sky.
It's special in January,
you'll never see kites like these again.
Go meet the people if you can
and if you want to know
about hunger, about suffering,
go live it for yourself.
When there's an epidemic,
when the doctor says
your brother may die soon,
your father may die soon—
don't ask me how it feels.
It does not feel good.
That's why we make
tea with tulsi leaves,
that's why there's always someone
who knows a good story.

SUJATA BHATT

MULIEBRITY

I have thought so much about the girl
who gathered cow dung in a wide, round basket
along the main road passing by our house
and the Radhavallabh temple in Maninagar.
I have thought so much about the way she
moved her hands and her waist
and the smell of cow dung and road-dust and wet canna lilies,
the smell of monkey breath and freshly washed clothes
and the dust from crows' wings which smells different—
and again the smell of cow dung as the girl scoops
it up, all these smells surrounding me separately
and simultaneously—I have thought so much
but have been unwilling to use her for a metaphor,
for a nice image—but most of all unwilling
to forget her or to explain to anyone the greatness
and the power glistening through her cheekbones
each time she found a particularly promising
mound of dung—

SUJATA BHATT

AT MUKTINATH   *CHITRA DIVAKARUNI*

I.

When they finally found us
wandering, aimless, on the ice below the Thorong La,
stares frozen blank
it must have been the fifth day
or was it the sixth?
Reaching across cracks in the memory
bottomless as that crevasse, concealed, dark,
into which our young sherpa fell
I connect with nothing.
One instant he was with us, laughing
kicking up sprays of new fallen snow
white as his teeth
then his dreadful wail
ricocheting from rock faces
finally, more dreadful silence.
For hours we lay with our mouths
against that black ice-mouth, breathing death.
Shone useless flashlights,
dangled rope, calling his name.
All night the mountains flung back at us
Angtarkay, Angtarkay-ay-ay.
In the morning we had to go on.

II.

Was it the third day
when we sank knee-deep in slush with every step,
pushed ahead as in a dream, not advancing?
Surely before that was the rain
insidious fingers thrusting through our clothing
with the sharpness of hypodermic needles,
bringing pain, then numb release.
Then the smoking torches, the leathery faces
of villagers, arms around us, carrying,
the agony as they soaked our hands and feet

in steaming buckets.
Somewhere in between
a woman throwing herself down
on snow, its comforting blanket
waiting to enfold her in jasmine sleep
and someone pulling at me to get up, get up.
All around, the sky
spinning in blinding white spheres.
They wrapped us in whatever they had—
blankets and sacks, their own yakskin coats.
In the kitchen, our backs against the stove,
they steadied our heads as we drank.
The hot tea with yak's milk and jaggery
flowed through me, strong and sweet, a glowing.

III.

When I could walk again, an old woman
took me to the temple.
Together, silent, we approached the *lingam*
the inscrutable black stone
gleaming flame-ringed from the alcove.
Outside, a fountain with a cow's head.
I knelt and put my lips against the grainy stone
let the water fill my mouth.
Its clear, cold, mineral taste.
The many-colored temple flags
fluttered like bright wings inside me.
When I opened my eyes,
beyond the calm stone profile
the sky had unfolded itself
pulsing electric and blue
shining as though the day would never die.

CHITRA DIVAKARUNI

Masa stepped into the kitchen in her grey kimono and turned on the light. Her granddaughter Yuki was sitting at the table, putting on and pulling off her yellow mittens. At seven in the morning in mid-March, the sun had not yet come through the two narrow windows. In the yellow light from the single bulb, Yuki's red sweater and blue jeans looked unnaturally bright against the wooden table and chair. Masa's eyes stung from the bright colors and the cold air; sometimes in the mornings she felt her left eyelid flutter almost imperceptibly. Yuki did not look up from the magazine that lay open on the table. On the floor by her chair were her suitcase and the violets she had dug up by the river the day before. Packed in plastic bags with air holes, the flowers reminded Masa of butterflies in a jar, the vividness gone from them as though they had turned into colored bits of paper.

"Up so early? The bus won't be here for two hours yet," Masa said.

"I know," Yuki said. She took off the mittens and hit them off against each other.

"Do you want breakfast?"

"No."

Masa went to the sink all the same and measured the rice and water into the saucepan. She filled the tin kettle with fresh water and placed the kettle and the saucepan side by side on the gas stove. Then she struck the match and watched the blue flames appear around the gas rings. Her arms felt especially heavy this morning. The house, too, was heavy with the smell of incense. The previous evening, a small gathering of relatives and neighbors had met with the priest for the third anniversary of her daughter Shizuko's passing on and joining the spirits of her ancestors. Only three years, Masa thought, and already Yuki acts as if she'd forgotten her mother and wants to forget us, too.

Masa sprinkled a small handful of tea leaves into the kettle and sat down opposite Yuki. Yuki continued to read the magazine. It was one of the many she had brought with her on this weekend visit—all of them the kinds of magazines city girls read about make-up, movies, dresses, boys. The yellow mittens lay on the table between Masa and Yuki. They were awkward and crooked, one much larger than the other. Yuki had told her that she'd made them herself in a home economics class at the high school. Masa wondered why she had needed mittens in mid-March. It was warm outside; there were spring mums and early strawberries in the yard, violets and clovers by the river. In the afternoon, right before the ceremony, Yuki had gone out in her black dress to dig up the violets by the river. She had come into the house with soiled hands while the guests were arriving to celebrate her mother's third anniversary and the priest was already burning the preparatory incense. "I didn't want to wait till it got dark," Yuki had said to no one in particular. "I want to transplant these to our backyard in the city. I'm going home tomorrow morning. I don't like the countryside very much." She washed her hands and sat through the ceremony, her back absolutely rigid, her posture too perfect. Her face had shown no grief, no regret, while the others, some of them not even relations, had sobbed during the priest's chanting. Now all the guests were gone and Masa was alone with Yuki until her husband Takeo would get up and come to the kitchen. Masa wished that he would hurry.

"Are you sure you don't want breakfast?" Masa asked again.

"I'm sure," Yuki said. She kept her eyes on the magazine.

"If you don't like rice, I can borrow bread from the neighbors and make some toast."

"I'm not hungry."

She'll be starved by the time she's on the train, Masa thought. She thought of the long bus ride from her village into the city of Himeji, and then the three-hour train ride from there to Kobe, the seaside city where Yuki lived with her father and stepmother. Masa had seldom been away from her village; it hadn't been necessary. All her children would come home to see her and Takeo every year. She remembered how Shizuko used to come home to them every summer, bringing Yuki with her, and stay for at least a month. Every year, Yuki would do something that the neighbors in the village would talk about for months. Masa thought of the afternoon Yuki had climbed up the chestnut tree and been too frightened to come down. The firemen from a near-by town had come and spread a net under the tree for her to jump into. Then there was the morning when Yuki had run clear through the glass screen in chase of a dragonfly. She had come through with small scratches and cuts all over the side of her face, her arms and knees, but nothing serious, nothing that had to be stitched up later, and in any case, she had continued running until she'd caught the dragonfly. And for days she bragged about having more scars than anybody she knew, just as she'd bragged the year before about being the only child in the village to jump into the firemen's net. That was Yuki as a child—cheerful and talkative—and people had always liked her for that. But she had changed, Masa thought, during the three years after Shizuko's death, while Shizuko's husband had remarried and allowed Yuki to visit Masa and Takeo only on special occasions.

Masa took two thousand-yen bills out of her wallet and laid them on the table next to the mittens.

"You'll want to have lunch on the train," she said to Yuki.

"I don't plan to," Yuki said. "If I do, I have enough money anyway. Lunches on trains don't cost this much."

"Then you can buy something else when you get back to Kobe. Get new mittens for next winter."

"I like these mittens. I told you I made them myself."

"They're too large for you."

"I like them this way. Tight mittens cut off my blood circulation. Besides, *she* said she'd buy me new gloves and I told her I didn't want any. I couldn't buy new ones with your money after that."

"So she is good to you?" Masa felt that her own voice sounded prying, awkward, the voice of a gossipy old woman.

"Of course she's good to me," Yuki said. "What else did you expect? But what I like best about her is that she lets me do things on my own. I don't like to be coddled. I like to be on my own." Yuki paused and stared Masa right in the eyes. "And she and Father get on so well. I think Father's happier now than he's been in a long time."

Masa stood up and took the saucepan off the stove. She dished the first spoonful of rice into a small bowl used for the family altar and poured the tea from the kettle to its companion cup. She placed the bowl and cup on a tray and turned to Yuki.

"Why don't you take these to the altar?" she said. "You should burn another stick of incense and tell the spirits of our ancestors that you've come to say good-bye."

"I'd rather not," Yuki said. She closed her magazine and looked up. "There's no one to say good-bye to."

Masa stared for a moment at the photograph of a model on the magazine cover. She was dressed in a red ski jacket and black pants. A tall foreign boy stood next to her, his large hand on her waist. The photograph looked flat, like a painted image.

"You shouldn't say things like that," Masa said. "You'll anger the spirits and they won't watch over you any more."

"You know as well as I do," Yuki retorted, "that the spirits of the ancestors, even if such things really existed, couldn't care less about whether I burn incense and tell them anything or not, and Mama, wherever she really might be, isn't in that little black box."

"Of course she isn't *in* the altar," Masa said. "But the altar is there so you can show respect for all the deceased members of our family who watch over you day and night. That includes your mother's spirit, too, and you must show respect, especially for your own mother."

"How can I respect someone who was coward enough to kill herself?" Yuki picked up the magazine and began to page through it quickly.

Before Masa could think of an answer, the kitchen door opened and Takeo came in in his short brown kimono and long brown underwear. If he had heard Yuki's words, his face did not show it.

"What time does the bus come?" he asked.

"In about an hour," Yuki said.

"Let's have breakfast then," Takeo said. "There's plenty of time."

"Everybody's trying to make me eat," Yuki said. "Don't you see I'm just not hungry?"

"I'm going to the yard to pick some strawberries," Takeo said, as if he hadn't heard Yuki. "Are you coming with me?"

"No. I don't want to eat them in the first place. And if I have to eat them, I'd rather not see them in the dirt. Maybe there are bugs on them."

"Suit yourself," Takeo said. "You don't have to see them until I wash them and put them on your plate."

Masa watched him as he picked up a colander and walked out the back door from the kitchen. Then she took the tray and went to the family room, where the altar was, leaving Yuki alone in the kitchen with her magazines, mittens, and violets wrapped in plastic.

At the altar, Masa thought of Shizuko's pale face. There was no sign of pain on that face. But with the faint smell of gas still clinging to the curtains, Masa had not been able to say, "She did not suffer much," not even after her son-in-law said that at least she had not chosen a painful way to die—with gas, one simply passed out and did not feel pain. Masa had stayed at the house of mourning for three days: the first day, the house was closed to all but the nearest relations; the second day, close friends and other relations attended the wake; and on the third day, crowds of neighbors, friends, and relatives on all sides came to the funeral. Masa remembered Yuki standing by the kitchen sink, washing her hair over and over. She said that it first smelled of gas, and then of cigarette smoke, and then of incense, that her hair would never smell the same again. Shortly before the funeral began, in the house filled with strangers, Masa came across Yuki in the narrow passageway by the kitchen. They embraced and the water dripped from Yuki's hair onto Masa's shoulder. Masa could still remember the cold, aching feeling that lingered in her shoulder for hours.

My thoughts are troubled this morning. Grant me peace, Masa prayed to the spirits of her ancestors. She bowed her head and closed her eyes tighter.

After a while, she opened her eyes, collected the bowls with yesterday's rice and tea and replaced them. She lit a stick of incense and stood up. She felt a dull ache in her hips as she walked toward the kitchen. From the hallway just outside the kitchen, she saw a white flash of intense morning light as the back door swung open. Takeo's tall figure blocked the light. Masa remembered what he had written in his diary, the small black notebook with narrow black lines and the dates printed in, on the day of Shizuko's death: "We are thankful for the peacefulness of her face." It was such an obvious platitude. Thankful for the peacefulness, Masa repeated to herself almost with resentment as she stepped into the kitchen and put the tray on the table, where Yuki was still reading her magazine. Then the next moment Masa watched in horror as Takeo tripped over the doorstep and fell forward, the strawberries flying in a red blur. His body hit the floor with a dull thump and he remained motionless. Masa took a step toward him and then froze. Behind her, she heard the scraping of the chair legs against the floor and the footsteps. Then the door swung to and fro again and intermittently Masa saw Yuki sprinting down the dirt road away from the house.

Slowly, Masa walked to where Takeo lay on the floor and knelt down beside him. He was slumped over the doorstep face down. I must not move him, she told herself. Afraid to touch, she stared at his motionless body. The strawberries had stained the fingers of his right hand. There was no cut, no blood anywhere, and Masa thought again of Shizuko's white face, how there had been no blood then either. Suddenly Masa realized that it was this absence of blood that had puzzled her then; the violence of self-inflicted death had left no mark on Shizuko's body, as though in the prime of her life she had died a natural death, so that her husband might explain away the pain of suicide, and her father might be thankful for the peacefulness of her face (but, Masa thought now, it was only absence of pain, not real repose) and record it in his diary where he kept a faithful account of the weather and temperature. But you must have suffered, too, Masa thought as she stared at Takeo's stained fingers. Then she pictured Yuki digging up the violets by the river, a solitary figure in a black dress in the early spring; she remembered Yuki washing her hair again and again in the cold sink, in the shivery darkness of the kitchen before the funeral. Masa laid her palm on Takeo's neck. His flesh was warm and moist with perspiration. She watched her own hand rocking gently with his breathing. He was still unconscious. Nothing about him stirred except the rising and falling of his neck and chest caused by his breathing.

Masa was still kneeling on the floor when Yuki returned with the doctor. The doctor opened his bag and knelt over Takeo, taking his pulse, listening to his heart, and then carefully checking his arms and legs for broken bones, and then Masa was watching Yuki and the doctor lift Takeo. Yuki's knuckles stuck out painfully white around Takeo's legs. Masa knelt a while longer on the floor, where the strawberries had been scattered, most of them crushed. Then she followed the doctor and Yuki into the bedroom. Takeo had been laid on his futon; his eyes were open. His lips formed a weak, apologetic smile. Masa heard herself sobbing. The doctor was telling her that it was all right now, nothing but dizziness caused by stooping in the sun and getting up to walk too soon, old people should never do that. There were no broken bones, the doctor continued, just a few bruises, nothing serious. Masa continued to sob. Her face felt warm, as though her flesh would melt with the tears.

After the doctor was gone, Takeo fell asleep, his face a little flushed, but his breathing easy and even. Yuki was sitting on the floor opposite Masa, across from Takeo's sleeping body.

"I'm going to call home," she said. "I should tell them that I'm taking the afternoon bus and train instead." She paused and looked Masa full in the face. "I forgot all about the phone when I saw Grandpa fall. It was like when I was small and you didn't have a phone. I was halfway to the Yamadas' house to use theirs, like we used to, when I realized. So I ran all the way to the doctor's instead."

"It was as well," Masa said. "He was here so soon."

"I told him that it was an emergency. He took his motorcycle and made me ride on the back. I think I kept screaming in his ear. My throat feels scratchy." Yuki touched the edge of Takeo's futon with her fingertips. "Just as we were getting off the motorcycle, the doctor told me that in the three years he hadn't seen me, I'd come to look more like Mama, except, he said, my nose was a little too thin. What a thing to say at a time like that. He also asked me if I still chased dragonflies and ran into glass screens." She looked at her watch. "I'd better go and call. Then I'm going to pick more strawberries. The doctor and I stepped all over the ones Grandpa picked. You want some, don't you?"

Masa nodded, but Yuki had already sprung to her feet and gone out of the room. Masa sat trying to shake the dull fatigue out of her eyes.

Takeo was now sleeping deeply. The flush had gone from his face; his forehead felt comfortably cool and dry. Masa stood up and walked to the kitchen. Yuki was washing the strawberries under the faucet. Masa went in and stood beside her at the sink.

"The bus doesn't come for two hours again," Yuki said. She stopped the faucet and turned to Masa. In the sink, half the strawberries were drying in the colander; the other half, still on their stems, floated in a large washing basin. "I was scared that Grandpa would never speak again," Yuki said.

"He'll be all right now," Masa said. She felt weak. Her own voice sounded fuzzy.

Yuki dipped her hands in the basin. "I want to tell you something," she said, her fingers moving the strawberries around in the water. "It's about Mama." She looked up at Masa for a moment and then again looked down at the strawberries in the washbasin. "The afternoon Mama died, I went to the skating lesson after school, like I always did on Wednesdays. My skating teacher had left a message and said she was going to be late. So I called Mama to tell her that I was going to be later than usual. It must have been right before she was going to do it." Yuki paused. "Would you rather if I didn't talk about this?" Her hands continued to swim in the water among the strawberries, like a pair of white fish.

"It's all right. Go on," Masa said. Her throat felt tight.

"She sounded kind of strange over the phone," Yuki said. "Just before she hung up, she said, 'Be good. You know I love you.' I can still hear her voice saying that now. It wasn't anything she wouldn't say on any other day. It's just the way she said it, like she meant it for more than that one afternoon. It bothered me, the way she said it. But I didn't go home right away. You know, I even thought about it."

"You shouldn't blame yourself," Masa said. She thought of the nights she stayed awake feeling that somehow she could have prevented the tragedy, although she could never think of how.

"I don't blame myself about that," Yuki said. "I'd have been too late even if I'd left the rink then. But what bothers me is something else. When I got home, Mama was unconscious. Soon I noticed that she wasn't breathing, she was turning cold. Father came home with the doctor in about a half hour, but she never spoke again. So there I was listening to her voice earlier over the phone but not seeing her. And then a few hours later, I was seeing her body but no voice ever came again. It's like I can't remember her whole." Yuki pulled her hands slowly out of the water. "I remember the voice without the body and the body without the voice. Sometimes I dream that my mother's voice had been trapped in the telephone line somewhere, and I try but I can't help her. I just can't help her." She stared at her hands for a moment. "I wanted so much to help her." She shook her head and covered her face with her hands. She began to cry.

Masa felt her chest and throat go tight. She fumbled for a towel and handed it to Yuki. "I'm sorry," she said. "I'm sorry, Yuki."

Yuki wiped her face vigorously and looked up. "But I didn't tell you all this so you'd feel sorry for me. What I started to say was that *I* was sorry." She dropped the towel in the sink and rubbed her eyes with her knuckles. "When I saw Grandpa fall, I thought I'd never hear his voice again, just like I won't hear Mama's. And I'd been so awful to him and to you."

Yuki was crying into her hands again. Masa remembered the tight feeling in her stomach as she had stood in the yard and watched the small child fall from the chestnut tree into the firemen's net—and the moment when, frozen in helplessness, she had watched the same child run through the glass screen.

"I've been so awful," Yuki was saying, "ever since Mama died. I don't know why. It's like I just can't stop being that way. Everything seems so terrible I just don't know what to do except be awful myself. But I do love you and Grandpa. I really love you. Do you believe me?"

"Of course I do," Masa said. She saw again the child running through the clear glass after a brilliant dragonfly, the glass shattering into shiny droplets of light. "I do."

Masa put her hand lightly on Yuki's back. Yuki dropped her hands from her face and leaned fiercely into Masa's shoulder. She was still crying. Masa held her tight. Yuki's tears were warm on her shoulder and her hair smelled of sunlight and early spring.

KYOKO MORI

TEARS OF AUTUMN   *YOSHIKO UCHIDA*

Hana Omiya stood at the railing of the small ship that shuddered toward America in a turbulent November sea. She shivered as she pulled the folds of her silk kimono close to her throat and tightened the wool shawl about her shoulders.

She was thin and small, her dark eyes shadowed in her pale face, her black hair piled high in a pompadour that seemed too heavy for so slight a woman. She clung to the moist rail and breathed the damp salt air deep into her lungs. Her body seemed leaden and lifeless, as though it were simply the vehicle transporting her soul to a strange new life, and she longed with childlike intensity to be home again in Oka Village.

She longed to see the bright persimmon dotting the barren trees beside the thatched roofs, to see the fields of golden rice stretching to the mountains where only last fall she had gathered plum white mushrooms, and to see once more the maple trees lacing their flaming colors through the green pine. If only she could see a familiar face, eat a meal without retching, walk on solid ground and stretch out at night on a *tatami* mat instead of in a hard narrow bunk. She thought now of seeking the warm shelter of her bunk but could not bear to face the relentness smell of fish that penetrated the lower decks.

Why did I ever leave Japan, she wondered bitterly. Why did I ever listen to my uncle? And yet she knew it was she herself who had begun the chain of events that placed her on this heaving ship. It was she who had first planted in her uncle's mind the thought that she would make a good wife for Taro Takeda, the lonely man who had gone to America to make his fortune in Oakland, California.

It all began one day when her uncle had come to visit her mother.

"I must find a nice young bride," he had said, startling Hana with this blunt talk of marriage in her presence. She blushed and was ready to leave the room when her uncle quickly added, "My good friend Takeda has a son in America. I must find someone willing to travel to that far land."

This last remark was intended to indicate to Hana and her mother that he didn't consider this a suitable prospect for Hana who was the youngest daughter of what once had been a fine family. Her father, until his death fifteen years ago, had been the largest landholder of the village and one of its last *samurai*. They had once had many servants and field hands, but now all that was changed.

Their money was gone. Hana's three older sisters had made good marriages, and the eldest remained in their home with her husband to carry on the Omiya name and perpetuate the homestead. Her other sisters had married merchants in Osaka and Nagoya and were living comfortably.

Now that Hana was twenty-one, finding a proper husband for her had taken on an urgency that produced an embarrassing secretive air over the entire matter. Usually, her mother didn't speak of it until they were lying side by side on their quilts at night. Then, under the protective cover of darkness, she would suggest one name and then another, hoping that Hana would indicate an interest in one of them.

Her uncle spoke freely of Taro Takeda only because he was so sure Hana would never consider him. "He is a conscientious, hard-working man who has been in the United States for almost ten years. He is thirty-one, operates a small shop and rents some rooms above the shop where he lives." Her uncle rubbed his chin thoughtfully. "He could provide well for a wife," he added.

"Ah," Hana's mother said softly.

"You say he is successful in this business?" Hana's sister inquired.

"His father tells me he sells many things in his shop—clothing, stockings, needles, thread and buttons—such things as that. He also sells bean paste, pickled radish, bean cake and soy sauce. A wife of his would not go cold or hungry."

They all nodded, each of them picturing this merchant in varying degrees of success and affluence. There were many Japanese emigrating to America these days, and Hana had heard of the picture brides who went with nothing more than an exchange of photographs to bind them to a strange man.

"Taro San is lonely," her uncle continued, "I want to find for him a fine young woman who is strong and brave enough to cross the ocean alone."

"It would certainly be a different kind of life," Hana's sister ventured, and for a moment, Hana thought she glimpsed a longing ordinarily concealed behind her quiet, obedient face. In that same instant, Hana knew she wanted more for herself than her sisters had in their proper, arranged and loveless marriages. She wanted to escape the smothering strictures of life in her village. She certainly was not going to marry a farmer and spend her life working beside him planting, weeding and harvesting in the rice paddies until her back became bent from too many years of stooping and her skin turned to brown leather by the sun and wind. Neither did she particularly relish the idea of marrying a merchant in a big city as her two sisters had done. Since her mother objected to her going to Tokyo to seek employment as a teacher, perhaps she would consent to a flight to America for what seemed a proper and respectable marriage.

Almost before she realized what she was doing, she spoke to her uncle. "Oji San, perhaps I should go to America to make this lonely man a good wife."

"You, Hana Chan?" Her uncle observed her with startled curiosity. "You would go all alone to a foreign land so far away from your mother and family?"

"I would not allow it." Her mother spoke fiercely. Hana was her youngest and she had lavished upon her the attention and latitude that often befall the last child. How could she permit her to travel so far, even to marry the son of Takeda who was known to her brother.

But now, a notion that had seemed quite impossible a moment before was lodged in his receptive mind, and Hana's uncle grasped it with the pleasure that comes from an unexpected discovery.

"You know," he said looking at Hana, "it might be a very good life in America."

Hana felt a faint fluttering in her heart. Perhaps this lonely man in America was her means of escaping both the village and the encirclement of her family.

Her uncle spoke with increasing enthusiasm of sending Hana to become Taro's wife. And the husband of Hana's sister, who was head of their household, spoke with equal eagerness. Although he never said so, Hana guessed he would be pleased to be rid of her, the spirited younger sister who stirred up his placid life with what he considered radical ideas about life and the role of women. He often claimed that Hana had too much schooling for a girl. She had graduated from Women's High School in Kyoto which gave her five more years of schooling than her older sister.

"It has addled her brain—all that learning from those books," he said when he tired of arguing with Hana.

A man's word carried much weight for Hana's mother. Pressed by the two men she consulted her other daughters and their husbands. She discussed the matter carefully with her brother and asked the village priest. Finally, she agreed to an exchange of family histories and an investigation was begun into Taro Takeda's family, his education and his health, so they would be assured there was no insanity or tuberculosis or police records concealed in his family's past. Soon Hana's uncle was devoting his energies entirely to serving as go-between for Hana's mother and Taro Takeda's father.

When at last an agreement to the marriage was almost reached, Taro wrote his first letter to Hana. It was brief and proper and gave no more clue to his character than the stiff formal portrait taken at his graduation from Middle

School. Hana's uncle had given her the picture with apologies from his parents because it was the only photo they had of him and it was not a flattering likeness.

Hana hid the letter and photograph in the sleeve of her kimono and took them to the outhouse to study in private. Squinting in the dim light and trying to ignore the foul odor, she read and reread Taro's letter, trying to find the real man somewhere in the sparse unbending prose.

By the time he sent her money for her steamship tickets, she had received ten more letters, but none revealed much more of the man than the first. In none did he disclose his loneliness or his need, but Hana understood this. In fact, she would have recoiled from a man who bared his intimate thoughts to her so soon. After all, they would have a lifetime together to get to know one another.

So it was that Hana had left her family and sailed alone to America with a small hope trembling inside of her. Tomorrow, at last, the ship would dock in San Francisco and she would meet face to face the man she was soon to marry. Hana was overcome with excitement at the thought of being in America and terrified of the meeting about to take place. What would she say to Taro Takeda when they first met, and for all the days and years after?

Hana wondered about the flat above the shop. Perhaps it would be luxuriously furnished with the finest of brocades and lacquers, and perhaps there would be a servant, although he had not mentioned it. She worried whether she would be able to manage on the meager English she had learned at Women's High School. The overwhelming anxiety for the day to come and the violent rolling of the ship were more than Hana could bear. Shuddering in the face of the wind, she leaned over the railing and became violently and wretchedly ill.

By five the next morning, Hana was up and dressed in her finest purple silk kimono and coat. She could not eat the bean soup and rice that appeared for breakfast and took only a few bites of the yellow pickled radish. Her bags, which had scarcely been touched since she boarded the ship, were easily packed for all they contained were her kimonos and some of her favorite books. The large willow basket, tightly secured by a rope, remained under the bunk, untouched since her uncle had placed it there.

She had not befriended the other women in her cabin, for they had lain in their bunks for most of the voyage, too sick to be company to anyone. Each morning Hana had fled the closeness of the sleeping quarters and spent most of the day huddled in a corner of the deck, listening to the lonely songs of some Russians also travelling to an alien land.

As the ship approached land, Hana hurried up to the deck to look out at the gray expanse of ocean and sky, eager for a first glimpse of her new homeland.

"We won't be docking until almost noon," one of the deck hands told her.

Hana nodded. "I can wait," she answered, but the last hours seemed the longest.

When she set foot on American soil at last, it was not in the city of San Francisco as she had expected, but on Angel Island, where all third-class passengers were taken. She spent two miserable days and nights waiting, as the immigrants were questioned by officials, examined for trachoma and tuberculosis and tested for hookworm by a woman who collected their stools on tin pie plates. Hana was relieved she could produce her own, not having to borrow a little from someone else, as some of the women had to do. It was a bewildering, degrading beginning, and Hana was sick with anxiety, wondering if she would ever be released.

On the third day, a Japanese messenger from San Francisco appeared with a letter for her from Taro. He had written it the day of her arrival, but it had not reached her for two days.

Taro welcomed her to America and told her that the bearer of the letter would inform Taro when she was to be released so he could be at the pier to meet her.

The letter eased her anxiety for a while, but as soon as she was released and boarded the launch for San Francisco, new fears rose up to smother her with a feeling almost of dread.

The early morning mist had become a light chilling rain, and on the pier, black umbrellas bobbed here and there, making the task of recognition even harder. Hana searched desperately for a face that resembled the photo she had studied so long and hard. Suppose he hadn't come. What would she do then?

Hana took a deep breath, lifted her head and walked slowly from the launch. The moment she was on the pier, a man in a black coat, wearing a derby and carrying an umbrella, came quickly to her side. He was of slight build, not much taller than she, and his face was sallow and pale. He bowed stiffly and murmured, "You have had a long trip, Miss Omiya. I hope you are well."

Hana caught her breath. "You are Takeda San?" she asked.

He removed his hat and Hana was further startled to see that he was already turning bald.

"You are Takeda San?" she asked again. He looked older than thirty-one.

"I am afraid I no longer resemble the early photo my parents gave you. I am sorry."

Hana had not meant to begin like this. It was not going well.

"No, no," she said quickly. "It is just that I . . . that is, I am terribly nervous . . ." Hana stopped abruptly, too flustered to go on.

"I understand," Taro said gently. "You will feel better when you meet my friends and have some tea. Mr. and Mrs. Toda are expecting you in Oakland. You will be staying with them until . . ." He couldn't bring himself to mention the marriage just yet and Hana was grateful he hadn't.

He quickly made arrangements to have her baggage sent to Oakland and then led her carefully along the rain slick pier toward the street car that would take them to the ferry.

Hana shuddered at the sight of another boat, and as they climbed to its upper deck she felt a queasy tightening of her stomach.

"I hope it will not rock too much," she said anxiously. "Is it many hours to your city?"

Taro laughed for the first time since their meeting, revealing the gold fillings of his teeth. "Oakland is just across the bay," he explained. "We will be there in twenty minutes."

Raising a hand to cover her mouth, Hana laughed with him and suddenly felt better. I am in America now, she thought, and this is the man I came to marry. Then she sat down carefully beside Taro, so no part of their clothing touched.

YOSHIKO UCHIDA

Emiko Oyama thought the Imperial Valley of California was the loneliest place she had ever seen. It was just like the Topaz Relocation Camp, she told her husband Kiyo, but without the barbed wire fence and crowded barracks. Miles of bleached desert punctuated sparsely by creosote bush and abandoned debris faced her from almost every window in their small house. Only the living room had a view of the dirt road which ended in front of their home, and across it, a row of squat faded houses where other farmers' families lived. They waved to her and Kiyo in passing, and Jenny played with the Garcia children, but Emiko's Spanish and their English were too limited for more than casual greetings.

Emiko felt a tug of anticipation on the day the moving van pulled up at the Ishikawas' place across the road—the house which in her mind had become inextricably linked with friendship. She had felt its emptiness as her own when Sats, Yuki and their three children gave up farming and departed for a life which came to her in delicious fragments in Yuki's hastily scrawled letters. Yuki, who made the best sushi rice in the world and had given her the recipe; who could draw shy Kiyo into happy banter. Yuki, whose loud warm laugh made the desert seem less drab, less engulfing.

She had been thinking about Yuki that morning as she weeded the yard and vegetable plot in preparation for planting. Sats and Yuki had advised her to plant marigolds around the vegetables to draw away nematodes, and she liked the idea of a bold orange border. Emiko liked bright colors, especially the flaming scarlet of the bougainvillea which rose above the front door where Kiki their cat lay sunning himself. There was a proud look in the amber eyes, for Kiki the hunter had slain three scorpions and laid them in a row on the porch, their backs crushed and deadly stingers limp, winning extravagant praise from Jenny and Emiko. The scorpions still lay there, at Jenny's insistence, awaiting Kiyo's return that evening. Emiko shuddered every time she entered the house, glancing at the curved stingers and thinking of Jenny's sandaled feet.

Emiko had finished weeding the front border and was about to go inside to escape the heat when she saw the new neighbor woman plodding across the sand toward her. A cotton shift could not conceal her thinness, nor a straw hat her tousled gray curls. Her eyes were fragile lilac glass above the wide smile.

"Hello, I'm Mattie Barnes. I just thought I'd come over and introduce myself while Roy is finishing up with the movers. Your bougainvillea caught my eye first thing and I thought, 'Those are some folks who know what will grow in the desert.' I hope you'll give me some advice about what to plant in my yard once we get settled in."

They talked about adjusting to desert life and Emiko learned that Mattie's husband Roy had recently retired. "We decided to move here because the doctor said it would be better for my lungs," Mattie explained, wiping her brow.

"Would you like a glass of lemonade?" Emiko offered. "Or maybe later, after you've finished moving—"

"Oh, I'd love something cold," Mattie said, adding vaguely, "Roy will take care of everything—he's more particular about those things than I am."

Emiko preceded Mattie into the house, hoping that Jenny was not lying on the cool linoleum, stripped to her underwear. As she crossed the threshold Mattie gave a shriek and stopped abruptly, eyeing the scorpions lined up neatly on the porch.

"What on earth are those things doing here?"

"Our cat killed them," Emiko said, feeling too foolish to admit her pride in Kiki's prowess. "Jenny wants me to leave them to show her father when he comes home from the field."

"Awful creatures," Mattie shuddered. "Roy can't stand them, but then, he can't abide insects. He said to me this morning, 'Of all the places we could have moved to, we had to choose the buggiest.' "

There was no buggier place than the Imperial Valley, Emiko agreed, especially in the summer. In the evening the air was thick with mosquitoes, gnats and moths. The cicadas buzzed in deafening chorus from every tree. They danced in frenzied legions around the porch light and did kamikaze dives into the bath water. All of them came in dusty gray hordes, as though the desert had sapped the color from them, but not their energy. Late at night, long after Kiyo had fallen into exhausted sleep, Emiko would lie awake, perspiring, listening to the tinny scrabble of insects trapped between the window glass and screen.

". . . but I like the desert," Mattie was saying, dreamily clinking the ice cubes in her glass. "It's so open and peaceful. As long as I can have a garden, I'll be happy."

Within a few weeks after their arrival, the Barneses had settled into a routine: Roy making daily trips to the local store and the Roadside Cafe; Mattie tending her garden and walking to church once a week with Emiko and Jenny. By the end of June Mattie had been enlisted with Emiko to make crêpe paper flowers for a church bazaar.

"My, your flowers turned out beautifully," Mattie exclaimed one morning, looking wistfully at the cardboard box filled with pink, yellow, scarlet and lavender blossoms set on wire stems. "They'll make lovely corsages." She sighed. "I seem to be all thumbs—my flowers hardly look like flowers. I don't know how you do it. You Japanese are just very artistic people."

Emiko smiled and shook her head with a polite disclaimer, but the bright blur of flowers suddenly dissolved into another mass of paper blooms, carrying her more than a decade into the past. She was a teenager in a flannel shirt and denim pants with rolled cuffs, seated on a cot in a cramped barrack room helping her mother fashion flowers from paper. Her own hands had been clumsy at first, striving to imitate her mother's precise fingers which gave each fragile petal lifelike curves, the look of artless grace. The only flowers in Topaz when elderly Mr. Wakasa was shot by a guard were those that bloomed from the fingertips of *Issei* and *Nisei* women, working late into the night to complete the exquisite wreaths for his funeral. Each flower a silent voice crying with color; each flower a tear.

"I did a little flower-making as a teenager," Emiko said.

"Will you come over and show me how?" Mattie asked. "I'm too embarrassed to take these awful things, and I've still got lots of crêpe paper spread all over the kitchen."

"Sure," Emiko nodded. "I'll help you get started and you'll be a whiz in no time. It isn't too hard; it just takes patience."

Mattie smiled, a slight wheeze in her voice when she said, "I've got plenty of that, too."

They were seated at the Barnes' small table surrounded by bright masses of petals like fallen butterflies, their fingers sticky with florist's tape, when Roy returned from shopping. When he saw Emiko he straightened and pulled his belt up over his paunch.

"A sight for sore eyes!" he boomed, giving her a broad wink. "What mischief are you ladies up to?"

"Emi's teaching me how to make flowers," Mattie explained, holding up a wobbly rose.

"Always flowers! I tell you," he leaned over Emiko's chair and said in a mock conspiratorial voice, "all my wife thinks about is flowers. I keep telling her there are other things in life. Gardening is for old folks."

"And what's wrong with that?" Mattie protested, waving her flower at him. "We *are* old folks."

"Speak for yourself," he winked at Emiko again. "What's so great about gardens, anyway?"

"I hold with the poem that says you're closest to God's heart in a garden," said Mattie.

"Well, I'm not ready to get that close to God's heart yet." There was defiance in Roy's voice. "What do you think about that, Emi?"

"I like working in the yard before it gets too hot," she said carefully. Her words felt tight and deliberate, like the unfurled petals on the yellow rose in her hands. "I don't have Mattie's talent with real flowers, though—aside from the bougainvillea and Jenny's petunias, nothing ever seems to bloom. The soil is too dry and saline for the things I used to grow. Now I've got my hopes pinned on the vegetable garden."

"Vegetables—hmph!" Roy snorted, stomping off to read the paper.

"Oh, that Roy is just like a boy sometimes," Mattie said. "I tell you, don't ever let your husband retire or you'll find him underfoot all day long."

"Doesn't Roy have any hobbies?" Emiko thought of her father and his books, his Japanese brush painting, his meetings.

"He used to play golf," Mattie said, "but there's no golf course here. He says this town is one giant sand trap."

"There have been times when I felt that way, too," Emiko admitted lightly.

"Well, don't let Roy hear you say that or you'll never get him off the topic," Mattie chuckled. "The fact is, Roy doesn't much know how to be by himself. I've had forty years to learn, and I've gotten to like it. And I suppose maybe he will too."

Her voice trailed off, and Emiko suddenly realized that Mattie didn't much care whether he did or not.

One day while Emiko was engrossed in pinning a dress pattern for Jenny she suddenly heard a tapping on the screen, like the scrabbling of a large beetle. She half-turned and felt a jolt of alarm at the sight of a grinning gargoyle hunched before the glass, hands splayed open on either side of his face, the caricature of a boy peering covetously into a toy store.

"Hey there! I caught you day-dreaming!" he chortled. "Looks to me like you need some company to wake you up."

"I'm not day-dreaming; I'm trying to figure out how to make a two-and-a-half yard dress out of two yards," she said. "Jenny is growing so fast, I can hardly keep up with her."

Roy walked into the house unbidden, confident of a welcome, and drew a chair up to the table. He fingered the bright cotton print spread over the table and gazed at Emiko, his head cocked to one side.

"You must get pretty lonesome here by yourself all day. No wonder you're sitting here dreaming."

"No," she said, her fingers moving the pattern pieces. "There's so much to do I don't have time to be lonesome. Besides, Jenny is here, and Kiyo comes home for lunch."

"But still—cooped up with a kiddie all day . . ." Roy shook his head. He chose to disregard Kiyo, who had no place in his imagined scenarios, and was hard at work miles away.

Emiko delicately edged the cotton fabric away from Roy's damp, restless fingers. I'll be darned if I offer him something to drink, she thought as he mopped his brow and cast an impatient glance at the kitchen. "I haven't seen Mattie outside this week. How is she feeling?"

"Oh, 'bout the same, 'bout the same," he said, his irritation subsiding into brave resignation. "She has her good days and her bad days. The doctor told her to stay in bed for awhile and take it easy."

"It must be hard on Mattie, having to stay indoors," Emiko said, thinking of her peering out through the pale curtains at the wilting zinnias and the new weeds in the back yard.

"I suppose so—usually you can't tear Mattie away from her garden." Roy shook his head. "Mattie and me are real different. Now, I like people—I've always been the sociable type—but Mattie! All she cares about are plants."

"Well, Kiyo and I have different interests," Emiko said, "but it works out well that way. Maybe you could learn a few things from Mattie about plants."

Even as the suggestion passed her lips, she regretted it. Roy viewed the garden as the site of onerous labor. To Mattie, it was the true world of the heart, with no room for ungentle or impatient hands. It was a place of deeply sown hopes, lovingly nurtured, and its colors were the colors of unspoken dreams.

"Plants!" Roy threw up his hands. "Give me people any time. I always liked people and had a knack for working with them—that's how I moved up in the business."

"Why don't you look into some of the clubs here?" Emiko tried again. "The Elks always need people with experience and time . . ."

"Sweetheart, I'm going to spend my time the way I want. I'm finished with work—it's time to enjoy life! Besides, how much fun can I have with a bunch of old geezers? That's not for me, Emily, my dear." She stiffened as he repeated the name, savoring the syllables. "Emily . . . Emily . . . Yes, I like the sound of that—Emily."

"My name is Emiko," she said quietly, her eyes as hard as agate. "I was named after my grandmother." That unfaltering voice had spoken the same words in first, second, third, fourth, fifth and sixth grades. All the grammar school teachers had sought to change her name, to make her into an Emily: "Emily is so much easier to pronounce, dear, and it's a nice American name." She was such a well-mannered child, the teachers were always amazed at her stubbornness on this one point. Sometimes she was tempted to relent, to give in, but something inside her resisted. "My name is Emiko," she would insist politely. I am an American named Emiko. I was named for my grandmother who was beautiful and loved to swim. When she emerged from the sea, her long black hair would glitter white with salt. I never met her, but she was beautiful and she would laugh when she rose from the waves. "My name is Emiko, Emi for short."

"But Emily is such a pretty name," Roy protested. "It fits you."

"It's not my name," she said, swallowing a hard knot of anger. "I don't like to be called Emily!"

"Temper, temper!" He shook his finger at her, gleeful at having provoked her.

"Well, I guess I'll be in a better temper when I can get some work done," she said, folding up the cloth with tense, deliberate hands. She raised her voice. "Jenny! Let's go out and water the vegetable garden now."

If Jenny thought this a strange task in the heat of the afternoon, it did not show in her face when she skipped out of her room, swinging her straw hat. It still sported a flimsy, rainbow-hued scarf which had been the subject of much pleading in an El Centro dime store. At that moment, Emiko found it an oddly reassuring sight. She smiled and felt her composure return.

"Tell Mattie to let me know if there's anything I can do to help," she told Roy, as he unwillingly followed them out of the house and trudged away across the sand. After they went back inside, Emiko locked the door behind them for the first time. When Kiyo returned home, his face taut with fatigue, she told him it was because of the hoboes who came around.

Emiko went to see Mattie less and less frequently, preferring instead to call her on the phone, even though they lived so close. Roy, however, continued to drop by despite Emiko's aloofness. His unseemly yearning tugged at her with undignified hands, but what he craved most was beyond her power to give. She took to darning and mending in the bedroom with the curtains drawn, ignoring his insistent knock; she tried to do her gardening in the evening after dinner when her husband was home, though it was hard to weed in the dusk. She was beginning to feel caged, pent up, restless. Jenny and Kiyo trod quietly, puzzled by her edginess, but their solicitude only made her feel worse.

Finally, one morning Emiko decided to weed the vegetables, sprouting new and tender. Surely the mid-morning heat would discourage any interference. Although the perspiration soon trickled down her face, she began to enjoy the weeding, pulled into the satisfying rhythm of the work. She was so engrossed that she did not notice when Roy Barnes unlatched the gate and stepped into the yard, a determined twinkle in his faded eye.

"Howdy, Emi! I saw you working away out here by your lonesome and thought maybe you could use some help."

"Thanks, but I'm doing all right," she said, wrenching a clump of puncture vine from the soil and laying it in the weed box carefully to avoid scattering the sharp stickers. Jenny was close by, digging at her petunias and marigolds, ignoring Mr. Barnes, who had no place in the colorful jungle she was imagining.

"If I had a pretty little wife, I sure wouldn't let her burn up out here, no sir," his voice nudged at her as she squatted on the border of the vegetable plot. If Mattie looked out of the window she would see only a pleasant tableau: Roy nodding in neighborly fashion as Emiko pointed out young rows of zucchini and yellow squash, watermelon, cantaloupe, eggplant and tomatoes. Mattie would not see the strain on Emiko's face, turned away from Roy, when he leaned over and mumbled, "Say, you know what I like best in this garden?"

Emiko grabbed the handle of the shovel and stood up before he could tell her, moving away from him to pluck a weed. "I know Mattie likes cantaloupe," she said. "So do I. Kiyo prefers Crenshaws, but I couldn't find any seeds this year. What do you and Mattie have in your garden?"

"Just grass," he said, undeterred. "Mattie's always fussing over her flowers—you know what she's like," he chuckled indulgently, "but I'd rather spend my time doing other things than slaving in the yard."

Emiko hacked away at the stubborn clumps of grass roots and the persistent runners with myriad finer roots, thread-thin but tough as wire. She worked with desperate energy, flustered, her gloved hands sweating on the shovel handle, forehead damp. She was groping for the language to make him understand, to make him leave her in peace, but he was bent on not understanding, not seeing, not leaving until he got what he wanted.

"You know what, Emi?" He moistened his dry lips, beginning to grin reminiscently. "You remind me of somebody I met in Tokyo. Have you ever been to Tokyo?"

"No," she said, digging hard. "Never."

"You'd like it, it's a wonderful place, so clean and neat, and the people so friendly. When I was in Tokyo, I met up with the cutest *geisha* girl you ever saw—just like a little doll. She'd never seen anybody with blue eyes before, and couldn't get over it." He chuckled. "I couldn't think who you reminded me of at first, and then it just hit me that you are the spitting image of her."

"Did Mattie like Tokyo too?" Emiko said, continuing to spade vigorously as his eyes slid over her, imagining a doll in exotic robes.

"She didn't go—it was a business trip," he said impatiently. Then his voice relaxed into a drawl, heavy with insinuation. "After all, I like to do some things on my own." He was moving closer again.

Then she saw it. Emiko had just turned over a rock, and as she raised the shovel, it darted from its refuge, pincers up, the deadly tail curved menacingly over the carapaced back. It moved a little to the left and then the right, beginning the poison dance. Emiko glanced to see where Jenny was and saw Roy jump back hastily; the scorpion, startled by his movement, scuttled sideways toward Jenny, lying on her stomach, still dreaming of her jungle.

The blood pounded in Emiko's head. She brought down the shovel hard with one quick breath, all her rage shooting down the thick handle into the heavy crushing iron. She wielded the shovel like a *samurai* in battle, swinging it down with all her force, battering her enemy to dust. Once had been enough but she struck again and again, until her anger was spent and she leaned on the rough handle, breathing hard.

"Mommy! What did you do?" Jenny had scrambled to Emiko's side, fear in her eyes, gazing at the unrecognizable fragments in the dirt.

"I killed a scorpion," Emiko said. She scornfully tossed the remains into the weed box, and wiped her brow on her arm, like a farmer, or a warrior. "I don't like to kill anything," she said aloud, "but sometimes you have to."

Roy Barnes recoiled from the pitiless knowledge in her eyes. He saw her clearly now but it was too late. His mouth opened and closed but the gush of words had gone dry. He seemed to age before her eyes, like Urashima-taro who opened the precious box of youth and was instantly wrinkled and broken by the unleashed tides of years.

"You'll have to leave now, Mr. Barnes. I'm going in to fix lunch." Emiko's smile was as quiet as unsheathed steel. "Tell Mattie I hope she's feeling better."

She watched him pick his way across the dirt, avoiding the puncture vine and rusted tin cans, looking as gray as the rags that bleached beneath the fierce sun. Jenny stared past him and the small houses of their neighborhood to the desert sand beyond, glittering like an ocean with shards of glass and mica.

"Do you think we might ever find gold?" she asked.

They gazed together over the desert, full of unknown perils and ancient secrets, the dust of dreams and battles.

"Maybe." Emiko stood tall, shading her eyes from the deceptive shimmer. "Maybe."

VALERIE MATSUMOTO

It was a mild morning for early November, sunny and cool with only a hint of frost. The heavy rains that had flooded the gutters for the past week were gone now. Patches of mud amid sparse wet spikes of grass made the yard treacherous. Along the cyclone fence clusters of sun-dappled brown and yellow leaves rustled in the light breeze. They drifted to the ground and skittered across the small yard, coming to rest against the splintered white wall of the dilapidated garage. The breeze became a steady wind.

Mariko Abe opened the screen door and shuffled onto her back porch, blinking in the bright sunlight. She moved over to a rusty lawn chair and sat down heavily, gasping from the effort. When she had caught her breath she sniffed the air, enjoying the tangy scent that made her think of dry crackling leaves and wood-burning stoves—the heady smell of autumn in New England.

As she exhaled with a long sigh, a sharper, more pungent smell intruded on her senses. It seemed to come from the laundry snapping on the line strung across her next-door-neighbor's porch. Mariko wrinkled her nose. Whatever kind of detergent that was, it reminded her of the starched uniforms of American soldiers.

As she settled herself in the chair and drew her sweater closer about her shoulders, she glanced at the porch railing and noticed that the paint was peeling badly. Better tell Paul to buy some sandpaper so he could scrape off the old paint before putting on a fresh coat. If he let it go until spring, it would probably never get done.

There never seemed to be enough time to do all the tedious little upkeep tasks that an old house required. Now that her asthma was worse, she found it even harder to manage. Paul was a big help, but he had his own family to mind on the weekends. Sometimes when he did odd jobs for Mariko he brought the children along, but not often. They were too wild for her, these *Sansei*. She and Paul had been raised with old-fashioned Japanese manners, but he seemed to have forgotten his when it came time to raising his own kids.

These days it was a rare luxury to just sit and think as she was doing now. Usually she preferred it that way. If she kept busy during the daytime hours she was more likely to sleep soundly at night, instead of tossing and turning with nervous thoughts or waking up screaming from a nightmare.

The sharp edges of folded paper in her pocket reminded Mariko of the letter. Slowly she withdrew it and smoothed it out on her lap, staring at the flowing handwriting until the words blurred and ran together. A sudden gust of wind threatened to pull the letter from her grasp. Her fingers tightened automatically and she rubbed her thumb across the slightly rough surface of the paper as she re-read the first page.

Dear Mariko:

How have you been this fall? I hope you've managed to stay well. I'm doing much better since my leukemia went into remission. Here's hoping it stays that way.

Recently I joined a group of hibakusha *who meet once a month to talk about our problems. It's not as terrible as it sounds! Sometimes we talk about the Bomb, but mostly we think about ways to make people aware of us.*

They want me to speak at the next Hiroshima anniversary event and tell about my life. It's going to be on television. Imagine that!

Mariko smiled and shook her head. Her friend Mitsuye was never one to turn down a chance to be in the spotlight. Mariko had told her many times that she should have been an actress. Mitsuye brought a dramatic flair to everything she did. And her scars were hardly noticeable.

The sound of a distant plane caused Mariko to raise her head and peer nervously at the sky. Scanning the milky blue expanse, she instinctively shielded her eyes from the sun's glare. A black dot appeared in the east. She followed the jet's white trail as it passed overhead, probably heading for the Air Force base twenty miles out of town. Only when the faint whine had completely faded did she sit down again and rub her eyes wearily.

"Stop this nonsense," she scolded herself. "You've been in America for nearly forty years. The war is over. Are you going to jump like a rabbit every time an airplane passes overhead?" For several minutes a painful tightness gripped her chest, then gradually subsided. Slowly her breathing returned to normal and she resumed reading the letter.

The group asked me if I knew of any other hibakusha *who would talk. I thought of you right away. You and I have never talked about what happened to us, but I have never forgotten and I know you haven't either. Marichan, will you join me?*

A chill passed through Mariko; she shut her eyes and shivered. The wind had grown stronger, picking up the leaves by the fence and relentlessly spinning them through the air. Fast-moving clouds obscured the sun and cast shadows across the yard. The mild sunny morning was rapidly turning into a gloomy afternoon, but Mariko hardly noticed the sudden change in weather conditions.

Her discomfort came from within.

Mitsuye knew her too well. The two women had been friends since child-hood. Both had lived on farms in California's San Joaquin Valley back in the thirties. Until they turned thirteen, the two girls were almost inseparable. Then their *Issei* parents had sent the girls back to Hiroshima to get a "good" Japanese education.

The girls ended up in different schools and seldom saw one another. After graduating from high school, Mariko had gone to Tokyo to receive training as a nurse. She moved back to Hiroshima in 1940 when a position opened at Taruya Surgical Clinic. Meanwhile, Mitsuye had married a restaurant owner and set-tled in the nearby town of Fukuyama. Mariko managed to visit her friend on occasion.

Mariko and Mitsuye were on opposite sides of Hiroshima the day the Bomb was dropped. Mitsuye had come to do some shopping at Fukuya's less than a mile from the explosion. Miraculously she managed to escape with only a few small burns. Aside from a persistent feeling of tiredness, she seemed to have no obvious problems. It wasn't until thirty years later, after her husband had died of radiation sickness, that she began to suffer symptoms of leukemia.

Mariko had just begun her day at the clinic on the outskirts when the *pika* flashed over downtown, two miles away. Falling debris knocked her to the ground and flying shards of glass left her with several cuts on her face. There was no time to wonder what had happened. She and the few surviving doc-tors and nurses were soon caught up with taking care of others who had been more badly injured.

Like Mitsuye, she seemed to have survived the Bomb with no serious ef-fects. Then when she was forty-two she began to experience sharp pains in her face. Tiny pieces of glass had worked their way through her skin and had to be picked out. Several facial nerves were damaged by the emerging glass. When they healed, her mouth was stretched to one side, giving it a permanent cyni-cal twist.

Lately her health had taken a turn for the worse. The asthma she'd had since childhood was becoming more severe. She often woke up in the morning gasping for breath. Whether it was in any way related to the Bomb, she could only speculate. Her trips to the doctor were much more frequent these days, and she dared not tell him the full truth. She knew she would lose her medical benefits if it were known she was an A-bomb survivor.

After the war Mariko had returned to the United States. She was unpre-pared for the all-pervasive hatred of the Japanese in California. Her family had been interned in one of the so-called relocation camps ordered by President Roosevelt to contain all the "traitorous" Japanese American citizens. Her parents and brothers were released in 1944 and sent east to Boston and New York. Mariko joined them shortly after her return from Japan. After her parents died she settled in Boston near her brother Paul and his family.

Mariko never married. She was always aware of the scars on her face and blamed them for making her unattractive. They were also a constant reminder of what she'd been through. Over the years the memories had never faded. When an occasional man did show interest in her, she quickly backed off from getting involved. She was afraid to get too close to anyone, not wishing to burden anyone with her memories and her nightmares. Her only real friend was Mitsuye, whose silent understanding helped Mariko feel she was not totally alone.

Through some cousins in New York Mariko had learned that Mitsuye had also returned from Hiroshima and was living in Queens. They quickly renewed their old friendship, although they seldom talked about their years in Hiroshima. Every two or three months Mariko would visit Mitsuye in New York, or Mitsuye would come up to Boston.

And now Mitsuye was asking her to get up in front of a TV camera and relive the awful events she had spent years trying to forget. She would also risk losing her insurance. Brave, foolish Mitsuye . . . how could she even think of doing such a thing since her bout with leukemia? What purpose would it serve?

With difficulty Mariko got to her feet and put the letter back in her pocket. She pursed her lips as she made her way down the porch steps and towards the garage. Mitsuye was a dear friend but there were limits to what one could do, even for a friend. Tomorrow she would write back and say no.

Today was for chores, raking the leaves and perhaps some weeding. She didn't want to think anymore. As she tugged open the creaking garage door just wide enough to squeeze through, she felt a growing irritation. How could Mitsuye consider speaking about such private things? The guilt for still being alive when so many had died. The horror of crawling half-naked and bloody through rubble that only moments before had been a gleaming modern clinic, the pride and joy of its staff. And all the years since then. She often felt as if she were neither dead nor alive, only an organism living out her allotted time-span because fate had chosen not to take her life that day.

Mariko groped about the dim interior of the garage and put on an old jacket and a pair of gardening gloves. Now where had Paul left the rake last

Saturday? She found she was trembling and suddenly anxious to get out of the small dark room. In her haste, she tripped over something and nearly fell. It was the long handle of the rake. Paul must have carelessly tossed it there. Suddenly she was unreasonably angry with him. Didn't he care whether his sister got hurt?

The sudden upwelling of emotion caused Mariko to gasp for breath. She forced herself to calm down and breathe more slowly. It would do no good to have an asthma attack in this miserable shed where no one could hear her or come to her aid. A survivor of something as catastrophic as the atom bomb deserved a more dignified end. She shook free of her self-pity long enough to smile at her own joke. Then she picked up the rake and went outside.

The cool fresh air cleared her head. The wind had died down and scattered its hapless burden of leaves across the wet grass. Mariko began to rake them into a neat pile. The slow mechanical action of swinging the rake helped further to calm her down. For a while, her mind was at ease.

Calmly, she began to reminisce about her years as a nursing student at Tokyo's General Hospital. How she had enjoyed the lively debates she had engaged in with her girlfriends! They cheerfully argued medical ethics in what little spare time they could find between nursing rounds and academic studies. Their favorite topic was what one would call "lifeboat ethics"—making choices in dire circumstances. Playing God—or Buddha, as it were—with their patients' lives.

If you were trapped in a bomb shelter with a very sick child and a feeble old man and you only had enough food and medicine for one of them, whom should you try to save? Was it more important to honor one's elders and preserve a life that was a dying ember, or should one invest in the future and fight to keep alive the newer spark? Whose life was more valuable? Did mere human beings have the right to decide such a thing?

Mariko shook her head ruefully as she recalled the ease with which she and her friends had argued the question, arrogantly confident that they would be able to make such a decision if forced to. None of them ever expected to encounter such a situation in real life. Yet she had, during the nightmarish aftermath of the Bomb. She was haunted by the faces of those she had passed by because their wounds looked far too difficult to deal with.

Mariko stopped raking. She leaned on the handle and bowed her head. Oh, Mitsuye, you are asking too much of me. How could I tell strangers what I did—leaving people to die because I couldn't deal with their awful injuries? She wasn't sure if there were words to describe the stunned faces, some with lips locked against pain, others contorted in anguish. She had felt over-whelmed and frustrated as a lone nurse working with meager supplies salvaged from the ruins of the hospital. She did what she could to stem a never-ending tide of burns and wounds and dysentery.

The bandages and ointments were depleted within an hour after the Bomb was dropped and still the people came, clutching their torn bleeding faces and carrying dying family members, friends or co-workers on their backs. She had to resort to treating burns with cooking oil, animal fat, and even sliced cucumbers. All through that first night and for the next two days, she and the few surviving nurses and doctors had struggled to ease the pain of those who came begging for help. It was a losing battle.

Paradoxically, some of the victims with the worst injuries eventually recovered, while others who appeared unscathed suddenly died. Making decisions based on conventional medical knowledge became impossible in the face of this strange radiation sickness. Mariko knew she had done her best in the horrifying circumstances, but her feelings of guilt lingered nonetheless.

It had been almost a relief when the last of her improvised bandages and salves had run out and she could no longer even attempt to treat the many victims that still came seeking help. Though it was agonizing to have to abandon people in pain, the burden of choosing who would live and who would die had been lifted from her shoulders.

Exhausted by her round-the-clock nursing and in pain from the cuts on her face, Mariko had finally left the clinic and caught a ride on an army truck to her uncle's house in Tomo Village several miles away. Her cuts became infected and refused to heal for months. She was ashamed to show herself in public. The villagers thought she brought bad luck with her, and avoided her whenever she went out. At last her skin healed enough for her to return to work. As soon as she had saved the money to return to America she left Japan with a sigh of relief.

Mariko was brought back to the present by the loud barking of her neighbor's German Shepherd on the other side of the wire fence. She glanced at her watch—it was nearly two. The dog always barked at the jabbering groups of schoolchildren streaming past on their way home from the bus stop. You could set your clock by that foolish dog's daily howling and pawing at the fence.

She was surprised to see that she had been outside since eleven-thirty. Her bones were beginning to feel the autumn dampness. Winter would be coming soon, but the flowerbeds could use some weeding. She looked forward to spring when she would plant chrysanthemums along the side of the house.

They reminded her of her father's garden.

As she put the wire rake in a corner of the garage, making sure that no one would trip over it, she paused to deliberate. Should she start working in the flowerbeds today? The rest of the afternoon stretched before her and she felt a need to fill it with activity. Her friend's letter had unsettled her. She needed time to push aside the ghosts of the past. Something fell from her pocket and fluttered to the floor. Huffing with the effort, Mariko stooped to pick it up. Her hand trembled. Somehow the folded letter had opened up as it fell to the ground. The words "speak for the dead" caught her eye, and she shivered as she straightened up. She read the rest of the letter.

. . . I know I'm asking a lot of you. These things are painful to remember. But we hibakusha *are the only ones who've seen firsthand what the* gembaku *can do to human beings. The world needs to hear from us, but we're getting old. Pretty soon there won't be anyone left who was actually there.*

You and I owe it to all those people who lost their lives. They can't speak for themselves. I firmly believe that that is why some of us have survived. If we don't speak for the dead, none of it will mean anything to anyone anymore. Does that make sense?

"We can speak for the dead . . ." Mariko had never thought of it in that light before. Was that why her life had been spared? Could she find a purpose to her seemingly empty existence? The letter blurred before her eyes.

I guess you could call this "bearing witness," as the Jewish people did to get through the concentration camps. Oh Mari, I can't tell you how much better I feel to be doing something like this. After all those years of wishing I'd never survived, now I feel I'm doing something worthwhile.

Well, please think about it. Call me when you can, or I'll call you. I miss you. My love to Paul.

Sayonara,
Mitsuye

Mariko slowly squatted in front of her empty flowerbeds and began pulling weeds, her mind turning over her friend's words. She said aloud, *"Kuri kaesa-nai . . .* it should never be repeated." She saw once again the child who had died in her arms, his bewildered eyes asking her how it had come to pass that one minute he was playing in the street, the next he lay dying. The young mother who tried in vain to keep her baby alive by nursing it even as she herself was bleeding to death. And the man whose entire body was one raw burn. There were more faces than she could count. Perhaps with Mitsuye's help, Mariko could pass on their memories.

She folded the letter and put it carefully back into the pocket of her work pants. Her hands in their thick cotton gloves cleared away the weeds with smooth, strong motions, deftly untangling them and tossing them aside. The mid-afternoon sun reappeared and warmed her back as she patted the rich moist soil and prepared it for the flowers that she would plant there next spring.

SIU WAI ANDERSON

Obachan *Hatta,*   *LORI KAYO HATTA*
Kailua-Kona Fields, 1983
        black and white photo

These photos were taken during the filming of my first documentary short, "Obachan."
Taking the internment experience as the point of departure (one went through the ordeal,

Obachan *Hatta, Kaimalino Housing, 1983*   *black and white photo*   *LORI KAYO HATTA*

the other did not), this personal film was an attempt to understand my grandmothers'
lives and personalities and world outlooks in the context of their contrasting histories
and experiences as Issei *women of that period.*

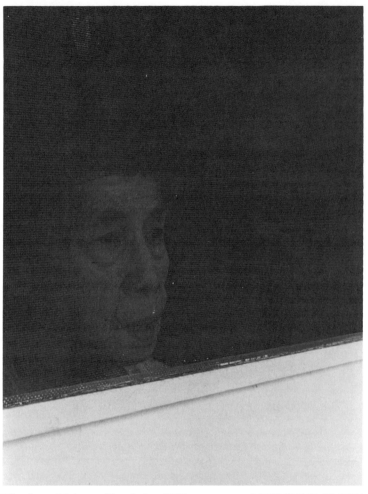

Obachan *Matano, Honolulu, 1983*   *LORI KAYO HATTA*
black and white photo

Self Portrait   *mixed media on paper*   TOMIE ARAI
                                    22" x 30"
                                    photo by D. James Dee

As a third generation American of Japanese ancestry—a **Sansei**—*I have tried to incor-
porate the influences of both cultures in my work as my part in a collective effort to
create an Asian American calligraphy or artistic language based on the unique experience
of Asians in America.*

Portrait of A Japanese Girl   *etching*   *TOMIE ARAI*
photo by D. James Dee

Rice Eaters   *mixed media on paper*   TOMIE ARAI

Garden   *mixed media on gessoed paper*   *TOMIE ARAI*
                                        30" x 44"
                                  photo by D. James Dee

Portrait of Chinese Family   *silkscreen*   *TOMIE ARAI*

Back of the Bus, 1953

drawing
23" x 39"

YONG SOON MIN

My work in art is reflecting my changing awareness as a "born-again" Korean digging deeper into my roots. It is beginning to reflect more of my sociopolitical concerns especially in the realm of the interface between the personal and the political.

American Friend mixed media/paper YONG SOON MIN
39" x 55"

Such a generous friend! You were our father's American friend who sponsored his immigration to the States after fighting together in the Korean War. Upon our father's request from America, you also got our mother a job on a U.S. army base in Seoul with which she supported her kids during the tough times just after the war.

Since our liberation from Japan, you influenced our political development by supporting the autocrat Syngman Rhee, and the military dictatorships of Park and Chun. You continue to share with us your economic and military might. You've even given us your valuable nuclear missiles!

You've given us far more than we bargained for! How could we ever reciprocate?

Echoes of Gold Mountain
Different Name, Same Game

mixed media wall installation

YONG SOON MIN

Whirl War   *mixed media room installation*   YONG SOON MIN
                        photo by Mark Towner

All Orientals Look Alike   *installation*   ROBERTA MAY WONG
photo by David Martinez

"All Orientals Look Alike" is the confrontation of myth and reality using the realism of photography to invalidate the myth of racism which generalizes that people identified by color are indistinguishable as individuals. I use humor to conjure the image of that mythological person that "all" orientals look like.

The four black and white photographs are interwoven into a single image, the central portrait, that symbolizes the myth. The installation is set as a funerary altar where we begin the process of healing as we mourn the loss of identity imposed by stereotypes. Ancestral offerings of nourishment are provided through spiritual and physical empowerment of the people, gained by the collective power of the individuals who act to shatter that myth.

All Orientals Look Alike   ROBERTA MAY WONG
(detail)   *installation*
              photo by David Martinez

75

The Last Supper   installation   ROBERTA MAY WONG

"The Last Supper" underlines the relationship of men and nations involved in the pro-liferation of nuclear arms. Defined in the context of Christian symbolism and modern cynicism, "The Last Supper" epitomizes the duplicity that exists among men and nations who pursue war as a vehicle to reach peace. Death is the prevailing element of "The Last Supper," surrounding the fragility of life whose sustenance we share both physically and spiritually, with all human beings.

FAMILY PHOTOS: BLACK AND WHITE: 1960

the light slides through lace panels on the window
on the dark sofa sit two children
the baby propped up like a five-pound rice sack
leaning against a little girl.
she smiles, the white curve of baby teeth
a geometric contrast to her straight china doll bangs.
the father stands with a slight smile
in pinstriped suit, hand on hip
his hair shiny with pomade
three flowers or brilliantine
a handkerchief points out of his breast pocket
even though you cannot see his shoes
you know they are polished.
the mother, young and plump, from eating
american food: candy bars, baked potatoes
she sits in a flowered dress
hair marcelled in waves
her face open and full
no longer the shy village beauty
she crosses her legs casually
and laughs at the photographer
she hopes her mother in the philippines
will be very proud.

VIRGINIA R. CERENIO

THE HANDBOOK OF SEX OF THE PLAIN GIRL

She calls herself the plain girl, but I
am plainer. Nothing is homelier
than the floor of my breasts; this house
of bones. Everything I know of sex
is large-breasted, blue-eyed, and blonde.

> I am woman learned in these ways—
> lie still, I will teach you.
> I have pulled back the quilts,
> swept clean the pillows, softened
> the lamp. I will unfasten my robe,
> set my hair free. Quietly
> let me smooth your skin into peace.
> This is how you please a man.

I ran away from the first boy who said I
was beautiful. What do I know
of pleasing a man? Mother will not answer
my questions, and these pictures she gives me—
do men and women really do this?

> Come into my red—let white
> iron burn, reshape and find its form
> in heat. My Master,
> my Emperor. I am yours tonight.

On the page, she crouches to receive him
as a glove enfolds the hand.
But this man beside me—who is he?
He calls my plainness beauty, and I,
who have little enough to give, will find
this reason enough to give
everything.

Men know nothing of sex—ask a man
what sex is and he will show you
his penis—we have much to teach:
my Master, my child, let me teach you
about your lips, your thighs,
your cheeks, the bones
of your hip.

But what can you teach about the pain
of his entrance, and later, the ache
of his departure? You, who taught
the Emperor to live forever,
teach me what to do with love.

MARIAN YEE

WINTERMELONS

Why are you standing there, Mother,
alone in the garden?
What is there behind the shy palms
of leaves that glow like white
wings in the moonlight? Come to bed—
these are only your melons.

Every summer you've planted wintermelons,
fussing there as if you were their mother,
smoothing the stems into their beds.
I've thought of you in your garden
when I was alone in distant places
and had only the wind to hold between my palms.

Once you held out your calloused palms
and talked of working among the rows of melons
grown at home in China. Here, where all is foreign
do you remember your own mother
as she bent to whisper charms over her garden?
You've kept those whispers—I've heard you listing.

Those words are in movement,
though today you sift bonemeal between your palms
and spread lime around your garden:
your words bring forth the melons.
Yet we haven't spoken much for years.
When I told you that I loved a foreign

man, you said that I was foreign
too. The first time I went to bed
with him, I wondered what you would say,
whether you knew the touch of palms
upon your breasts. Have you known
all along of this hidden garden?

Though I've left behind your garden
to discover things still new
to me, I always return to your melons
shaped in moonlight, round, imbedded
in their net of vines. Let me rest my palm
here a little longer. Tomorrow I am leaving, Mother.

MARIAN YEE

HEAT IN OCTOBER

The first day the radiator
kicks in, the air through the vent
smells of the white shirts my mother
ironed, of steam and starch, stiff
pointed collars. Rainy winter afternoons,
the flames of the gas heater burned
a jagged blue crown while she ironed
and I made paper cranes with every
square sheet except the black ones I'd
set aside, patches of night sky. On
clear nights she showed me the winter
constellations: the Orion guarding
the low sky in the early evening,
the Pleiades I could only count four of,
Sirius the burning dog's eye.

That was before winter began to trouble
her and every November she'd contemplate
the basketful of yarn she no longer
wanted to knit. I found them, all those balls
of yarn, the spring after her death, wound
tight as cocoons. On the floor they
unwound rainbows I would not trust; in
the yard her perennials bloomed—
false colors of hope.

Hot air whirrs through the gridiron
painted black. There is a distant
groan that never quite subsides. I look
away from the wall. The window ledge
swims with potted plants. White spider flowers
hang cautious on shoots of new growth. Spotted
aloe leaves glisten like water lizards
sprawled flat in the sun. The hibiscus daily
unwinds the flame-red lipstick of its bud.

Another winter, I trust these omens of hot air
no more trustworthy perhaps than my mother's
perennials, and keep them in the window,
amulets against cold spells.

KYOKO MORI

THE CLUB

He beat me with the hem of a kimono
worn by a Japanese woman
this prized
painted
wooden statue
carved to perfection
in Japan or maybe Hong Kong.

She was usually on display
in our living room atop his bookshelf
among his other overseas treasures
I was never to touch.
She posed there most of the day
her head tilted
her chin resting lightly
on the white pointed fingertips
of her right hand
her black hair
piled high on her head
her long slim neck bared
to her shoulders.
An invisible hand
under the full sleeve
clasped her kimono
close to her body
its hem flared
gracefully around her feet.

That hem
made fluted red marks
on these freckled arms
my shoulders
my back.
That head
inside his fist

made camel
bumps
on his knuckles.
I prayed for her
that her pencil thin neck
would not snap
or his rage would be unendurable.
She held fast for me
didn't even chip or crack.

One day, we were talking
as we often did the morning after.
Well, my sloe-eyed beauty, I said
have you served him enough?
I dared to pick her up with one hand
I held her gently by the flowing robe
around her slender legs.
She felt lighter than I had imagined.
I stroked her cold thighs
with the tips of my fingers
and felt a slight tremor.

I carried her into the kitchen and wrapped her
in two sheets of paper towels
We're leaving
I whispered
you and I
together.

I placed her
between my clothes in my packed suitcase.
That is how we left him
forever.

MITSUYE YAMADA

FOR AN ASIAN WOMAN WHO SAYS MY POETRY GIVES HER A STOMACHACHE

You would rather scream out your anger in a workshop
and then you would find peace
and you ask if I find peace
by becoming more angry in my poetry

You turn to my sister-poet and say she's found peace
because her style is soft
and mine shouts

I jokingly say that I do find peace
when I sleep for at least 6 hours
but I give you my one true answer:

Peace does not exist
not while a woman is being raped
a child is being abused
a lesbian is being beaten
a man is denied work because of his race

and if I could document my life in snapshots
I would take hours to describe the pains
of being a girl and a young woman
who thought beauty
was being white
        useless
        a mother
        a wife

seen only in the eyes of the racist beholder
wrapped in the arms of the capitalist media
starved in the binds of patriarchal culture

and how I screamed in silence for years
beating myself down, delirious in my victimization
preferring the cotton-spun candy I thought was life

and now in my hours of awakening
as my hair turns white
my anger moves, a storm into the sunlight
where women and men fight alongside each other
in the battles against degradation, poverty, manipulation, fear
where anger is pure as the love I have for freedom
where desire is the catalyst for action
where the possibilities are rice and flowers and children
growing strong everywhere

NELLIE WONG

LEGACY   *STEPHANIE SUGIOKA*

This is the eldest daughter
of wind and of wood.
Her words are as irrelevant
and as lost
as the broken song
of wind and bamboo.

The boys,
only three and five,
are unaware that I
am a species of ghost
in this their high glass house.
(The older one still insists
his mother must be mine.)
So when I arrive
they run figure eights around me,
triumphantly announcing
that I am there
(and, gullible as always,
I believe them).

This is the eldest daughter.
A small sound gnaws at her sleep,
a tedious, uneasy creaking
of pine branches
crossed
against one another.

This is the day, for some reason,
my father and stepmother
want to discuss their wills.
It is understood that the boys
should inherit the house.
Of an oriental design,
made to let in as much light
as the dogwoods, maples, and oaks
will allow,

it manages, somehow,
to look like an airport.
This is the house
that sprang phoenix-like
from the ruins of the former,
(my other) family.
(I've never lived there myself.)

> This is the eldest daughter.
> Music pierces her skull
> like twirling needles.
> It is the Japanese flutes
> that sing the panicked movement
> of her hands
> like broken-winged birds.

We finish our discussion
with a wicked stepmother joke,
and I take my leave.
Then out with the boys
to the rock garden
to learn who has watered
which crocus.

And they shall inherit
a house of light.
I believe in their small round lives
as I believe
in the round white stones
at our feet.

> This is the eldest daughter
> of wind and of wood.
> Her legacy is a house
> where no light shines.
> The reeds sing it
> whispery lullabyes,
> and hemlocks stroke
> its splintered sides.

She is the black wind
that haunts the house—
rushing, always rushing
out of the room
down the hall
around the corner
to find the mother
to find the father
who do not own the house
who are not there.

STEPHANIE SUGIOKA

FATHER'S BELT

Closing first the front door, and then the patio,
side, garage and back doors, her father
has brought her back to the green and orange
family house; this time from the Metro
bus stop which he circled in the Pinto,
until she, anemic and dizzy, wise
at sixteen, returned with her untidy suitcase.

Rolling against the wall, Eva pushes
him away from her as if to make room
for the roar seeping up. Then, she stops.
She shuts down as if a tranquilizer
entered her blood, closing down
like a factory at five; she leans
forward to listen to him avidly, now.

The belt flips, loosens, clatters
to the carpet. Looking at her father's belt,
she recalls how it striped her face
like birthmarks, or how it moved like a snake
from the loops of his pants to settle
on his discarded shirt, and his pants,
half-remembering his shape—warm
and deflating, on top.

Afterwards, thoughts like worms eating their way
out, she smoothes the cracks on the leather,
presses the buckle to her hot throat.

SHALIN HAI-JEW

I really didn't think twice about the two letters I got from Hawaii. One was from an aunt, the other from an old high school friend. Both said they were glad I was moving back home. I thought it was just a simple misunderstanding. My eldest sister Dar and I were both going home for Christmas but it was just for a visit. I had a job and an apartment full of furniture in Oregon which I had no intention of leaving.

When I arrived in Hawaii, I gave my friend Lydia a call. She suggested that we spend a day at the zoo. We walked along the black asphalt paths surrounded by the caws and squawks of tropical birds and looked at the listless hippos and lions and tigers languishing in their dusty fenced yards. We stopped at the gibbons' cage and watched the slender apes chatter and scramble nervously about. Lydia asked, "Did you find a job here? Or are you going to stay home with your mother during the day?"

"I'm not moving back. I'm just here for a visit."

"Oh, really?"

One of the apes grabbed onto the metal bars of the cage and peered at us with its enormous eyes.

"Dar said that you were moving home to help take care of your mother's house."

I watched Lydia as she shelled a peanut to throw into the cage. A little sign posted in front of the cage read: "Please do not feed me. I am on a special diet."

I remembered a phone conversation I had had with Dar about a month ago. She had just talked to Mama on the phone. Mama was depressed. She's getting old and especially now that Dad is gone she can't keep up with the house. Her three girls are all so far away; they all live on the mainland. She wished one of them cared enough about her to come home and help with the house but of course, Elizabeth is married and has a baby so she can't be expected to pick up and move . . .

Nothing new really, except that it upset Dar. She felt that Mama was seriously depressed and she needed professional help.

"Mama really needs one of us around her. But we all know Elizabeth has a family and she can't just uproot herself and move. . . . "

I had known what she was thinking. I had also known that if I said, "Well, why don't you move back home?" Dar would get indignant and declare that it wasn't all that easy and if I really cared I would make an effort to go back and not put all the responsibility on her.

Now after talking to Lydia, it seemed that my silence had told Dar I took Mama's plight to heart. Dar convinced herself that I was going home to stay.

That night as Mama, Dar and I were eating dinner, I mentioned that I had spent the day with Lydia.

"She had the impression that I was going to stay here, but I told her that I had to be at work the Monday after Christmas."

There was a silence in which Dar seemed to be engrossed in mixing her rice and beef curry.

"I wonder why she thought that," Mama said.

As I was washing the dishes, Dar came up beside me. She started to rinse the dishes and put them in the rack.

"I never told you I was going to stay," I said.

"When Mama picked me up at the airport she said that you had quit your job and were going to move back home."

Mama didn't always tell the truth. I'm not sure when I discovered this. When I was in elementary school I had always believed her when she woke us up in the morning and told us that we were late—it was already a quarter to eight. I always leapt out of bed, got dressed and rushed into the kitchen, to discover it was only seven o'clock.

I had believed Mama when I had snuggled up to her in bed, and she'd put down the newspaper she was reading and told me stories about people who were cut in half by elevators because they were too slow, or about children who ate too much dried fruit and then exploded when they drank a glass of water.

Mama could tell lies in the most peculiar ways. There were times when she'd scream, her neck veins popping out like an iguana's. I'd be crying, crying and she'd slap me. Then the phone would ring. Mama would pick it up and say in her low, receptionist's voice, "Hello?" If it were one of her friends she could sit and chat and laugh for half-an-hour and then resume her sour mood the moment she hung up.

There were days when she'd cuddle me and see the bruises that she had given me the day before and she'd cluck, "You should be more careful."

One Christmas I had pneumonia, and after I opened my presents I crawled back into bed.

Mama came and stood in my bedroom doorway. "Don't you want to ride your new bicycle?"

"Not now."

"You should go out and get some air. It'll be good for you."

I shook my head and burrowed deeper under the covers.

"Stubborn. Don't know what's good for you!"

She stomped down the hall and started cooking, clanging pans and slamming cupboard doors.

That evening we were going to Auntie Alicia's for dinner. I didn't want to go. I still felt sick. But I was made to put on my bright pink, long muumuu and brush my hair. Dad had washed our new Ford LTD so that you could see the bits of gold glitter in its paint. He had on his dark blue aloha shirt and Mama, Dar and Elizabeth were also dressed in long muumuus. We three girls sat in the back. The seats of the LTD were overpadded velveteen. You really couldn't sit on those seats. You sank into them as they embraced and absorbed you.

It was twenty-eight miles over the Pali Highway to my aunt's house. The Pali is carved in the Koolau mountain range. It is a thin, chiseled strip that winds around steep red cliffs and overlooks the Maunawili valley. The LTD hummed around hairpin turns and curves. I sat, drowning in the plush executive seat, every passageway in my head choked with mucus. My sisters' animated chatter seemed to filter through a wad of gauze—all I could hear was a hum. I tried focusing on a patch of blue sky, but I couldn't contain the greenish-yellow pudding surging up from my stomach, filling my mouth . . .

"What? Pull over to the side, Daddy!" Mama yelled.

Even before the car came to a complete stop, Mama leaped out, threw open my door and yanked me out. She stood with her hands on her hips as I retched and vomited on the side of the road, squatting in the gravel.

"God damn it," she said through her teeth.

Dad had found a MacDonald's napkin and was wiping the car mat.

"If you had gotten some air like I told you, you wouldn't have thrown up."

I began to dry heave. Mama watched me, shifting her weight, her arms folded like a matronly Buddha. She shook her head. "Didn't even have enough sense to roll down the window." She couldn't contain herself anymore. She slapped me hard on the ear. My head swam.

When we pulled into Auntie's driveway, my two cousins ran out from the yard and waved their arms. "Auntie Katie and Uncle Richard are here!"

Mama waved and smiled. Auntie Alicia came out of the house as we were getting out of the car. She smiled at us and asked, "How's my girls?"

Mama had turned toward me and, still smiling, put her arm gently on my shoulder.

This Christmas was a quiet one with just Mama, Dar and me. Elizabeth called that evening. I heard Mama ask, "Do you want to talk to Sarah?"

"I'll get it in the bedroom," I yelled.

"Liz," I said after I heard Mama hang up, "do you remember that Christmas I threw up in the car?"

"No."

I could hear her cooing to her baby Jeffery.

"Can you hear him? You should have seen him today. We got an aquarium and he was just fascinated by the fish."

When she was in junior high, Elizabeth had bred guppies. Not the ordinary gray-drab ones that darted in and around the sea grass like mosquitoes—the guppies Liz bred couldn't survive anywhere else but in an aquarium. They were beautiful blues and reds; their eyes were ringed provocatively with black. Some had tails twice as long as their bodies. These fish swam leisurely, dragging their veined and translucent trains behind them.

One afternoon I walked into the living room and noticed the fish had disappeared. I walked closer to the aquarium. Dar came up behind me and tapped me on the shoulder. She startled me and I gave a little cry.

"Shh. I'm just cleaning the tank. Don't tell anyone, O.K.? I want it to be a surprise."

The next morning Elizabeth discovered her guppies floating at the top of the aquarium, their silver bellies exposed. She sat beside the base of the aquarium, huddled in a little ball, her face pressed to her knees. Dar stood by her.

"You can always get some other guppies," Dar said. "Sarah probably overfed them. She was always feeding them."

I hadn't ever fed them. Dar had told me that she was going to clean the tank. No one else had heard her. There had been no one else in the room.

The guppies drifted in a circle, their large black eyes staring, their tails drooping; the little ceramic frog still burping tiny spheres of air, the sides of the aquarium still plated with deep-green algae.

There had been no one else home that day, that day when I was nine. Elizabeth and Dar had gone to their swimming lesson; Dad and Mama were at work.

"Stay inside," Mama said every morning when she left. "Don't answer the door and keep them all locked."

When the doorbell rang, I ran into the bedroom and peered out the louvers. There was a white van in the driveway so I knew it was Mr. Winston. He rang the bell again and had started toward his van when I opened the door.

"Is your dad home?"

I shook my head.

"Ummm." Mr. Winston looked towards his van. He was a big, red-faced man who lived just down the street. He had a Chinese wife and a little two-year-old girl named Heather. "I just need an Allen wrench 'cause I'm working on my van. Do you know where he keeps his tools?"

I nodded. "Under the laundry sink."

As he was pulling out hammers and wrenches from my dad's tool box, Mr. Winston asked about my school. He asked what I liked to do. He was friendly and kind. He was funny and told funny stories. I had seen his motorcycle. He was going to take a ride on it. He was making a place to cook and eat and sleep in his van. Yes, I would like to see it.

Mr. Winston had an anchor tattooed on his arm, and big stubby, hairy fingers. What he did to me that day had reminded me of Mama's fingers as she stuffed the Christmas turkey. She would jam a fistful of stuffing into the bird's cavity and smash it with her palm. Her gold wedding band would be coated with raw egg and milk as she'd pull the bird's flap of skin over more and more stuffing, stretching it, stretching it until it tore. Then she'd lace the cavity shut with steel tines so that nothing could spill out.

Dar woke up the morning after Christmas and called to Mama, "After Christmas sales!"

Mama was in the bathroom spraying her hair. I stood in the doorway and asked, "Do you remember Mr. Winston?"

"Who?"

"Never mind."

"Oh, you mean that little family that used to live down the street," Mama said.

"Oh, I remember," Dar said. "They had that cute little girl that we'd babysit sometimes. What about them?"

"Sarah was asking about them," I heard Mama say as I walked out of the bathroom.

Before they left, Mama ran through her ritual of checking the stove burners and locking all the doors. She walked out and then stuck her head back in and called, "Don't let anyone in while we're gone."

"I won't."

I heard the car back out of the driveway and then the house was quiet. There was a big cardboard box on the top shelf in Mama's bedroom. I had found it one day when I was looking for wrapping paper. Mama made carbon copies of all the letters she wrote to us and kept them in that box, along with all our letters to her. I got a stool from the kitchen and got the box down. Most of the letters were mundane, about the weather, improvements to the house, parties we had gone to. But in a letter Dar wrote to Mama about a month ago, I found this:

> *I spoke to Sarah on the phone a few days ago. She seemed scattered and con-*
> *fused and couldn't pay attention when I was talking to her. She's a good kid*
> *but she needs psychiatric help. I think it would be best if she lived at home, or*
> *somewhere she could be attended to . . .*

I felt my face growing hot. I could keep this letter and tonight I could put it on the table. I could confront them with it. Tell Mama what was really said in that phone conversation. But then, they would ask me where I got that letter. They would accuse me of being a thief, a conniving spy. They would say by my actions I proved that I couldn't be trusted, that I was a child. I folded the letter up and put the box back on the shelf.

I went into the kitchen and started to clear away the breakfast dishes, when it occurred to me that Mama would know. Even though I thought I put the box and letters back exactly as I found them, she would know. The letters would be slightly out of order, or one envelope would be facing the wrong way, and she would know. But she wouldn't say anything. Not until the time was right for her.

My face was flushed, the skin on my arms red. I was hot, glowing hot. I realized: they wanted me to be afraid. They were the spies, watching me, knowing my thoughts, my fears. They wanted me to find that letter, to read it, to put it back secretly. They would want me to pretend I hadn't seen it. It would be the first step, my initiation, in becoming like them.

I wouldn't let that happen. I would make them know I read this letter. I would demand answers. I am not a child. I am not a spy.

I found a roll of Scotch tape in the kitchen drawer, went back into the bedroom and took the box down. I took all the letters out of their envelopes and taped each sheet to the closet door. I taped up Mama's carbon copies, Christmas cards, Mother's Day cards, postcards, Dad's old love letters written fifty years ago. They marched in straight rows around the bedroom walls, oblivious to the grooves in the wood panelling. They papered the ceiling and covered the light fixture and surrounded the headboard. I turned on the light which illuminated the blue ink loops and dots and wagging tails. I pulled back the curtains and opened the louvers wide. The pages fluttered in the breeze.

I sat cross-legged on the bed, closed my eyes and listened to the pages rustling, murmuring their lies.

SUSAN K.C. LEE

The village of Bagong Silang is an untidy assortment of a half dozen palm-thatched houses, about a hundred kilometers north of Manila. It falls under the jurisdiction of the municipality of San Pablo, a town of a few hundred people, a day's walk away. The people of Bagong Silang have lived for generations along a narrow strip of mud road that borders the rice paddies. They are, as a rule, thrifty and industrious folk. When not toiling in the rice fields, they tend vegetable gardens. They own a few pigs, a few chickens, nothing much else of value.

Aling Saturnina used to live in the last house on the left, the one behind the *santol* tree. Last year, she and her married daughter were taken to San Pablo in a military jeep, and since then no one has seen or heard from them. The villagers don't like to talk about the events that led to Aling Saturnina's disappearance. When asked, they will cross themselves and their eyes will slide sideways and perhaps one or two will invoke the name of the town's patron saint, as though the saying of it had the power to protect them from all harm. If the questioner becomes too persistent—as lately some of these newspapermen from San Pablo have been—they will escape to the rice fields, and wait there till nightfall to return to their homes. They are simple folk and don't bother with things they cannot understand.

Everyone remembers Aling Saturnina because she had a temper. She had eight children, was always cursing and beating one or the other with the back of her wooden slippers. She was fond of *tuba*, the potent drink made from fermented coconut juice. Whether or not she had money for the children's supper, she would send one of her sons to the *tiyanggi* for a bottle. The eldest son, Lando, ran away when he was fourteen. A few years later, Isagani left. Then, in quick succession, Prospero, Lina, Catherine, and Rey, too, disappeared.

Siko stayed until he was nearly full-grown. When he finally left, he took the last of his mother's savings with him—a few crumpled pesos, which she had kept in a tin tucked away under the eves of the house. When Aling Saturnina discovered the loss, her curses could be heard all over the village.

Now there was no money for *tuba*, and the youngest child, Ana, was a skinny, sickly girl, not much use out in the rice fields. The villagers avoided Aling Saturnina then because she would pace the street restlessly with feverish, yellow eyes, like a bitch in heat. They felt sorry for Ana, but what could they do? Sometimes they would press a few eggs into her hands, a few clumps of spinach. No one was surprised when, soon after Siko's departure, Ana took Poldo as a husband. There was no money for a church wedding, so Poldo simply moved in. Poldo proved to be a good son-in-law, a hard worker. He and Ana lived peacefully together in Aling Saturnina's house for many years.

One day, Aling Saturnina learned that Siko had been killed. It was Ana who brought her the news, Ana who came stumbling down the narrow street, crying and blowing her nose into her skirt. At first, Aling Saturnina was confused. Hands knotting her dress in anxiety, she ordered Ana to compose herself.

"Ah, *Ina!*" Ana cried. "Siko has been shot! He was caught breaking into a colonel's house in San Pablo."

Aling Saturnina sighed. She was not sad, no. She had not seen him in such a long time, and sometimes it pleased her to think that she could no longer remember his face, not even when, in those moments when she was without *tuba*, she wrinkled her forehead and tried hard to concentrate. He had hurt her, how he had hurt her! The memory of that bitter day when, with trembling fingers, she had reached up to the roof and lifted down the old tin can where she had ten, perhaps fifteen pesos lovingly stored, and, prying open the cover with her anxious fingers, had seen only emptiness staring back at her—ah! That memory rushed over her once again with overwhelming clarity. She remembered the helpless feeling, as though she had been hit in the belly, that had accompanied her discovery. She had not had *tuba* all that day, and the next, and her body had been wracked by chills, she had been in a fever of want. Over and over again, on those sleepless nights when she had found herself pacing the village like a restless animal, she had asked herself, "How could he do this to me?" She had thought, for a time, that of all her children, Siko loved her the most. She had kept him warm beside her on cold nights, she had taken care never to beat him, not even when he had done something that angered her, preferring instead to beat Lando, because Lando was the eldest and should have been responsible for the behavior of his younger brothers and sisters. She had never suspected him of stealing, though after he had gone she began to hear stories from the neighbors, stories of how Siko had been caught more than once filching tomatoes from their vegetable gardens, and how when baby chickens disappeared, they all thought instinctively of Siko. How was it that she had never known? A son of hers—a thief! Aling Saturnina was ashamed. And now this horrifying deed—breaking into someone's home, and that someone no less than a colonel! It was beyond Aling Saturnina's comprehension. She should have known, she berated herself, she should have known all along. Her heart was thudding painfully. The ingrate! She wanted to curse, beat the air with her fists. She looked at Ana crying helplessly in a corner.

"That's enough!" she cried. "You'll make yourself sick. Your brother was a fool, may lightning strike me, but he was. I would have beaten any of you with my *tsinelas* if I had caught you stealing so much as a twig from a neighbor's garden!"

Then she went to the shelf where she had kept a bottle of *tuba*, and took it with her to the rice fields.

As her feet trod the worn paths threading the rice paddies, Aling Saturnina's spirit remained cold and unforgiving. Her mind gnawed ceaselessly at the fact of Siko's betrayal; that fact had assumed the hardness and blackness of a kernel, lodged at the front of her forehead, between her eyes. On this she focused all her attention. She was oblivious to the fresh green of the rice saplings that blanketed the wet earth, the brilliant, blue arch of the sky, the birds gliding soundlessly overhead. The silence wrapped itself around her like a cloak. The village dropped farther and farther behind until it was no more than an indistinct blur on the horizon.

Aling Saturnina grew tired. She decided to sit and rest for a while in one of the bamboo thickets that sprouted up here and there, forming pockets of dry land among the paddies. As she stretched out on the hard, packed earth and looked around her, her eyes beheld the great, blue bulk of The Mountain, rising straight up out of the plain. The Mountain made her think contemptuously of the legend the villagers told their young children, the legend of the enchantress, Maria Cacao, who was said to live in a palace of gold on The Mountain's highest peak. Now and then, the villagers said, she ventured down to the lowlands and lured men away from their homes and families. Aling Saturnina had stopped believing this story a long time ago. She knew now that when sons and husbands disappeared from the village, as her own had done, they had been lured away by more dangerous enchantments, such as were to be found in the big city of Manila, not far to the south. Her husband had left her after one such trip to the city, never to return. And the rest of her sons, the ones who were still living—they were probably there, too, probably living in the shantytown of Tondo, which she had heard was twice as large as the municipality of San Pablo. Some day, Aling Saturnina thought, some day I'll go after those bastards.

She sat in the fields letting the wind riffle through her long, gray hair and calm her aching nerves. Now and then she took deep, long gulps of the *tuba*. She sat there a long time, until it grew dark and the rice paddies, filled with water, began to reflect the light of the moon. A cold wind rose and parted the bamboo thickets. Still she sat and stared. After a while, she thought she could hear a great clamor of barking dogs arising from the village, and she rose, suddenly expectant. She looked towards the general direction of the village, ears straining. The clamor increased in ferocity. She could imagine the village dogs, twisting and straining on their hind legs, jaws agape. She had seen them bark in unison like this many other times, and always, always, the sleepy villagers, rushing to their windows in the dead of night, had seen, coming down the street, strange, pale figures—ghosts, spirits, goblins. The last time, they had seen the ghost of Aling Corazon's daughter. She had drowned herself in the Agno River after her husband left her. She had walked slowly down the middle of the street, crying silently and wringing her hands. At intervals she would stop and look around her with imploring eyes. The villagers had watched Aling Corazon, to see what she would do, but she remained dry-eyed at her window, and, after the wraith had passed, she closed her shutters and went to bed, like all the rest.

In a little while, Aling Saturnina thought she could hear Siko's voice, breaking through a gust of wind. The clumps of bamboo trembled and swayed. Aling Saturnina wondered what form her son would take in coming to her. Would he come as a huge black dog or a pig? She had heard that spirits liked to assume such disguises. Would he appear as one of those bat-like creatures who fly through the air with only the upper halves of their bodies? Several of the villagers had sworn they had seen such things hovering over the rice fields. Just then, something dark dropped from the sky and landed before her with a soft thud. Aling Saturnina saw that it was a man, squatting on his haunches, head lowered, palms pressed against the earth. The creature raised its head, revealing a blood-spattered face. It was Siko.

Even with his face so disfigured by blood, there was no mistaking the gap between his two front teeth, almost exactly like the one her husband had. Siko squatted, grinning, in the moonlight. He was wearing blue jeans and a white cotton T-shirt, and there were dark, purplish patches of clotted blood across his chest. After she recovered from her initial surprise, Aling Saturnina wanted to hit him. But what is the use of hitting a ghost? Instead she cried: "*Walang hiya ka*! How dare you take my money, leave me and your sister to starve to death!"

As soon as she said those words, she felt her limbs stiffen and become curiously immobile. She wanted to cry out but her tongue lay leaden in her mouth. She could not even reach for the bottle of *tuba* at her feet. Siko stopped grinning. He stood up and approached her, scrutinizing her face. He came so close that she could distinctly smell the odor from his rotting gums.

"*Kumusta ka, ina?*" he said in a teasing tone of voice, a tone he might have used if he had seen her once a week all his life. "I am very pleased to see you again. It's good to see you looking so well."

He laughed soundlessly and Aling Saturnina shuddered. She wondered if he had returned to do her harm. She had nothing to defend herself with, not even one of those pictures of the Holy Family which the other old women of the village wore on cords around their necks, not even a bit of ginger pinned to her dress.

"Don't be alarmed, *ina*," Siko continued. "I've forgiven you everything. Even for the fact that you seemed to care more for the *tuba* than for any of your children. Perhaps you couldn't help it. No one wants to be poor. Mud between your toes all your life, *nipa* hut blown down with every typhoon. What a life!"

You bastard, Aling Saturnina thought. Who told you to go and kill that man?

"Let me tell you about that man," Siko went on. "He was rich. You know how it is: after years in the army you become a *padron*. People come to you for special favors, and of course you would not be so stupid as to help without getting anything in return. It's why everyone wants to enter the army in the first place. Take any poor boy from the provinces, give him twenty years in the army, and at the end of that time he ought to have enough to retire comfortably in a mansion—two, if he's any kind of operator."

But you did not have to kill him, Aling Saturnina thought.

It became quiet—so quiet that Aling Saturnina could hear the dogs of the village barking again. Far off she could make out one or two lights against the darkness of the rice paddies. So there were a few people awake. But they would not venture outside on a night like this, not with the dogs warning them away.

Siko was squatting on the ground again, staring morosely at his wounds. He seemed to be remembering something. When he spoke again, his voice was sad:

"You remember *Ate* Lina? Little, snot-nosed Lina who was always falling into a pile of *karabaw* dung when she was young?

Ah, Aling Saturnina thought. Lina.

"You're frowning," Siko continued. "You look uncertain. Perhaps you don't remember? No matter. She'd changed her name so many times. At one time she was *Fleur-de-lis*, a waitress at The Fishnet in Manila. Later, when she became a taxi dancer, she changed her name to 'Pepsi.' Pepsi Perez. When I met her again, last year, she was working the bars in Olongapo. She had gone back to using her own name because it didn't seem to matter to her anymore, what she did. She had a regular customer, this colonel. 'In a little while,' she told me, 'this life will be over for me. I'll be a straight woman.'"

No, Aling Saturnina thought. No, that doesn't sound like Lina.

"Let me tell you, let me tell you, *ina*," Siko said. "The colonel was not the first man I killed. There was another one in Aliaga. But he was only a minor official with the Bureau of Land Transportation. After a few days, the case was closed. His wife and two children lived way out in Cagayan de Oro. What could they do? No one worth anything comes from Cagayan de Oro."

Ah, how evil! Aling Saturnina thought.

"I admit that I felt sorry about that man afterwards," Siko went on. "He was only doing his duty and not even getting rich by it. But this lousy colonel . . ."

Siko paused. His face became momentarily indistinct. Then he said: "I'll tell you how it was. This colonel was a dog, a real dog. I don't know what gutter he crawled out from. I could have killed him when I first saw him touch my sister. But Lina begged me not to. She said she had a plan, that I should be patient. 'One day,' she said, 'we'll come into our own.'

"So I waited. I was patient. Lina became the colonel's mistress. He took her up with him to San Pablo and I did not even try to follow. Now and then, I heard things. I heard that this colonel had a wife, a real shrew. She was used to her husband bringing home girls and she was not fooled when the colonel introduced Lina as his masseuse. Later I heard that she had threatened to go after Lina with a knife. Things were getting bad for Lina, but every time I wanted to go and get her she said, 'Wait.' Well, the day came when she said, 'Come.' And when I saw her again she had a broken nose and bruises all over her chest and back. The colonel had gotten tired of her and stood by while his wife did this to her. She was crying and saying, 'Let's get out of here.' I said, 'Not before getting what's our due.' So that night I went up to the colonel's house. It was a mansion right at the edge of town, with tennis courts in the back and a swimming pool a mile long. You see how these dogs live!

"I had just gotten over the garden wall when—bang!—I heard a shot and part of my right ear flew off. A fat woman with hair all done up in curlers was standing a little way off. I guessed she must be the colonel's wife. She was very angry. 'Get him, you fool!' she kept shouting. I turned and saw the colonel behind me, preparing to shoot again. But he was having trouble—his gun had jammed. I started laughing then, because he was cowering in front of me like a frightened rat. I took his gun and cracked his skull with it. That's when the other one, the one with the curlers, came up behind me with a knife. The next thing I knew, I was lying on the ground, and the last thing I saw before the world went black was the ugly face of the colonel's wife, leering over me."

Siko stopped, took a deep breath, and shuddered. Aling Saturnina moaned and closed her eyes. She was crying. She had not cried for years—not even when her husband had left her, not even when her parents had died, not even when, right after Siko had left, the days of going without *tuba* had left her weak and silly as a child. When she opened her eyes, a few moments later, she was alone. Siko had disappeared.

Aling Saturnina got up slowly. Her legs were stiff. Her back ached. The thought struck her that she was already very old, that she would not have long to live. She hurried back to the village. How long had the dogs been silent? It was dark and peaceful in the little hut she shared with Ana, Poldo, and their two children. In a corner of the one room, a votive candle cast its reddish light on the painting of Christ which Ana had propped up on a table. Garlands of dried flowers hung from the painting's upper corners. Carefully, so as not to wake the sleepers, Aling Saturnina groped her way forward. Kneeling before the makeshift altar, Aling Saturnina gazed long and hard at the face, so foreign in its whiteness, staring back at her. The nose was long and sharp, the lips thin and straight. The long, brown hair fell in fantastic curls past the white-robed shoulders. Aling Saturnina clasped her hands. She wanted to pray for Siko and Lina, and for the rest of her children, who she imagined must be suffering, just as Siko and Lina had suffered.

"Ama namin," she prayed. *"Ama namin . . . "*

But that was as far as she went, for she had forgotten the rest of the words to the Lord's Prayer. She gazed, helpless and mute, at the painting before her. Ah, she was unworthy, she had not been taught the proper words with which to couch her requests. For a little donation, perhaps the priest in San Pablo could be induced to say a mass for her children. How had she dared to raise her voice to God—she, who had proven to be such an unfit mother! For such impertinence she should be struck by lightning! She cowered for a few moments before the amiable glance of the Christ in the painting, filled with remorse.

Slowly, before she realized it, her eyelids began to droop. Then she gave a tired sigh and her shoulders sagged. Aling Saturnina was fast asleep.

Early the next morning, a cloud of dust could be seen travelling at high speed down the narrow road that led to the village. The cloud would stop suddenly before a particularly deep pothole, the dust would subside, and the outlines of an army jeep could be briefly seen before being swallowed up again in a fresh cloud of dust. Just before the village, the jeep stopped, and four men in tight-fitting military uniforms stepped out. The villagers remained in their homes, peering watchfully from the windows. The four men paused at the first house they came to, the home of *Mang* Tomas. After briefly stopping to ask for directions, they continued down the street until they arrived at the house of Aling Saturnina. One of the men approached the ladder leading up to the house. The other three remained standing near the road. Before the man near the ladder could ascend, Aling Saturnina's face, stiff with suspicion, appeared at a window.

"What do you want?" she said.

"Are you the mother of Francisco Dawang?" the man by the ladder inquired.

"I have no son by that name," Aling Saturnina said angrily, and made to shut the window.

"Wait, *Ale*! Don't be so impatient. We know that Francisco Dawang, also known as Siko, was indeed your son. We just need you to answer a few questions."

"I have not seen Siko in over 10 years," Aling Saturnina said. "And I curse the day I bore him."

"He was shot breaking into someone's house last night in San Pablo. We have another one of your children, Lina, in the jail. Won't you please come along quietly now?"

At the mention of Lina's name, Aling Saturnina seemed to waver. She disappeared from the window a moment and the men could hear her speaking to someone inside the house. Finally she reappeared at the door, tying a worn bandanna around her head.

"All right," she said. "I'll come. But I have to be back by nightfall, you hear?"

"Of course, *Ale*," one of the men said. "It's only a formality."

They tried to help her down the stairs, but she waved them away angrily. Then she walked quickly away from the house, not bothering to glance at any of the neighbors, who were peering from their windows.

When they had almost reached the jeep, they heard a voice calling, "Wait! Wait!" They all turned and looked. It was Ana, running down the road with her youngest child balanced on her hip.

"I'm coming, too!" Ana cried. "I can't let my mother go alone."

"*Stupida!*" Aling Saturnina shouted. "Go home and wait for Poldo to get back from the fields."

Ana paused only long enough to hand her child to the astonished wife of Mang Tomas, who had been watching from her front gate.

"*Ale*, tell Poldo I've accompanied *ina* to town. Tell him not to worry about me, I'll be back this evening."

Aling Saturnina continued to protest. "Idiot!" she berated her daughter. "You'd leave your own children!"

"Quiet!" one of the soldiers said. "We'll bring her along, too."

Aling Saturnina grew dazed and silent. She and Ana got into the jeep, the engine roared to life, the soldiers leaped in, and soon they were far away, soon there was nothing to see along the narrow road but the dust steaming up from the potholes. It was quiet in the village again. *Mang* Tomas's wife cradled Ana's baby in her arms. "Shush, shush," she whispered, for it was crying.

The next morning, when Aling Saturnina and Ana had still not returned, Poldo went into town to make inquiries. That night he returned alone, looking like a much older man than the one who had set out in the morning. He had been directed to various military offices, and at each one he had been told that the two had been turned over to the National Bureau of Investigation "for further questioning." The time for harvesting rice came and went, and still Aling Saturnina and her daughter did not return.

Poldo and his two children live alone now in the house behind the *santol* tree. The children, seven and four, are very thin and are always crying for their mother. Poldo continues to go into town to make inquiries, but his trips are becoming more infrequent.

Poldo himself is gaunt and quiet, not at all like his former self. The villagers can remember a time when he could plant more rice saplings in a day than any other man in the village. Now they look sadly at him as he toils alone in the fields and note how, when he presses against the heavy wooden plow, his ribs create ridges on his chest and back. He is too thin, almost tubercular. Who will take care of his children if he goes?

In the meanwhile, Siko's ghost continues to roam the village. Several times the villagers have begged the parish priest from San Pablo to come and exorcise him, but each time the parish priest replies that he is too busy. The ghost can sometimes be seen dancing across the rice paddies on nights when there is a full moon, or sitting on the roof of someone's house, glaring with reddish eyes. In the beginning, the villagers tried to chase him away with holy water and crucifixes. He would disappear for a few days and then return. Now they merely shrug their shoulders. He has been absorbed into the pattern of their everyday existence. He is as familiar to them now as the air they breathe or the water they drink. They tell their children that he is a *tikbalang*, a creature half monkey and half man, who swings from the branches of trees and makes his home in the forest. They avert their eyes from the shadows when walking alone at night. They have learned to live with the ghost, as they have learned to live with everything else, as they have learned to smile, to shrug, when pigs or chickens disappear, saying only, "It is Siko."

MARIANNE VILLANUEVA

"Ta' malu!"

Mei Sim wriggled at her mother's words.

"You no shame! Close your legs."

Mother was standing five steps below the landing, the soft straw broom in one hand and her head on a level with Mei Sim's shoulders.

Mei Sim stared down at her legs, which she had spread apart the better to balance her body, as she half-lay on the smooth wooden landing and thought her thoughts to herself.

Up came the broom and thumped against her knees. She pulled them together and tugged at her short skirt.

"What you do here all day? Go ask Ah Kim to give you a bath." Her mother's round pretty face was troubled. She had had a perm just last week, and the fat curls sat like waxed waves over her brow, wrinkled with vexation. "We're going to visit Tua Ee. And don't sit with your legs open there. She think I bring you up with no shame."

"Ya, ma." Mei Sim sidled past her mother's solid body down the stairs, glad for something to do. Every day was a problem for her until her brothers came home from school at three when they would shout at her to go away but could still be persuaded to give her a piggy-back ride or to let her hold their legs in a wheel-barrow run. The house was empty and dull until then, containing only chairs, tables, beds, cupboards, photographs and such like, but no one to play with.

Ah Kim was scrubbing her brother's uniform on the ridged washboard. Drub, drub, drub, slosh, slosh. Mei Sim squatted beside her. Ah Kim's stool was only a few inches high and she had her legs thrust straight in front with the wooden board held firmly between. Her *samfoo* sleeves were rolled up high and the pale arms were wet and soapy up to the elbows. Taking the chunk of yellow laundry soap in her right hand, Ah Kim scrubbed it over a soiled collar. Then, seizing the collar in a fist, she pushed the cloth vigorously up and down the ridges. Her knuckles were red and swollen, but her face was peaceful. "You wait," she said, not turning away from the washboard. "I wash you next."

Bath-time was directly under the tall tap in the corner of the open-roofed bathroom. Mei Sim was just short enough to stand under the full flow of water pouring in a steady stream from the greenish brass tap while Ah Kim scrubbed her chest, legs and armpits with LifeBuoy. She was six and soon would be too tall for this manoeuvre. Soon, Ah Kim said, she would have to bathe herself with scoops of water from the clay jar in the other corner of the bathroom. Dodging in and out of the water, Mei Sim thought she would not like to have to work at her bath.

Mother dressed her in her New Year's party frock, an organdy material of pink and purple tuberoses with frills down the bib and four stiff layers gathered in descending tiers for a skirt. She picked a red and green plaid ribbon which Ah Kim threaded through her plaits and, her face and neck powdered with Johnson Talc, she waited for the trishaw, pleased with herself and her appearance.

Mother had put on her gold bangles, gold earrings, and a long heavy chain of platinum with a cross as a pendant. Her *kebaya* was a pale blue, starched and ironed to a gleaming transparency under which her white lace chemise showed clearly. Gold and diamond *kerosang* pinned the *kebaya* tightly together, and the brown-gold sarong was wrapped tightly around her plump hips and stomach. She had to hitch herself up onto the trishaw and, once seated, carefully smoothed the sarong over her knees. When Mei Sim climbed in, Mother gave her a push to keep her from crushing her sarong.

Grand-aunty's house was all the way in Klebang. Usually father took them there for visits in the evening after their meal. It was enough of a long way off for Mei Sim to always fall asleep in the car before they reached home.

The trishaw man pedalled vigorously for the first part, ringing his bell smartly at slow crossing pedestrians and hardly pausing to look before turning a corner into another narrow road. At Tranquerah he began to slow down. There was much less motor traffic, a few bicycles, and now and again a hawker's cart got in his way. Mei Sim watched his brown legs pedal up and down. Green snaky veins zig-zagged up his calves. His shaven coconut-round head was dripping with sweat. He didn't stop to wipe it, so the sweat ran down his forehead and got into his eyes, which were deep-set and empty, staring vaguely down the long road.

Mei Sim grew bored with watching the trishaw man pump the pedals after a while. She leaned forward to stare at the houses on both sides of the road. What interesting things to see that she had missed on their evening car rides! Here was a small stall with bottles of *chinchaloh* and *blachan* neatly mounded on shelves. She glimpsed through an open door a red and gold altar cloth and bowls of oranges and apples before a dim sepia portrait. Two *neneks* in shabby sarong and *kebaya* sat on a long bench by the covered front of another house. Each woman had a leg pulled up under her sarong, like one-legged idols set for worship. Here was a pushcart with a tall dark *mamak* frying red-brown noodles in a heavy *kwali*. How good it smelled. Mei Sim's stomach gave a little grumble.

Now they were passing the Baptist Gospel Hall where on Sunday evenings she had seen many people standing in rows singing sweetly. In the morning glare the shuttered windows were peeling paint and a crack showed clearly on the closed front door which had a huge chain and lock on it.

"*Hoy!*" the trishaw man shouted. The wheels swerved suddenly and bumped over something uneven. Mei Sim hadn't seen anything.

Her mother gripped her arm and said aloud, "You *bodoh*. Almost fall off the trishaw. Sit inside all the way."

"What was that, *ma'*?"

"A puppy dog."

She turned her head to peer behind but the canvas flaps were down.

The trishaw man was talking to himself in Hokkien. A small trail of saliva was trickling down the side of his mouth. Mei Sim could only hear mumbles like "*hey . . . yau soo . . . chei. . . .*"

"What is he saying, *ma'*?" she whispered, alarmed.

"Never mind what he say. He angry at puppy dog, bring him bad luck."

Mei Sim looked at the bare brown legs again. They were moving much more slowly and the mumbles continued, sometimes louder, sometimes quieting to a slippery whisper. Her mother didn't seem to mind the trishaw's pace or the man's crazy talk. She had been frowning to herself all this time and turning the three thick bangles round and round her right wrist. Her agitated motions made a gentle jingle as the bangles fell against each other, like chimes accompanying the slow movements of the trishaw pedals.

They were on a deserted stretch of Klebang before the sandy rutted path on the left that led to Grand-aunty's house and the shallow sloping beach facing the Malacca Straits. Wood-planked shacks roofed with rusty galvanized iron alternated with common lots on which grew a wild profusion of morning glory, *lallang*, mimosa and sea-grape. A few coconut and areca palms leaned in jumbled lines away from the hot tarmac. The sky was a blinding blue, barren of clouds, and arching in a vast depth of heat under which the dripping trishaw man mumbled and cursed. The bicycle lurched forward and the attached carriage, on which Mei Sim crouched as if to make herself lighter, moved forward with it jerkily.

"*Aiyah! Sini boleh,*" her mother said sharply, and almost at the same moment the man's legs stopped and dangled over the wheels. She pushed Mei Sim off the sticky plastic seat and stepped down carefully so as not to disarrange the elaborately folded pleats of her skirt.

The man had finally taken a ragged face towel from his pocket and was mopping his face without looking at them. Mrs. Chung clicked the metal snap of her black handbag, zipped open an inner compartment, extracted a beaded purse from it, unbuttoned a flap and counted some coins which she clinked impatiently in one hand, waiting for the man to take the change. Pouring the different coins into his calloused palm, she walked up the path without a word. Mei Sim stood for a moment watching him count the coins, then, at her mother's annoyed call, ran up the narrow lane just wide enough for a car to go through.

Waddling ahead of her, her mother was singing out, "Tua Ee, Tua Ee." A wooden fence, newly whitewashed, separated Grand-aunty's house from the lane which suddenly petered out into a littered common compound shared with some Malay houses on low stilts. Beneath the houses and through the spaces between the concrete blocks on which the wood stilts were anchored, Mei Sim could see the grey coarse sand grading to a chalky white for yards ahead clumped by tough beach grass and outlined at stages by the dark, uneven markings of tidal remains, broken driftwood, crab shells, splinters of glass, red-rust cans, and black hair of seaweed.

Grand-aunty came out through the gap in the fence in a flurry of *kebaya* lace. Her gleaming hair was coiffed in a twist, and a long, gold pin sat on top of her head, like the nail on the fearsome *pontianak*, Mei Sim thought.

"What's this?" she said in fluent Malay. "Why are you here so early without informing me? You must stay for lunch. I have told that prostitute daughter of mine to boil the rice already, so we have to cook another pot."

Grand-aunty had four sons, of whom she loved only the youngest, and a daughter whom she treated as a bought slave. She was not a woman for young girls and showed Mei Sim no attention, but she tolerated Jeng Chung as the niece whose successful marriage to a rich *towkay's* son she had arranged ten years before.

Mei Sim's mother visited her at least once a week with gifts of fruits, *pulot* and *ang-pows,* and consulted her on every matter in the Chung family's life. At six, Mei Sim was allowed to listen to all their discussions; she was, after all, too young to understand.

It was in this way she learned what men liked their women to do in bed, how babies were made and how awful giving birth was. She knew the fluctuations in the price of gold and what herbs to boil and drink to protect oneself from colds, rheumatism, overheat, smallpox, diarrhea, or female exhaustion.

It was in this way she found out that women were different from men who were *bodoh* and had to be trained to be what women wanted them to be, like *kerbau* hitched to their carts.

This morning she settled on the kitchen bench behind the cane chairs on which her mother and grand-aunt were sitting close to each other sharing the *sireh* box between them, chatting and scolding in Malay and snatches of English, and she listened and listened without saying a word to remind them of her presence.

". . . and Bee Lian saw Hin at the cloth shop . . . she told me he's been going there every afternoon when he's supposed to be at the bank . . . that slut is probably taking all his money but I haven't said a word to him. I thought maybe you can help me; what should I say to him. Oh, that swine, useless good-for-nothing. I scratch his eyes out / better still if take a knife and cut her heart. These men always walking with legs apart / what does he want from me / three children not enough / but she is a bitch / otherwise why would he even look at her—black as a Tamil and hairy all over her / I keep myself clean and sweet-smelling / a wife he can be proud of / so itchified / never enough, always wanting more, more / that's why now he won't give me more money / say business bad / ha! bad / we know what's bad / I'll get some poison and put it in her food / and all my friends talking behind my back / she's making a fool out of me but what can I do / I tell them better than a second wife / not even a mistress / just loose woman smelling like a bitch any man can take, so why not my Peng Ho."

It was Father Mother was complaining about! Mei Sim scrubbed her ears hard to clear them of wax, but quick tears had risen and clogged her nostrils, so her ears were filled with a thick air of sorrow. She knew all about second wives. Hadn't Second Uncle left his family to live in Ipoh because their Cantonese servant bewitched him, and now he has three boys with her and Second Aunty is always coming to their house to borrow money and to beg for the clothes they've outgrown for her own children? And little Gek Yeo's mother had gone mad because her father had taken another wife, and she is now in Tanjong Rambutan where Mother says she screams and tears her clothes off and has no hair left. Poor Gek Yeo had to go to her grandmother's house and her grandmother refuses to let her see her father.

Mei Sim wiped her nose on the gathered puff sleeve of her dress. Grand-aunty had risen from her chair and was shaking the folds of her thickly flowered sarong. Her Malay speech was loud and decisive. "All this scolding will do you no good. Men are all alike, itchy and hot. You cannot stop him by showing a dirty face or talking bad all the time. You will drive him away. The only thing women have is their cunning. You must think hard. What do you want, a faithful man or a man who will support you and your children? Why should you care if he plays around with this or that woman? Better for you, he won't ask so much from you in bed. No, you must be as sweet to him as when you were first courting. Talk to him sweet-sweet every time he comes home late. This will make him feel guilty, and he will be nicer to you. Make him open the purse strings. Tell him you need money for prayers at Hoon Temple to bring luck to his business. He will appreciate you for your efforts. Some men have to be bullied, like your grand uncle, but . . ."

She stopped to take a breath, and Siew Eng, her skinny dark daughter crept up beside and whispered, *"Na' makan, 'ma'?"*

"Sundal!" Grand-aunty shouted, and slapped her sharply on her thin bare arm. "Who asked you to startle me? You know how bad my heart is. You want me to die?"

Siew Eng hung her head. Her *samfoo* was faded and worn at the trouser bottoms, and the thin cotton print didn't hide her strange absence of breasts. She was already sixteen, had never been sent to school but had worked at home washing, cleaning and cooking since she was seven. All her strength seemed to have gone into her work, because her body itself was emaciated, her smile frail, and her face peaked and shrivelled like a *chiku* picked before its season and incapable of ripening, drying up to a small brown hardness.

Mei Sim had never heard her cousin laugh, had never seen her eat at the table. She served the food, cleaned the kitchen and ate standing up by the wood stove when everyone had finished.

Mother said Siew Eng was cursed. The fortune teller had told Grand-aunty after her birth that the girl would eat her blood, so she wouldn't nurse or hold the baby, had sent her to a foster mother and taken her back at seven to send her to the kitchen where she slept on a camp bed. Mei Sim was glad she wasn't cursed! Her father loved her best, and Mother bought her the prettiest dresses and even let her use her lipstick.

"Now your uncle . . ." Grand-aunty stopped and her face reddened. "What are you waiting for, you stupid girl? Go serve the rice. We are coming to the table right away. Make sure there are no flies on the food."

Her daughter's scrawny chest seemed to shiver under the loose blouse.

"Ya. 'mak," she mumbled and slipped off silently to the kitchen.

"Come, let's eat. I have *sambal blachan* just the way you like it, with sweet lime. The soy pork is fresh, steaming all morning and delicious."

Grand-aunty gobbled the heap of hot white rice which was served on her best blue china plates. She talked as she ate, pinching balls of rice flavoured with chilies and soy with her right hand and throwing the balls into her large wet mouth with a flick of her wrist and thumb. Mother ate more slowly, unaccustomed to manipulating such hot rice with her hand, while Mei Sim used a soup spoon on her tin plate.

"Your uncle," Grand-aunty said in between swallows of food and water, "is a timid man, a mouse. I used to think how to get male children with a man like that! I had to put fire into him, everyday must push him. Otherwise he cannot be a man."

"Huh, huh," Mother said, picking a succulent piece of the stewed pork and popping it into her mouth whole.

"But Peng Ho, he is an educated man, and he cannot be pushed. You must lead him gently, gently so he doesn't know what you are doing. Three children, you cannot expect him to stay by your side all the time. Let him have fun."

"Wha . . ." Mother said, chewing the meat hard.

"Yes. We women must accept our fate. If we want to have some fun also, stomach will explode. Where can we hide our shame? But men, they think they are *datoks* because they can do things without being punished. But we must control them, and to do that we must control their money."

Mei Sim thought Grand-aunty was very experienced. She was so old, yet her hair was still black, and her sons and husband did everything she told them. She was rich; the knitted purse looped to her string belt under her *kebaya* was always bulging with money. Father had to borrow money from her once when some people didn't pay for his goods, and she charged him a lot for it. He still complained about it to Mother each time they drove home from Grand-aunty's house.

"But how?" protested Mother, a faint gleam of sweat appearing on her forehead and upper lip as she ate more and more of the pork.

Grand-aunty began to whisper and Mei Sim didn't dare ask her to speak up nor could she move from her seat for she hadn't finished her lunch.

Mother kept nodding and nodding her head. She was no longer interested in the food but continued to put it in her mouth without paying any attention to it until her plate was clear. "*Yah, yah. Huh huh. Yah, yah,*" she repeated like a trance-medium, while Grand-aunty talked softly about accounts and ton-tins and rubber lands in Jasin. Mei Sim burped and began to feel sleepy.

"Eng!" Grand-aunty called harshly. "Clear up the table you lazy girl. Sleeping in the kitchen, nothing to do. Come here."

Siew Eng walked slowly towards her mother, pulling at her blouse nervously.

"Come here quickly, I say." Grand-aunty's mouth was drib' 'ing with saliva. She appeared enraged, her fleshy nose quivering under nai.owed eyes. As Siew Eng stood quietly beside her chair, she took the sparse flesh above her elbow between thumb and forefinger and twisted it viciously, breathing hard. A purple bruise bloomed on the arm. "I'll punish you for walking so slowly when I call you," she huffed. "You think you can be so proud in my house."

Siew Eng said nothing. A slight twitch of her mouth quickly pressed down was the only sign that the pinch had hurt.

"What do you say? What do you say, you prostitute?" Grand-aunty raised her handsome head and yelled, spraying saliva around her.

"Sorry, *'mak*," Siew Eng whispered, hanging her head lower and twisting the cloth of her blouse.

Only then did Grand-aunty get up from the table. The two women returned to the chairs beside the *sireh* table, where two neat green packages of *sireh* rested. Sighing happily, Grand-aunty put the large wad in her mouth and began to chew. Mother followed suit, but she had a harder time with the generous size of the *sireh* and had to keep pushing it in her mouth as parts popped out from the corners.

Mei Sim sat on her stool, but her head was growing heavier, her eyes kept dropping as if they wanted to fall to the floor. She could hear the women chewing and grunting; it seemed as if she could feel the bitter green leaves tearing in her own mouth and dissolving with the tart lime and sharp crunchy betel nut and sweet-smelling cinnamon. Her mouth was dissolving into an aromatic dream when she heard chimes ringing sharply in the heavy noon air.

For the briefest moment Mei Sim saw her father smiling beside her, one hand in his pocket jingling the loose change, and the other hand gently steering an ice cream bicycle from whose opened ice box delicious vapours were floating. "Vanilla!" she heard herself cry out, at the same moment that Grand-aunty called out, *"Aiyoh!* What you want?" and she woke up.

A very dark man with close-cropped hair was carefully leaning an old bicycle against the open door jamb. Two shiny brown hens, legs tied with rope and hanging upside down by the bicycle handles blinked nervously, and standing shyly behind the man was an equally dark and shiny boy dressed in starched white shirt and pressed khaki shorts.

"'*Nya*," the man said respectfully, bowing a little and scraping his rubber thongs on the cement floor as if to ask permission to come in.

"*Aiyah*, Uncle Muti, *apa buat*? You come for business or just for visit?"

"*Ha*, I bring two hens. My wife say must give to *puan*, this year we have many chickens."

"Also, you bring the rent?" Grand-aunty was smiling broadly, the *sireh* tucked to one side of her mouth like a girlish pucker. "Come, come and sit down. Eng, Eng!" Her voice raised to a shriek till Eng came running from behind the garden. "Bring tea for Uncle Muti. Also, take the hens into the kitchen. Stupid girl! Must tell you everything."

The boy stayed by the bicycle staring at the women inside with bright frank eyes.

Curious, Mei Sim went out. He was clean, his hair still wet from a bath. "What school you?" she asked. He was older, she knew, because he was in a school uniform.

He gave her a blank stare.

"You speak English?" she asked.

He nodded.

"You want to play a game?" She ran out into the compound, motioning for him to follow.

Mei Sim had no idea what she wanted to play, but she was oh so tired of sitting still, and the white sand and brown seanuts and blue flowers on the leafy green creepers on the fence seemed so delicious after the crunch, crunch, crunch of Grand-aunty's lunch that she spread her arms and flew through the sky. "Whee, whee," she laughed.

But the boy wouldn't play. He stood by the sweet smelling *tanjong bunga* and stared at her.

"What you stare at?" she asked huffily. "Something wrong with me?"

"Your dress," he answered without the least bit of annoyance.

"What to stare?" Mei Sim was suddenly uncomfortable and bent down to look for snails.

"So pretty. *Macham bungah*."

She looked up quickly to see if he was making fun of her, but his brown round face was earnestly staring at the tiers of ruffles on her skirt.

"Want to play a game?" she asked again.

But he said, "My sister no got such nice dress."

Mei Sim laughed. "You *orang jakun*," she said, "but never mind. You want to feel my dress? Go on. I never mind."

He went nearer to her and stretched out his hand. He clutched at the frills around the bib, staring at the pink and purple tuberoses painted on the thin organdy.

"Mei Si-i-m!" Her mother's voice brayed across the compound. There was a confusion as the boy rushed away and the woman came running, panting in the sun, and pulled at her arm. "What you do? Why you let the boy touch you? You no shame?"

Grand-aunty stood by the door, while the dark man had seized his son by the shoulder and was talking to him in furious low tones.

Mei Sim felt tears in her mouth, and wondered why she was crying, why her mother was shaking her. Then she saw the man pushing his rusty old Raleigh through the gate, without the hens, still holding the boy by his shoulder. She saw the look of hate which the boy threw at her, and suddenly she felt a hot pain in her chest as if she knew why he must hate her. A huge shame filled her and she was just about to burst into noisy weeping when she saw her mother's red, red eyes. "He did it, he pulled at my dress," she screamed, stretching her body straight as an arrow, confronting her lie.

SHIRLEY GEOK-LIN LIM

AFTER DELIVERING YOUR LUNCH

Empty-handed, I return home
along the same path above the Kamo's west bank.
I am trying to whistle, that sort of day.
Today the nurse will try feeding you,
her chopsticks efficient, insistent;
you will clench your face, swallow.
This last week I have watched every mouthful
feed the bandage thickening around your neck.

I stop to choose three persimmon leaves,
slide them into a breast pocket, walk
past the steps descending to river
to where the crooked limb of the middle-aged pine,
like the entrance to a tea room, asks everyone to bend.
This time before I duck I clasp
the rough bark to my cheek, lean into wind.

The leaves, one red, two yellow,
garnish a Kutani plate I brought you from summer one year.
I arrange the fish on them, three bites
now twelve translucent morsels you can swallow.
A cobalt-brushed porcelain dish holds five young spinach leaves,
boiled to peak color in salted water, chopped fine, mounded.
I add six drops of soy sauce.
Into a bowl smaller than your cupped hand
I slip a cube of tofu;
into a second, muskmelon ripe to melting,
the softest, juiciest bits.
I think I know just how little you will eat, how few
times I can watch you swallow.
Tonight, in the shopping bag I delivered your lunch in,
dishes will rattle as I carry your leftovers home in a cab.

LYNNE YAMAGUCHI FLETCHER

HIGASHIYAMA CREMATORIUM, NOVEMBER 16, 1983

We are called.
Eight of us, two taxis' worth.
We follow the director,
tuxedoed as for a banquet,
through heavy glass doors
briefly into fall.
A maple leaf
withered to a brown fist
skitters across the walk.
We are gabardine, thick-haired, tailored.
Black becomes us.

Through a steel door,
a chamber like a bank vault.
You are not here.
Chunks of chalk
parody your form.
At one end of the cart
rice-straw sandals
put on you for your journey
lie, kicked off,
charcoal but whole.
Only these.
I lift your hip, ilium, left.
It smells like eggshell.
Your bones cluck and shift coolly.
We whisper.
This is not our show.

The director speaks,
his tone combed back like his hair.
To honor Buddha.
Kokugo.
I understand.
Before the altar in the corner,
he pulls on white gloves,
lifts chopsticks,

balances a tray on his left hand.
Maitre d', he selects daintily, reciting:
Nodobotoke, throat Buddha, *meditating*.
Atlas, a ring, karmic circle.
From the skull—collapsed by heat,
the fragments snap neatly;
coccyx, index finger, tarsal.
His tray fills.

The urn.
Stark porcelain, scalp-white by your bones,
molded, mechanical.
You would not have considered it.
In turn we fill it, a bone each.
I am third.
I lift your finger,
close my lips.
The chopsticks weigh more.
Tomorrow I will crop my hair.

LYNNE YAMAGUCHI FLETCHER

Kokugo: "national language." What the Japanese call their own language among themselves, believing no foreigner can ever truly master it.

THE WAY APRIL LEADS TO AUTUMN

Kiss me.

Even in your own tongue the words would have been foreign.
You weren't laughing.
I couldn't see your eyes behind your bottle-thick lenses
but joy hung in your voice
ruddy as a ripe peach
a breeze could pluck.
Your cheek smelled of sun-dried flannel and
I blushed,
bashful as a new lover
in a wrinkled nightgown.
A window opened.
I kissed you again.

Your death has withered my shyness.
Your lips are softer than your cheek,
your forehead polished, salty.
Your hands kiss me back.
I stop one kiss short of comfort.

LYNNE YAMAGUCHI FLETCHER

ON BEING IN THE MIDWEST

Don't you feel it's like being in the midst of a long novel?
Have I ever known anything about beginnings and endings?

Or is what I feel like marriage
with precariousness receding in a rear-view mirror?

Where was it I once steadied myself for sudden dawnings
and the earth could collapse like a cape?

I try out my thoughts in order to understand:
If I go far in any direction
would I find I have remained?
There must be ways to leave oneself behind

This is experience where light is broad
and daybreak and dusk support one like land

I remember how the edge takes the body away
and burning water puts out the sun

and seas begin to travel
in silver shaken out,
stars scattering,
shores moved by hungry weather

Here, parole has been revoked
and this, with me in its tidelessness,

has come down with an even breathing of massed secrets

DIANA CHANG

ON THE FLY

You reconnoiter. Following, I swat and sulk.
You're in my hair.

Go, go!
You lay causeways through the air,
return to touch my wrist,

rise on your smile.

Now where are you?
I search bare lanes,
hold out honey.

We while away the night.
My knee, my cheek
exist because of you.
You bank through my arms.
As though in love, I career after you.

Again, I tear you out of my hair.
Wings akimbo, you bite hard.
This—my live-in—is a falling out.

At last I know to throw open windows.
Either you will or won't
. . . stay.

The cup we shared is filled with moonlight.
As at an amphitheater
when the music was new,
I sat like you rubbing your hands—
so much to relish together.

Is the silence now saying
you were staking only air?

You took up no room, really,
now high, then there.

Largeness now
has me residing

unkissed
unsettled

no longer flying

and nowhere

DIANA CHANG

ZHOUKOUDIAN BRIDE'S HARVEST

Greeting you on the street that day
In May, my heart leaped and quartered.
Now, with you in Beijing and I
Here in Oakland, my head demands proof
Of what I'll name as Love that moment.

If you have a wife, *mei guanxi*.
My disorderly thinking shames me.
In the sun's light, I see you/
Face, in the moon's light, also.

All my life, I train and work
Honoring the Five Relationships, yet
At this hour, I know the me—
Nightsoil, pandering fields, convinced
A yield is as good as gods permit.

If *xiang* means the heart of eye
Looking through trees;
The head attached to shoulders,
And also, under feet, that day
In pink-cheeked springtime sun,
I felt the Fragrance of Antiquity:
The face of a man flying with his head
In thought. While a whole body
Of woman reached out. Almost
Touching you.

Now, in Oakland, under winter's mist,
I imagine you, face, floating through seasons.
Each time, different tones. Once,
A caged bird/tiger.
As usual, with earth requiring water.

For a man who digs and studies teeth and bones,
What do you notice in a woman
Who smells in tortoise shells and shoulder bones of sheep
A fragrance and re-names species?

With light abundant on our bodies,
Wind and water flowing calmly,
Capable of invigorating *xiang* instead of *xiang*,
Xiansheng, just what do you propose?

CAROLYN LAU

Zhoukoudian: Beijing Man
Xiang: Resemblance: a flock of pigs marching: an elephant

CURRENTS

Each night a dark river flows over the edge
of your heart, its hard current
pulling you toward the pain at the end
of your dream. If I could,
I would give you fins, a streamlined body,
scales or a pair of gills, whatever
would help you swim back up that long rush
of water, home again.
I would walk along the river,
watch your shadow slide between rocks
that rake the water,
your gills filtering fragments of air.
Bright as coins, your scales would flash
in the chilled light.
Upstream is where I would wait.

But tonight, you ask only for quiet
in the curve of my arms, a space too small
for anything but breathing.
It is all I can give you.
Love's swift current roars
past me in the dark as you sleep.

TINA KOYAMA

DOWNTOWN SEATTLE IN THE FOG

All day, I wear a grey disguise that buttons
over half-toned dreams, and even scarves in my pocket
can't assert themselves better than my shoes.
They tick under me like a morning metronome,
but where is the time they keep? I steal time
at night and feel cheated when I dream without color:
Last night, the man I used to love
wore a cream-colored shirt as he does in real-life,
but my dress, the shade of distant fuchsias,
appeared as grey as this. Sometimes in dreams,
I don't remember red or how I got there.
Sometimes I write letters in red as if pages
need corrections even when they're white.
My breath is white today; it leads me
into morning better than my shoes,
for shoes sound red even when they're grey,
making check marks in the soft, fall air.

TINA KOYAMA

ON SUCH A DAY

When my heart becomes heavy with acute pain of life,
I'd rather be a plain stone in the field.
On such a day,
I'd pay a visit to a rocky field near the river.

When my feet ache and are weary from life's long journey,
Willfully
I'd put broken pieces of a stone together.
There and then
My searing heartache for life images
The sorrowful shape of a shattered stone.

In such time of trial when night descends gently,
My heart is clouded with unspoken sadness.
And I become a stone
That coughs out blood of sheer loneliness.
The art of opening up my heart wholly,
The art of sharing myself unconditionally,
I know nothing of such.
On such a day,
I become a stone bathed in the vast bed of
The long river that flows timelessly.

SONG-JOOK PARK
Translated by *HYUN-JAE YEE SALLEE*

UNTITLED

In the deepest night and a full moon,
at once riding the flying mare and being her
my own pumping broad wings, ascending higher—

My legs around that great horse's neck
not riding
but my body singing down under
in front of the beautiful dark head
feeling her moist tongue in my center—

I am risking my life for these moments,
My head possibly dashed against the rocks.

Now riding with our rhythms matching,
the exertion of her back's muscles and
the mounting pulsations between my thighs—

Higher and soaring through mist and above mountains
shaped like jagged spires
the cold thin air ripping through my lungs—

We finish.
And you lay your head on my thigh,
your wings enfolding my legs, and we rest.

MERLE WOO

WHENEVER YOU'RE CORNERED, THE ONLY WAY OUT IS TO FIGHT

Karen, comrade and sister poet, sends me this news article
about a woman warrior.
She includes a note that says:
    "We've got her philosophy and her strength, too.
    We'll get them all by the ears and let them have it."

The article is one I've been wanting
to slip into speeches, talks, poems, conversations.
The images we get from reality—
Those fighting-back images in the face of great adversity.

I saw another news article of the Voting Rights marchers.
Their banner, red, black and green—for Black liberation,
carried by Carrie Graves of Richmond, VA—mother of five teenagers.
Carrie says:
    "My arms are tired, my feet have blisters,
    but I'm fired up!"

So, what is *this* article?
The reporter must have loved writing it, the way it came out:

Beijing

A crippled grandmother caught a leopard by the ears, dragged it to
the ground and then helped kill it with her bare hands, official reports
said Tuesday.

Qi Deying, who can barely walk because her feet were bound from
birth, was gathering herbs with her niece and grandchildren on a mountain
in North China's Shaanxi Province when the six-foot leopard attacked her
and sank his teeth into her arm.

But the animal soon realized he had bitten off more than he could
chew.

The 77-year-old Qi grabbed the leopard by the ears, wedged its jaw
shut with her right shoulder and forced it to the ground, the Shaanxi
Daily said.

Their bodies locked in combat, the grandmother and the leopard
rolled more than 120 feet down the mountainside, bouncing off rocks

before coming to rest in a wheatfield.

Qi called out to her grandchildren, who were hiding behind a boulder, to come to her aid. They tore branches off a tree and helped her beat the animal to death.

Qi, only bruised, told the paper: "Whenever you're cornered, the only way out is to fight."

MERLE WOO

Manning the Shroud   PATTI WARASHINA
porcelain, low fire and mixed media
41" x 14" x 18" wide x 20" deep
photo by John Reich

I am interested in surrealism and stream of consciousness. I like to think of my art work as a visual journal of my life—they say art shouldn't be therapeutic but I do use my art

A Procession (detail)   *porcelain*   PATTI WARASHINA
10' long
photo by Roger Schreiber

to express my feelings and emotions. You cannot judge artists when they're still living, so we have to seek our own vision and play out that vision in our own time.

Cactus Heart	*clay, acrylics, sand*	JUDY HIRAMOTO
	18" x 15" x 15"	

"Magical realism" best describes my ceramic sculpture. They are real because they are concrete representations. And they are "magical" because they embody spirits from states of ecstasy and dreams. They evoke the mystery so prevalent in Bhutan, Bolivia, Bali, and even the Bay Area, if one knows where to look. . . . My sculptures are human-size . . .

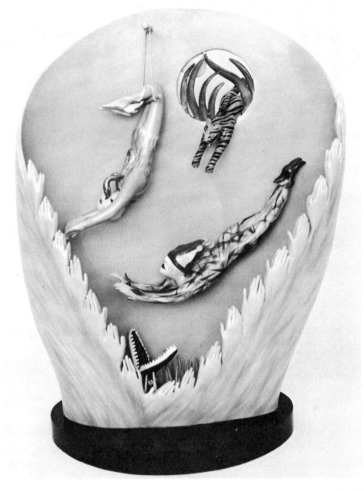

Fool's Play   *clay, acrylics, wood*   JUDY HIRAMOTO
22" x 15" x 8"

They are my shrines containing the essence of special people and places, the painful and exhilarating in life. These shrines are also milestones—they are memories frozen in stone of where I have been, and sometimes, even where I will go.

Desert   *glazed ceramics*   *JUDY HIRAMOTO*
                            16" x 24" x 9"

Piano Solo   *collage*   JUDY HIRAMOTO
                              11¼" x 12¼"

The collages were made while living in Tokyo. I feel they are an expression of the multi-cultural ambience which reflects contemporary Japan as well as my own lifestyle that has led me to travel in forty countries.

Fish Jumping   *glazed clay*   CAROL MATSUYOSHI
12½" x 5¼" x 8½"
photo by David L. Brown

Intuition is an essential part of my work. I usually do not have a plan but go with the flow. Handbuilding gives me the freedom to do this.

Ring of Forgotten Knowledge   *terra cotta and earth*   ELAINE SAYOKO YONEOKA
14" x 14" x 12"
photo by Seth Ansell

I am interested in mystery and what lies just beyond our understanding and my work may be inspired by the prehistoric past, city life, or nature. My desire is to create something naturally that transcends time through randomness and movement, out of being totally alive with head and heart.

SAN JUAN

The goat that used to bleat in our yard—
her throat slit, her hide burned
and scraped by the neighbors
for the feast of San Juan.

At the water pump in the sun
they wrenched coiled colors
out of the wound, and bared the ribs
of the ivory goat on the ground—
from a distance they were hanging
pearl necklaces on their arms.

When they held her neck
did she make a sound?
It was screaming, I thought,
when I had covered my ears
and heard myself.

The fires burst under the pots
and dogs fought over
singed hair and blood.

Later, from far away,
friends called my name, singing
with guitars to the sea.

MYRNA PEÑA REYES

TOADS MATE AND FATHER CLEANS THE POOL

Toads mate
and father cleans the pool.
While toads sit stringing eggs
like black bead necklaces
on lily pods and reeds,
he rakes the water with a stick
and drips a pile of toad eggs
on the ground.

But when it rains
the toads still come
to croak for mates—
while on the ground
their black seed pile will dry
and crumble in the sun.

MYRNA PEÑA REYES

THE SONG OF BULLETS   *JESSICA HAGEDORN*

Formalized
by middle age
we avoid crowds
but still
love music.

Day after day
with less surprise
we sit
in apartments
and count
the dead.

Awake,
my daughter croons
her sudden cries
and growls
my new language.
While she sleeps
we memorize
a list of casualties:

The photographer's brother
the doctor is missing.
Or I could say:
"Victor's brother Oscar
has been gone for two years . . .
It's easier for the family
to think of him dead."

Victor sends
a Christmas card
from El Salvador:
"Things still the same."

And there are others
who don't play
by the rules—

someone else's brother
perhaps mine
languishes in a hospital;
everyone's grown tired
of his nightmares
and pretends
he's not there.

Someone else's father
perhaps mine
will be executed
when the time comes.
Someone else's mother
perhaps mine
telephones incessantly
her husband is absent
her son has gone mad
her lover has committed suicide
she's a survivor
who can't appreciate
herself.

The sight
of my daughter's
pink and luscious flesh
undoes me.
I fight
my weakening rage
I must remember
to commit
those names to memory
and stay angry.

Friends send postcards:
"Alternating between hectic
social Manila life & rural wonders
of Sagata . . . on to Hongkong and Bangkok—
Love . . ."

Assassins cruise the streets
in obtrusive limousines
sunbathers idle
on the beach

War is predicted
in five years
ten years
any day now
I always thought
it was already happening

snipers and poets locked
in a secret embrace
the country
my child may never see

a heritage
of women in heat
and men
skilled at betrayal

dancing
to the song
of bullets.

JESSICA HAGEDORN

DURATION OF WATER

So that I make you a microcosm or symbolic center of the public
like a theatre, with hundreds of painted scenes combining and recombining
in order to exaggerate situations of joy or pain on stage, instead of
five short songs about you, accompanying dancers who seem to float on
                                                              their backs
in still water, as the empyrean. They would be the water motor.
                                                     Three stones
protrude from the water and three instruments combine and repeat a
                                                        simple scale,
but some passions only resolve with fire and weather catastrophes.
The orchestra nevertheless clears like foliage
for Yang Kue Fe's sigh, when she hears the emperor wants her.
There is a red line on the boards I can follow in the thick smoke
or mist. The shoulders of the man change scale, as if I had
been manipulating the field inside a small box, to see how light
can transform me into foliage, as a sexual punishment. The music
can take on the cold or heat of the air like blue chameleons on the limbs of
                                                              the tree,
as if you could look through the leaves into the empyrean. I can turn back
my sleeve with the multiplicity of detail of the battleground. The colors
combine into legible hues at a distance. There is a craft at work
to reconcile emotion in a purely speculative ambience,
tracking the last aria, like a duration of water
which is a piece of white silk.

MEI-MEI BERSSENBRUGGE

CHRONICLE

I was born the year of the loon
in a great commotion. My mother—
who used to pack $500 cash
in the shoulders of her fur gambling coat,
who had always considered herself
the family's "First Son"—
took one look at me
and lit out
on a vacation to Sumatra.
Her brother purchased my baby clothes;
I've seen them, little clown suits
of silk and color.

Each day
my Chinese grandmother bathed me
with elaboration in an iron tub;
amahs waiting in line
with sterilized water and towels
clucked and smiled
and rushed about the tall stone room
in tiny slippers.

After my grandfather
accustomed himself
to this betrayal by First Son,
he would take me in his arms,
walk with me
by the plum trees, cherries, persimmons;
he showed me the stiff robes
of my ancestors and their drafty hall,
the long beards of his learned old friends,
and his crickets.

Grandfather talked to me, taught me.
At two months, my mother tells me,
I could sniff for flowers,
stab my small hand upwards to moon.
Even today I get proud
when I remember
this all took place in Chinese.

MEI-MEI BERSSENBRUGGE

The float plane touched down so smoothly that it felt to Lucy as though the surface of the lake had risen to meet it. From below, the encircling mountains seemed more imposing than ever. The pilot taxied steadily across the reflection of the snow-flecked peaks toward the cluster of houses that formed the village of Kigiak, and Lucy saw a group of people waiting for them on the narrow beach.

As she clambered out of the cockpit and stepped onto the flimsy aluminum wing, she could see that her welcoming committee was mostly women. Many of them had brightly colored scarves tied over their long black hair, and all of them wore pants. Lucy felt conspicuous suddenly in her khaki skirt and tasseled loafers—clothes she had worn more to make a good impression than because she liked them. The women giggled and looked away when she tried to meet their eyes which added to Lucy's feeling of self-consciousness.

A smooth-faced young man stepped forward and offered to help her down. Their eyes met. Lucy smiled. His brows furrowed in a frown, and then he too looked away, but she thought from the way he held onto her hand a moment longer than necessary that he, too, had noticed their resemblance to each other.

She stepped down. He released her hand and murmured words she couldn't make out in a soft monotone. At first Lucy thought she hadn't understood him because her ears were still vibrating with the drone of the plane, but when he repeated his question, she realized that he must be speaking to her in Yup'ik.

"My name is Robert," he said in English, dropping his eyes again. "I thought you were Eskimo."

"Lucy," she said, extending her hand. "I'm Chinese-American. My grandmother was Chinese."

He studied her closely. His eyes were very intense. He was a handsome man, his dark skin so smooth that it seemed to shine. This time it was she who looked away.

Then the women and children overcame their shyness and pressed forward. Robert introduced his wife, a tall stringy woman, and their fat-cheeked baby. The villagers formed a procession to carry Lucy's luggage up the path to the trailer that was to be her office and home. Behind her, Lucy heard the plane's motor start up again as it took off across the water, gaining speed. She was really on her own now, she thought. Sink or swim.

From the air, the houses that dotted the shoreline of Lake Kigiak looked as though they'd been shaken out like dice and come to rest in loose clusters. From the ground, however, Lucy could see that most of the structures were government-issue: pre-fabricated wooden boxes on poorly constructed foundations. The village looked shabby to her, and the huge mountains that rose on all sides of the lake were intimidating: dormant creatures that might awaken at a moment's notice and send the houses tumbling into the water as carelessly as children's blocks on a piece of suddenly stretched fabric. But the mountains were also greener and more lush than anything she had been led to expect about the "far, frozen north," and it was actually warm here, almost hot. The mountainsides reflected the scattered sunlight, playing back every nuance of light and shadow.

Her welcoming committee left her at the door of the trailer. Lucy was grateful for the privacy; she needed to absorb this rush of impressions.

She'd made it. She was here, in the Alaskan "bush," away from the east coast and her own people for the very first time in her life. It was, in fact, a summer of firsts for her: just graduated from college, out here in this remote Eskimo village in western Alaska to undertake her first real job, as the region's new public health nurse. She'd been told that she'd probably experience "culture shock" the first few weeks, but right now she was more concerned about being accepted. She hoped that looking like a Native would work to her advantage.

The health department people in Anchorage had let her know in various ways—some making it sound like a warning, others like a joke—that she would very likely be mistaken for a Native. Now that she was out here, face to face, she felt a little overwhelmed by the similarity her skin coloring and features bore to theirs.

The trailer was furnished with tacky furniture, cheap acetate curtains and synthetic carpeting, but Lucy got the feeling that it was probably a cut above the villagers' housing, and it was hers, rent-free, courtesy of the state. She hadn't done too badly for herself on her very first job.

She carried her suitcases down the hall to the bedroom, and then returned to the front, which was one long room containing both kitchen and office. She lay her briefcase on the formica-topped table and pulled open the topmost drawer of the black metal filing cabinet, and then the two lower ones, in turn. Each contained rows of neatly labeled files, which Lucy flipped through. Everything seemed to be in order. She wondered again why her predecessor had left so abruptly. She had asked that question at the main office, and although no one seemed to know, neither had they seemed particularly concerned.

Lucy pulled open the drawers in the kitchen counter. The top one held a plastic silverware tray containing an assortment of cutlery. The bottom drawer, the deep one, held all kinds of medical paraphernalia: two blood pressure cuffs, stethoscope, bottles of medicine, disposable syringes. Feeling more comfortable, Lucy smiled and slid the drawer shut.

There was a soft tapping at the door, and muffled voices. She opened it to find two of the smaller children, a boy and a girl.

"Hello," she said. "Would you like to come in?"

The children looked at their feet and then at each other. Finally, the little boy mumbled towards the floor, "You want to come outside?"

"I'd like that. Let me change into some dungarees."

"Dungarees?"

"Blue jeans."

"Levi's?"

"Levi's."

They all laughed, and when she went down the hallway to change her clothes, the children followed her. They stood side by side in front of the double bed, watching her undress. The boy's name was Amos, his sister's Mary. Mary sucked her thumb with a serious expression and left the talking to her brother.

They led Lucy around the village, making special mention of the houses that had television. Theirs didn't. Three husky-type dogs with matted fur followed them around, even coming inside the schoolhouse. Amos assured her it was all right for them to be in there when Lucy tried to shoo them out. She asked him if they were sled dogs.

"What's that?"

Lucy had never seen a pool table in a schoolhouse before. Outside again, the kids pointed out the old Russian Orthodox church, perched peak-roofed and solitary on the upper hillside, its three-barred cross askew. Lucy wanted to take a closer look, but the kids were anxious to go down to the water.

By now Mary had a tight grip on Lucy's hand. Lucy stood beside her on the little beach and gazed out across the water. With the village at their backs, there was nothing in the vista to indicate what year, or even century, this was. The lake stretched for miles, flat and expansive, surrounded by mountains. The slopes themselves were mottled with sunlight and new growth. Lucy noticed a single house in a cleft in the hills, approximately a mile to the left.

"Who lives over there?" she asked.

"Abners," Amos said.

Mary spoke in her little voice. *"Gussuks."*

"Gussuks?"

"Missionaries," Amos explained.

The kids laughed at the puzzled look on Lucy's face. Amos ran around collecting pebbles and sticks from the shore, which he flung as hard as he could into the glassy water.

Later in the evening, although it was still fully light outside, Lucy was going through the files, making occasional notes on a yellow legal tablet. She was so absorbed in her work that the knock on the door startled her. When she opened it, Robert smiled at her from behind mirror sunglasses. Lucy had always disliked those glasses because they took unfair advantage.

"How's it going?" he asked.

"Fine. I think I'm going to like it here."

Amos and Mary came running up the path just then, jostling Robert as they pushed past him into the trailer. Amos spoke breathlessly; Mary reached for Lucy's hand.

"Mom says you eat with us."

"Looks like you're pretty popular with my niece and nephew already," Robert said, grinning.

"You're their uncle?"

"Their mom and my wife, they're sisters." He waved a hand as he walked down the trail.

Mercy was scraping Hamburger Helper around with some ground beef in an electric skillet when they arrived. She welcomed Lucy with a wide, mostly toothless, smile. "Hi, nurse!"

The house was cramped and cluttered. It smelled of food and cooking and the closeness of people in a small space. Lucy sat down stiffly at a rickety metal table, the surface of which was strewn with magazines, empty soda cans, and used paper plates. Mercy came over, gathered everything up in her arms, and dumped it in a large cardboard box that sat on the floor beside the stove. She served out two portions from the skillet onto paper plates, set them on the table, and told the kids to eat. Then she reached up on top of the refrigerator and brought down a green plastic cup of what she explained was seal oil, and a paper plate of dried fish, pale and fibrous and almost translucent where it was not encrusted with salt. Mercy set these dishes down on the table and proceeded to pick several dead mosquitoes out of the oil with her fingers. She wiped her hands on her polyester slacks.

She showed Lucy how to eat the fish, by first breaking off a portion, sucking on it to soften it, dipping it into the oil, and then biting off the oily part. She then redipped the remainder. Lucy wondered how long this particular cup of oil had been recycled for how many mouths, but she plunged a piece of the fish in and popped it into her mouth. Although all she could taste at first was salt and the bitterness of the oil, she came to enjoy the chewy texture.

"You like it? Want some more?" Mercy's chin and fingers were slathered in oil.

"Sure. It's good."

"You're all right, girl." Mercy grinned and handed Lucy another strip of fish.

Amos suddenly got up from the table, his food only half-eaten, and went over to a blue plastic utility bucket that stood in the farthest corner of the house. He casually unzipped his fly and peed into the bucket, watching them at the table the whole time, as if he didn't want to miss anything. Lucy realized that they had no plumbing, and that what was in the bucket was one of the odors she had smelled when she first walked in. Her throat constricted. She quickly broke off another piece of fish and put it in her mouth. She was glad her trailer had plumbing.

Amos stopped on his way back to the table to check the clock on the stove. "Mary!" he said sharply. "Nine o'clock!"

Mary's eyes widened. She set her fork on the table and slipped down from her chair. They ran out of the house.

Although Mercy shook her head, she didn't look particularly annoyed. "T.V.," she said. She looked at Lucy. "So you're a nurse, huh?"

"Well, I just graduated."

"College? Hey, you must be plenty smart."

Lucy laughed, relaxing for the first time. "I don't know about that."

"You like it here?"

"Yes." She reached for another piece of fish, which caused Mercy to smile in approval.

"That other nurse," Mercy shook her head with a disgusted expression, "she didn't belong here."

"Why'd she leave?"

"Who knows?" Mercy shrugged. They ate in silence.

"So where you been all your life? Anchorage?"

"No, Boston."

"Where the hell is that?"

"The east coast. New England."

"Then how come you look Native?" Mercy asked shrewdly.

"My grandmother was Chinese."

"And she ate lots of rice, right? With chopsticks!" Mercy tittered as though this was a big joke. Lucy smiled. "You sure don't look *gussuk*," Mercy went on.

"What does that mean, '*gussuk*'?"

"You know, white. Like those missionaries."

"Well, I'm probably *not* like them."

"No. You look Eskimo. Now you gotta act Eskimo."

"Okay," Lucy said, breaking off another piece of fish. "You can teach me."

Mercy got up from the table and went to the refrigerator.

"You want a pop?"

"No, thanks."

Mercy returned with a Pepsi Light, sat down, popped the top, and reached for a pack of Salems. She lit one of the cigarettes with a disposable lighter and resumed her interrogation. "So how come you're not married?"

Lucy laughed. "Because I'm not."

"How old are you?"

"Twenty-three."

"Brother. You gonna be an old maid?"

Mercy apparently found Lucy's indignation amusing. She started laughing again, coughing out smoke. She stared at Lucy for a minute without speaking, then she shook her head. "Damn, girl. You *look* Eskimo. Maybe not a hundred percent, but—" She thought for a moment, then said, *"Avuk!"*

"What's that mean?"

"Halfbreed." Mercy laughed at Lucy's expression. "Hey, it's a joke, you know? Don't get all bent out of shape."

Lucy told herself to calm down. Mercy didn't mean any harm. Maybe this was just Eskimo humor.

"You sure you don't want some pop?" Mercy offered her the can.

Lucy shook her head.

"Hey, you're not a virgin, are you?"

Lucy stared at her. This was going too far. She was on the verge of saying something, but Mercy had erupted in her high-pitched laughter again, slapping her lap to emphasize her mirth. "You're all right, girl. Eskimo, *Gussuk*, what the hell, right?"

"Right," Lucy said carefully. "What the hell." She reached for the can of soda and raised it to her mouth. "As a matter of fact," she said, not looking at Mercy, "I'm not."

"Good. That other one, I think she was."

It didn't much matter to Lucy that Mercy had a strange sense of humor, that the seal oil was a little bit rancid, or that the dried fish had gotten caught between her teeth. The point was that she was sitting in an Eskimo house, eating real Eskimo food. Her predecessor had probably holed up in that trailer night after night eating peanut butter and jelly sandwiches.

Lucy spent her first week reorganizing the filing system and visiting the older, housebound villagers. She communicated with those who didn't speak English by having their children act as interpreters. She set up office hours, took blood pressures, administered T.B. tests and polio vaccinations. She took pride in her efficiency.

It was almost solstice, staying light all night long now as dusk merged with dawn. Someone told her it wouldn't get dark again until August. The extended daylight made her feel energized and productive. She liked Kigiak; she wanted to stay there for at least a year.

The first of the green and red sockeye salmon entered the lake, swimming in soundless and inexorable procession to their spawning grounds. Day after day they'd been journeying, these silent swimmers, focussed on a single intent. The village children tossed stones and sticks into the water, but the fish merely passed around them, undeterred, too mesmerized and single-minded now to be startled or hurried or prevented from achieving their end. Lucy was fascinated by their strength, by their beauty and brightness.

She walked out beside the lake one night to watch them. She wandered along the shoreline, swatting at mosquitoes from time to time, enjoying the iridescent greenery and the breezes that wafted down from the snow-covered peaks. Occasionally, the dorsal fin of one of the fish broke the surface of the water with a faint splash.

She stopped when she came to a recess in the shore, where the alder ended and the ground gave way to peat and marsh. *"Muskeg"* was what they called it here. The mosquitoes were not so bad in this little cove, and the shallow water seemed to be some sort of resting place for the fish. They milled offshore in shadowy clumps, swimming in long, slow circles, as though gathering strength to resume their journey. Lucy sat down on a grassy hummock, brushing some insects away from her face.

Robert's approach was stealthy. She never even heard him until he stepped out of the shrubbery behind her and asked her if she wanted a cigarette. He was wearing his mirror sunglasses again.

"I don't smoke. Neither should you."

He grinned and sat down on the damp earth beside her. "You like it here?" he asked.

"I'm still not used to the mountains, but yes. It's so lovely, and peaceful."

"Just like a calendar picture, right?"

Something in his voice made her glance at him. "Don't you like it?"

He shrugged. "It's my home, you know? But I feel trapped here." When he spoke there were pauses between his sentences, and his voice was soft, unhurried. "I've only been to one other place, to live, I mean."

"Where'd you go?"

"Fairbanks."

"Did you like it?"

He shook his head. "Too cold. Too many *gussuks*. I got homesick." He was quiet for so long that she thought he'd exhausted the subject. "Now I want to go away again, but there's nowhere to go."

"But Kigiak's so beautiful. You're so lucky to live here—" Lucy hesitated, and when Robert didn't say anything more, she kept silent, too.

Instead, she watched the fish milling offshore, their fins sometimes breaking the sheen that was the surface of the water at this hour. She watched the water and felt Robert watching her. They sat like this, not speaking, for perhaps ten or fifteen minutes, and it struck Lucy that it was probably the longest period of time that she had ever shared silence with anyone. It surprised her when Robert spoke.

"These fish, they depress the hell out of me."

"Why's that?"

"I can't help thinking how they're all gonna die."

It hadn't occurred to Lucy that the salmon were already dying, having stopped eating once they entered fresh water. She considered the fact that none of these thousands of fish would ever swim in the ocean again, and would in fact be dead in a matter of weeks. It was an awesome thought.

Robert sighed and she glanced at him, thinking that he was going to say something else, but all he did was to reach for her hand, as casually as though they'd known each other for some time. She pulled away in alarm and stood up. She couldn't look him in the face.

"I have to get back," she said, starting off. She didn't like the way her voice sounded apologetic. She hurried away. Only when she had reached the curve in the shoreline did she dare to glance behind her. He was sitting exactly as she'd left him, gazing out across the lake. The mountains glowed with rose and violet light. It was hard to tell if it was sunset or dawn.

It was a few nights later that he came to her trailer, waking her with his insistent knocking. When she opened the door, wearing her nightgown, he stepped in without hesitation and sat down at the table. He was wearing the dark glasses, and this time she appreciated the irony of living in a place where you wore dark glasses in the middle of the night. She also noticed that he was really not much taller than she, and that he had a slight frame. She thought she could fight him if she had to. She also admitted to herself for the first time that she was attracted to him, in spite of the fact that he frightened her. Or maybe because of it.

She remained standing beside the door. "What do you want?" She had intended to sound indignant, or at least annoyed, but it didn't come out like that at all.

His face was turned towards her expectantly, his eyes unreadable behind the mirror lenses.

"Robert." Now her voice sounded firmer, more businesslike.

He took off the glasses then and looked at her standing there in her long flannel nightgown, her hands on her hips. He smiled.

"You'll have to leave," she said.

He hooked the glasses back over his ears and stood up. Lucy opened the door wide and then locked it behind him. As she got back into bed, she realized that he'd never said a word.

She took to locking her door every night after that, the only one in the village to do so, she was sure. If the others learned of it, it would make them feel bad, she knew. But she wasn't one of them; she had to look out for herself.

She didn't see Robert again for over a week and was beginning to think he'd lost interest. It was a relief, but she had to admit to feeling a little disappointed, too. She asked herself if she would have gotten involved with him if he hadn't been married, and decided that there were just too many cultural differences. She told herself that his interest in her was purely sexual, an extra-marital fling.

One day Mercy asked her, "Got your party dress ready, nurse?"

"What for?"

"The big bash. The glorious Fourth. Robert and them, they already went to Dillingham to get the booze."

The night before the holiday, she was awakened by a rhythmic tapping on her bedroom window. It came from the back of the trailer, the side that faced away from the village. Lucy always kept the blue curtains drawn across the glass.

"Who is it?" This time she was scared.

"Robert."

"What do you want?"

"Let me in." Then, as an afterthought, "Please."

She wondered if he was drunk. He continued to rap on the glass. "Go home, Robert. Go to sleep."

But he didn't go home. He tapped at her window for what seemed like hours, maybe all night. Lucy burrowed under the covers and piled the pillows and her clothes on top of her head. Still she could hear it. The sound seemed to have moved into her brain. She would doze for a time, and then awaken, and he would still be there, tapping. She was amazed by his persistence, and also by the fact that he didn't just smash the window with his fist or a piece of wood. Occasionally, along with the percussion on the glass, she would hear his voice, tired and patient, saying, "Let me in."

When she woke up, exhausted, in the morning, the noise had stopped. She stood to one side of the window and drew the curtain back cautiously. There was no one there.

The Fourth of July party was held in the one-room schoolhouse. All the desks and chairs had been pushed back against the walls to allow room for dancing. The music, played on someone's tape deck, was exclusively country-western: Waylon Jennings, Willie Nelson, Dolly Parton, and other voices Lucy didn't recognize.

There were cases and cases of beer. Lucy had never seen so much beer other than in a package store. Olympia, Hamm's, Rainier, Heineken, Budweiser. Cans and bottles, in sixpacks and cartons, ferried up by boat from Dillingham all week long, and all illegal, since Kigiak had been voted "dry" the year before. Lucy wondered if the presence of alcohol was responsible for the absence of some of the villagers.

The drinking had already started. Lucy noticed right away that these people drank fast, guzzling their beer, drinking to get drunk. The women drank as much and as deliberately as the men, and as the evening wore on several people crumpled to the floor, unconscious. The children had disappeared early, and now Lucy understood why.

She danced with some of the men, enjoying herself. At one point, someone suggested loudly that they sing the national anthem, and Mercy nominated Lucy to lead it, pushing her into the center of the room. Lucy protested in embarrassment. "I don't know the words. Honest."

Robert stood beside his wife all evening. For some reason, they struck Lucy as an Eskimo version of that "American Gothic" painting. Esther was a tall, skinny woman who seemed to derive no pleasure from either the occasion or the beer she sipped. Lucy realized she had never seen Esther smile. Robert looked preoccupied. He didn't seem to be drinking, which surprised Lucy, since even she was putting away her share of beer.

When she slipped out the door to make her retreat, Lucy was aware of two things. The first was that she had drunk a lot more that she'd meant to, and the other was that someone had followed her out.

Robert quickly caught up to her on the trail. He took her hand and asked her to go with him to his house, to talk.

Lucy took a deep breath. "I'll talk to you. But I don't want to hold hands."

But Robert's grip was firm and he wouldn't let go.

They sat side by side on the living room carpet, their backs against the sofa. Robert still hadn't let go of her hand, and he raised it now in a gesture of frustration before returning it to the floor. Then he tried to kiss her.

"You said you just wanted to talk," Lucy said. She felt flushed. She was worried that Esther would come home and see them.

Robert was silent for a long time. Then he looked at her and said, "Why do you hate me?"

They heard footsteps on the porch just then. Lucy jerked away from him and stood up.

Mercy kicked open the door with her foot and entered the kitchen. She stood in the middle of the linoleum floor, swaying unsteadily, beer spilling from an open can of Budweiser in one hand, a sixpack of Rainier dangling from the other. With an effort, she focussed on Robert and Lucy and smiled broadly. "Merry Christmas, kids! Merry Christmas!"

Lucy spoke in a tired voice. "It's not Christmas, Mercy. It's the Fourth of July. You know that."

"Yeah, yeah, yeah. Freedom and liberty and all that jazz." She hoisted the sixpack, as though to offer them some, gave a sudden lurch, and toppled over at their feet.

Lucy watched Mercy fall with utter detachment, and when it finally registered that she felt neither friendly nor professional concern, she knew that she was drunker than she'd thought. She looked at Robert. His eyes were closed.

She studied Mercy's broad, flat face, her right cheek crumpled against the beige carpet, her mouth all scrunched up and already leaking saliva. She was snoring. Lucy watched the pale, toothless gums appear and disappear with each rasping breath. Mercy's long black hair lay scattered around her head. Her blouse had ridden up around her stomach, exposing the faint, caterpillar-like trails of stretchmarks where her flesh folded against the top of her bluejeans.

Lucy sat down and reached for Robert's hand. He opened his eyes and leaned towards her, swivelling his torso awkwardly in the attempt to embrace her, crushing her knuckles into the rug as his weight shifted onto his arm. She turned her face to him, but then, losing nerve, pulled away. She tensed, anticipating his anger, but when she looked at him again, he was crying.

Her own eyes pooled with tears. "It's not that I don't like you, Robert. It's just that—Well, look, you *are* married, after all." I shouldn't even be here, she thought, looking down at their joined hands.

"I don't love her," he said quietly. "I love you."

"How can you love me? You don't even know me."

"Your world is different from mine."

"That doesn't mean it's better." Lucy paused. "What about your baby? Robert, you have to at least try."

He shook his head. Lucy felt utterly confused. She had only come out here to do a job. It wasn't *her* fault that he was unhappily married.

When she stood to go, he didn't protest or try to stop her. It required all of her concentration to get out the door and down the slanted steps without falling, and as she picked her way along the grassy path to her trailer, she felt the alcohol surging against the front of her skull like surf. My God, she thought, as she stumbled through the door, I'm really drunk. Another first.

Later, she couldn't remember even entering the trailer, let alone falling into bed fully dressed. But she would remember that Robert had come and tugged off her clothes, and that when they made love she had cried out—something she'd never done before.

When she awoke with a splitting headache late in the morning, he was already gone. She wondered if anyone had seen him leave, if there was going to be trouble, if she might lose her job. She'd acted recklessly, unprofessionally. She would make certain that it never happened again. At least she was reasonable sure that she hadn't risked pregnancy. She stayed in the shower a long time, until the throbbing in her head subsided.

When she went outside at last, to walk down to the lake, it was afternoon. It seemed to her that the volume of salmon had thinned, as if overnight, but there were still hundreds of them, proceeding silently, empowered with purpose. She saw a few kids on the public dock, jigging for fish with hand-held lines.

It was unnaturally quiet and subdued for that time of day. No one else was about. She thought of small western towns in movies, when disease struck and entire households were put under quarantine. She had an urge to go back to bed herself.

She noticed that the door of Robert's house was ajar, and before she thought about what she was doing, she was standing on the porch looking in.

Mercy was lying on the floor pretty much where she had fallen, but she lay on her back now, her hair still flung out around her head, her mouth open. Her blue jeans and pink underpants were bunched around her ankles. Her pubic hair was grey, Lucy saw, as shocked by that as by anything. A man Lucy had never seen before was snoring on the couch.

She pulled the door closed and made her way quickly back to the trailer, where she threw up in the sink almost as soon as she got inside. She locked the door and lay down on the sofa. She'd change the sheets on the bed when she felt better.

Robert came over around suppertime. He knocked politely, but firmly. No more tapping at windows, Lucy thought.

She opened the door and stood in the doorframe. He was wearing his dark glasses again. He smiled at her. "Just wanted to make sure you were okay."

"I'm fine," Lucy said. She didn't smile. "I'm very busy. Is there something I can do for you?"

Robert was happy. "How about a cup of coffee?" he said, stepping forward, expecting her to move. Her outstretched arm blocked his chest. He stopped smiling.

"I'm busy, Robert. Look, you can't go on bothering me anymore."

His face was expressionless as he turned and walked away. She could read no emotion in the set of his shoulders, in his walk.

Later, when he came rapping at her bedroom window again, she got quietly out of bed and went to sit in the front room. After a couple of hours, he left. Lucy realized later that this was the moment when she decided she would leave Kigiak at the end of the summer. She could see what Robert meant about it being too small, and for all her dark hair and coloring, she was and always would be a *gussuk*. She didn't belong here.

He didn't come anymore after that, and she learned that he had gotten a job in Dillingham.

She didn't see him again until late in August, when the nights were darkening and the very last straggling salmon, their skin tattered and infected with freshwater fungus, had passed beyond the village. Every now and then the pale carcass of a dead fish washed ashore. She heard that Robert had lost his job.

She'd taken to going down to the dock after supper, to sit and think. When she saw him, she held very still. He was some distance away, down by the river, straining to push a wooden skiff off the shore. When the boat was free, he stepped lightly into the stern, leaned from the waist, and pulled once on the engine's starter cord.

He turned the boat with a smooth, uninterrupted motion, gave it full throttle, and sped away across the darkening lake. He drove standing up. Lucy watched until his figure and the outline of the boat became one silhouette, and then she continued to watch until she could neither see the skiff nor hear the motor.

In September she left Kigiak and Alaska to go back to Boston. She'd decided to return to school. The administration in Anchorage told her she'd done an outstanding job, and said that if she ever wanted to come back they could always find a place for her.

Lucy was gone for two years. She'd been back in Anchorage less than three months, working for the health department, when a middle-aged Native woman approached her one night in the lobby of a downtown movie theatre. Lucy had planned to meet her boyfriend there, to see a foreign film.

"Hello," the woman said, approaching Lucy with a hesitant smile. "You probably don't remember me."

Lucy was sure she had never seen this woman before in her life.

"My name is Anna. I met you in Kigiak. On the Fourth of July, maybe three, four years ago. I'm Robert's cousin."

"I'm sorry, I don't remember." Lucy looked around. Rick was late. "I remember Robert, of course. How is he?"

Anna continued to smile, but her voice became very soft, almost a whisper. "He died. Last year. Drowned."

Lucy felt her face grow flushed. "Drowned?" Her voice sounded unnaturally shrill. "But he was so good with those boats. How could he—"

Anna reached out and touched Lucy's sleeve, giving her another gentle smile. "You look even more like him now than when I met you."

"Who?" Lucy looked desperately for Rick. For no reason at all, she felt exasperated with this woman. She wished that she would stop smiling, for one thing.

"Robert. You look like him."

Lucy was relieved to see Rick enter the lobby. She turned abruptly from Anna and went to meet him, taking his arm. They walked towards the theatre, where the lights were already going down.

"Who was that?" Rick asked.

"Just some Native woman. I really don't know what she was talking about." Lucy shrugged. Then she began to cry.

MEI MEI EVANS

When Hang Fong Toy finally awakens, she can't tell if the rhythmic pounding is one of her headaches or just the water pipes banging again. She looks around the room, listening. The street light falls through the Venetian blinds; the slanting lines make the room seem larger.

You Thin Toy sleeps curled toward the wall, a brush stroke on the wide bed. He's a retired merchant marine and has sailed the world. Now he spends afternoons at Portsmouth Square, playing chess and telling stories about himself as a young man. "Like a seagull," he says, "I went everywhere, saw everything."

His oldtimer friends like to tease him, "So, why do you sit around the Square now?"

"Curiosity," he says, "I want to see how you fleabags have been living."

You Thin knows all the terms for docking a ship; Hang Fong can name the parts and seams of a dress the way a doctor can name bones.

Hang Fong sews in a garment shop. She's only been outside of Chinatown for official business: immigration, unemployment and social security. When the children were young, they took her to Market Street, the Emporium and J.C. Penney's, but now, without translators, she's not an adventuress.

There was a time when her desire to return to China was a sensation in her belly, like hunger. Now she only dreams of it, almost tasting those dishes she loved as a young girl. Sometimes she says to You Thin before falling asleep, maybe a visit, eh?

After raising their children, Chinatown has become their world. They feel lucky to have an apartment on Salmon Alley. Louie's Grocery is around the corner on Taylor, and Hang Fong's sewing shop is just down the block. Their apartment is well situated in the back of the alley, far from the traffic fumes of Pacific Avenue.

Hang Fong and You Thin like their landlord, an old Italian lady, and her mute son so much that they have given them Chinese names. Fay-Poah (Manager Lady) and Ah-Boy (Mute-Son). Manager Lady wears printed pastel dresses that Hang Fong, a sewing lady, admires very much. Ah-Boy, a big man with a milky smell, works as a porter at the Oasis Club, but during the day he works around the building. When Hang Fong hears his broom on the stairs or the garbage cans rattling in the airshaft, she feels safe. It's good to have a strong man like Ah-Boy nearby. She tells You Thin, Ah-Boy is a good son, and You Thin nods. He likes to think that the anchor tattoo on Ah-Boy's arm makes them comrades of sorts.

Hang Fong thinks, maybe Manager Lady left her window open. But then the sound becomes erratic and sharp. Hang Fong gets up, leans toward the wall. You Thin lets out a long breath.

Hang Fong presses her ear against the wall, listening. Her eyes are wide open. Suddenly she rushes toward her sleeping husband and shakes him, "Get up! Get up! It's the Manager Lady, she's in trouble!"

You Thin stretches out and props himself up on one elbow. He rubs his eyes, trying to wake up. The banging comes again; and the old couple stare at each other. Outside, a car screeches to an urgent stop. They listen to the faint bubbly hum of the fish tank in the other room, and then hear the rumbling ice box motor shut off with a final click. You Thin and Hang Fong look at each other, the silence feels big.

The pounding comes again. Once. Twice.

"Something's wrong! Manager Lady is trying to tell us that!" Hang Fong throws off her covers. In one motion, her legs whip out and her slippers make a swishing noise as she moves across the room. The overhead fluorescent light flickers and snaps and then is quiet. The room is bright, glaring.

You Thin squints, reaches over, and raps sharply, one-two-three on the wall.

A sound knocks back in return.

Hang Fong slaps the wall with her open palm, the sound is flat and dull. She presses palm and cheek into the wall, and shouts, "Manager, Manager, are you all right? Nothing's wrong, is there?"

"SSHHH!!!" You Thin yanks her away.

"Don't talk loud like that, she don't know what you say, maybe she thinks that you yell at her."

You Thin is out of bed, pacing. Hang Fong remains sitting, she pulls her sweater closer around her neck, the sleeves hang limply at her sides.

"Let's see . . . wait a minute, where's Ah-Boy?"

"It's Tuesday, he's got the night shift."

"Oh. Tuesday. Right."

Last week, when You Thin was at Manager Lady's paying the rent, he looked out her kitchen window while waiting for her to come back with the receipt. He saw a Chinese pot beneath a pile of chipped plates. So, the next day, he returned with a blue vase, its floral pattern similar to many of Manager

Lady's dresses.

"I see?" he asked, pointing out the window.

Manager Lady opened her mouth wide, as her hand fluttered toward the window.

"Oh. *Si, si,*" she said.

You Thin pulled the window open. He moved the cream-colored plates and lifted the pot for Manager Lady to see. She nodded, cradling the blue vase to her bosom.

With two hands, You Thin carried the pot across the hall. Under the running faucet, Hang Fong scrubbed hard. Red, green and yellow, the palace ladies and plum blossoms came clean. You Thin scraped away the last of the dirt with a toothpick. The characters came clear. Good Luck and Long Life. You Thin and Hang Fong laughed, feeling lucky.

"Worth a lot of money, in time," You Thin said.

"Something to pass on to the children," Hang Fong added.

You Thin told everyone on the Square that the pot belonged to a hard-working old-timer who died alone. Hang Fong said that it was a good omen that they were chosen to house this valuable object. "It's very old," she told her sewing-lady friends.

"So, should we call the Rescue Car?" Hang Fong asks.

You Thin looks out the window, distracted. He shakes his head, ". . . but even if they get here in two minutes, best we could do is stand in front of the door with our mouths open."

Hang Fong knows that he wants to climb the fire escape and get inside Manager Lady's apartment. It's risky, she thinks. You Thin isn't a young man and his step isn't always steady. She won't say anything, because the long years of marriage have taught her one thing, he likes his way.

"Well, what do we do?" Hang Fong asks. On the fire escape, a pigeon sleeps, its beak in its chest feathers. Hang Fong watches it. She hears the big engines of the garbage trucks churning up the hill. Fog horns sound in the distance, like help on the way.

You Thin asks, "Well, you think I could make that big step across to their fire escape?"

Hang Fong shrugs her shoulders. "Don't know, how do you feel?"

You Thin raises the window, looks out and snaps back in. Before Hang Fong can speak, he's run to the bathroom and clattered his way out carrying the long wooden board they use as a shelf over the bathtub.

"This is how . . ." He slaps the board. "This will reach from our fire escape to theirs. You hold this end, just in case, and the rest I can do."

Hang Fong grips hard, but she keeps a harder eye on him. Inside, she repeats over and over, "Be careful . . . be safe . . . be careful . . . be safe . . ." You Thin is a brave man, she thinks, You Thin is a good man.

One leg, then the other, and he is over there. He peers through the window, knocks, and then tries to lift it open. Shut tight, he has to pull hard, two, three times before it comes open.

You Thin feels along the wall for the light switch. All along the way, he speaks to Manager Lady, softly, in Chinese, "You're all right, nothing's wrong, don't be frightened . . ." You Thin believes in the power of the voice: a well-meaning word spoken in the face of ill-fortune can turn luck around.

Manager Lady is a wide figure on the floor. Everything around her speaks of her age: the faded covers, the cluttered nightstand, the bottles of lotions and pills. You Thin takes her hands; he's happy hers are warm.

Hang Fong knocks in quick, urgent raps, and You Thin opens the door for her. She moves quickly through the entryway, kneels and takes Manager Lady's head onto her lap, whispering, "Don't be scared, don't be scared." Manager Lady's eyes open; she says something in Italian, the long vowels reach forth and hang heavy in the air. Hang Fong and You Thin look at each other. They understand.

You Thin says, "I go. Go to get Ah-Boy."

"You know where it is then?"

"Uh, let me think . . . where Lee's Rice Shop used to be?"

"No! Across from Chong's Imports."

"Yes, right, I know, I know."

The air outside is sharp. The street lamps cast an orange glow to the empty alley. You Thin moves quickly through Salmon Alley. But when he turns onto Pacific, he rests a moment, the long road before him is marked with globes of light. He runs his hand along the walls for support. On the steep hill, his legs feel strangely heavy when they land on the pavement and oddly light when they bounce off. He chants to himself, "Hurry. Important. Faster."

When he reaches Powell, he leans against the fire hydrant for a moment, glad that he's halfway there. He can see Broadway, it's still brightly lit. He's breathing hard by the time he gets to The Oasis. This late, it's been long closed. You Thin stands outside, banging on the big wooden doors and rapping on the windows. He cups his hands to the barred window, trying to see in. But with the glare from the street lamps, it's like looking into a mirror.

He takes a deep breath, "Ah-Boy, AAHHH-Boy-AAAHH! . . ."

Silence. Then the sound of flapping slippers, and Ah-Boy opens the door, mop in hand.

You Thin throws his arms about, waving toward Pacific. He slaps the restaurant wall, shouting, "Mah-mah, Mah-mah. Be sick. Be sick."

Ah-Boy opens his mouth; his head jerks back and forth, but there is no sound. He lets his broom fall with a clatter. The heavy door slams shut.

Ah-Boy is a big man and You Thin can't keep up for long. At Pacific, You Thin waves him on.

You Thin watches for a moment as Ah-Boy moves up the hill. Yes, he nods, Ah-Boy is a good son.

When You Thin gets to the apartment, Ah-Boy is sitting on the floor with his mother's head in his lap, her gray hair is loosened from its bun. She is speaking to Ah-Boy in a low voice.

You Thin and Hang Fong stand under the door frame, watching. "Just like last year . . ." Hang Fong says, ". . . just like Old Jue."

On the phone You Thin speaks loud. He pronounces the syllables as if each sound were a single character, "Numbah Two. Sah-moon Alley. Old Lady. Sick. You be the come. Now, sabei? I stand by downdaire, sabei? Numbah Two, Sah-moon Alley."

Hang Fong stands next to him, listening hard. She whispers something to him.

You Thin raises his head, and speaks even louder. "One minute. You know, Old Lady, she be . . . uh, uh . . . Old Lady she be come from Italy. You sabei? Lady not from China."

At the Square the next day, You Thin challenges the Newspaper Man to a chess game. You Thin plays with one leg raised on the cement stool. "My Car over your lousy paper Gun, and you're eaten!" The Newspaper Man's children fold *The Chinese Times* on the next table. Lame-Leg Fong tries to tell You Thin which pieces to move. The #15 Kearney bus inches down Clay, its brakes squeaking and hissing. Cars honk.

You Thin tells his story about last night in between chess moves. He describes the distance between Salmon Alley and Broadway. His running motions make his blue sleeves go vlop-vlop in the wind. He repeats all the English words he used, tries to use the ones he'd heard, and makes all the faces Ah-Boy made. He walks the line on the ground to show what he did in midair. Little boys run by on their way to the water fountain.

Hang Fong tells the story without looking up. The ladies listen with rounded backs and moving hands. Sheets of fabric run from the machines to the floor.

Clumps of thread knot around the chair legs; spools of color ripple above the ladies' bent heads. The overlock machines click; the steam irons hiss. Some ladies sing along with the drum and gong beat of the Cantonese opera playing on the radio. A voice booms over the intercom system, "LAST CHANCE TO HAND IN THOSE TICKETS, RIGHT NOW!" No one looks up. Some ladies cluck their tongues and roll their eyes. Others shake their heads and curse under their breath.

Many of the sewing-ladies want to hear Hang Fong's story, but missing a sentence here or there, they can't follow the drama. Is it a story or is it real? The women become heavy-footed; the needles stamp urgent stitches into the fabric. Trousers fly over the work tables; the colorful mounds of clothing clutter the floor.

Eventually the grumble of the machines drowns out the story. A young girl runs in to ask her mother for money as the fish peddler arrives, singing out her catch in a breath as long as thread.

FAE MYENNE NG

Connie couldn't remember whose party it was, whose house. She had an impression of kerosene lamps on brown wicker tables, of shapes talking in doorways. It was summer, almost the only time Connie has run into her since, too, and someone was saying, "You must know Lisa Mallory."

"I don't think so."

"She's here. You must know her."

Later in the evening, it was someone else who introduced her to a figure perched on the balustrade of the steps leading to the lawn where more shapes milled. In stretching out a hand to shake Connie's, the figure almost fell off sideways. Connie pushed her back upright onto her perch and, peering, took in the fact that Lisa Mallory had a Chinese face. For a long instant, she felt nonplussed, and was rendered speechless.

But Lisa Mallory was filling in the silence. "Well, now, Connie Sung," she said, not enthusiastically but with a kind of sophisticated interest. "I'm not in music myself, but Paul Wu's my cousin. Guilt by association!" She laughed. "No-tone music, I call his. He studied with John Cage, Varese, and so forth."

Surprised that Lisa knew she was a violinist, Connie murmured something friendly, wondering if she should simply ask outright, "I'm sure I should know, but what do you do?" but she hesitated, taking in her appearance instead, while Lisa went on with, "It's world class composing. Nothing's wrong with the level. But it's hard going for the layman, believe me."

Lisa Mallory wore a one-of-a-kind kimono dress, but it didn't make her look Japanese at all, and her hair was drawn back tightly in a braid which stood out from close to the top of her head horizontally. You could probably lift her off her feet by grasping it, like the handle of a pot.

"You should give a concert here, Connie," she said, using her first name right away, Connie noticed, like any American. "Lots of culturati around." Even when she wasn't actually speaking, she pursued her own line of thought actively and seemed to find herself mildly amusing.

"I'm new to the area," Connie said, deprecatingly. "I've just been a weekend guest, actually, till a month ago."

"It's easy to be part of it. Nothing to it. I should know. You'll see."

"I wish it weren't so dark," Connie found herself saying, waving her hand in front of her eyes as if the night were a veil to brush aside. She recognized in herself that intense need to see, to see into fellow Orientals, to fathom them. So far, Lisa Mallory had not given her enough clues, and the darkness itself seemed to be interfering.

Lisa dropped off her perch. "It's important to be true to oneself," she said. "Keep the modern stuff out of your repertory. Be romantic. Don't look like that! You're best at the romantics. Anyhow, take it from me. I know. And *I* like what I like."

Released by her outspokenness, Connie laughed and asked, "I'm sure I should know, but what is it that you do?" She was certain Lisa would say something like, "I'm with a public relations firm." "I'm in city services."

But she replied, "What do all Chinese excel at?" Not as if she'd asked a rhetorical question, she waited, then answered herself. "Well, aren't we all physicists, musicians, architects, or in software?"

At that point a voice broke in, followed by a large body which put his arms around both women, "The Oriental contingent! I've got to break this up."

Turning, Lisa kissed him roundly, and said over her shoulder to Connie, "I'll take him away before he tells us we look alike!"

They melted into the steps below, and Connie, feeling put off balance and somehow slow-witted, was left to think over her new acquaintance.

*

"Hello, Lisa Mallory," Connie Sung always said on the infrequent occasions when they ran into one another. She always said "Hello, Lisa Mallory," with a shyness she did not understand in herself. It was strange, but they had no mutual friends except for Paul Wu, and Connie had not seen him in ages. Connie had no one of whom to ask her questions. But sometime soon, she'd be told Lisa's maiden name. Sometime she'd simply call her Lisa. Sometime what Lisa did with her life would be answered.

Three, four years passed, with their running into one another at receptions and openings, and still Lisa Mallory remained an enigma. Mildly amused herself, Connie wondered if other people, as well, found her inscrutable. But none of her American friends (though, of course, Lisa and she were Americans, too, she had to remind herself), none of their Caucasian friends seemed curious about backgrounds. In their accepting way, they did not wonder about Lisa's background, or about Connie's or Paul Wu's. Perhaps they assumed they were all cut from the same cloth. But to Connie, the Orientals she met were unread books, books she never had the right occasion or time to fully pursue.

She didn't even see the humor in her situation—it was such an issue with her. The fact was she felt less, much less, sure of herself when she was with real Chinese.

As she was realizing this, the truth suddenly dawned on her. Lisa Mallory never referred to her own background because it was more Chinese than Connie's, and therefore of a higher order. She was tact incarnate. All along, she had been going out of her way not to embarrass Connie. Yes, yes. Her assurance was definitely uppercrust (perhaps her father had been in the diplomatic service), and her offhand didacticness, her lack of self-doubt, was indeed characteristically Chinese-Chinese. Connie was not only impressed by these traits, but also put on the defensive because of them.

Connie let out a sigh—a sigh that follows the solution to a nagging problem . . . Lisa's mysteriousness. But now Connie knew only too clearly that her own background made her decidedly inferior. Her father was a second-generation gynecologist who spoke hardly any Chinese. Yes, inferior and totally without recourse.

*

Of course, at one of the gatherings, Connie met Bill Mallory, too. He was simply American, maybe Catholic, possibly lapsed. She was not put off balance by him at all. But most of the time he was away on business, and Lisa cropped up at functions as single as Connie.

Then one day, Lisa had a man in tow—wiry and tall, he looked Chinese from the Shantung area, or perhaps from Beijing, and his styled hair made him appear vaguely artistic.

"Connie, I'd like you to meet Eric Li. He got out at the beginning of the *detente*, went to Berkeley, and is assimilating a mile-a-minute," Lisa said, with her usual irony. "Bill found him and is grooming him, though he came with his own charisma."

Eric waved her remark aside. "Lisa has missed her calling. She was born to be in PR," he said, with an accent.

"Is that what she does?" Connie put in at once, looking only at him. "Is that her profession?"

"You don't know?" he asked, with surprise.

Though she was greeting someone else, Lisa turned and answered, "I'm a fabrics tycoon, I think I can say without immodesty." She moved away and continued her conversation with the other friend.

Behind his hand, he said, playfully, as though letting Connie in on a secret, "Factories in Hongkong and Taipei, and now he's—Bill, that is—is exploring them on the mainland."

"With her fabulous contacts over there!" Connie exclaimed, now seeing it all. "Of course, what a wonderful business combination they must make."

Eric was about to utter something, but stopped, and said flatly, "I have all the mainland contacts, even though I was only twenty when I left, but my parents . . ."

"How interesting," Connie murmured lamely. "I see," preoccupied as she was with trying to put two and two together.

Lisa was back and said without an introduction, continuing her line of thought, "You two look good together, if I have to say so myself. Why don't you ask him to one of your concerts? And you, Eric, you're in America now, so don't stand on ceremony, or you'll be out in left field." She walked away with someone for another drink.

Looking uncomfortable, but recovering himself with a smile, Eric said, "Lisa makes me feel more Chinese than I am becoming—it is her directness, I suspect. In China, we'd say she is too much like a man."

At which Connie found herself saying, "She makes me feel *less* Chinese."

"Less!"

"Less Chinese than she is."

"That is not possible," Eric said, with a shade of contempt—for whom? Lisa or Connie? He barely suppressed a laugh, cold as Chinese laughter could be.

Connie blurted out, "I'm a failed Chinese. Yes, and it's to you that I need to say it." She paused and repeated emphatically, "I am a failed Chinese." Her heart was beating quicker, but she was glad to have got that out, a confession and a definition that might begin to free her. "Do you know you make me feel that, too? You've been here only about ten years, right?"

"Right, and I'm thirty-one."

"You know what I think? I think it's harder for a Chinese to do two things."

At that moment, an American moved in closer, looking pleased somehow to be with them.

She continued, "It's harder for us to become American than, say, for a German, and it's also harder not to remain residually Chinese, even if you are third generation."

Eric said blandly, "Don't take yourself so seriously. You can't help being an American product."

Trying to be comforting, the American interjected with, "The young lady is not a product, an object. She is a human being, and there is no difference among peoples that I can see."

"I judge myself both as a Chinese and as an American," Connie said.

"You worry too much," Eric said, impatiently. Then he looked around and though she wasn't in sight, he lowered his voice. "She is what she is. I know what she is. But she avoids going to Hongkong. She avoids it."

Connie felt turned around. "Avoids it?"

"Bill's in Beijing right now. She's here. How come?"

"I don't know," Connie replied, as though an answer had been required of her.

"She makes up many excuses, reasons. Ask her. Ask her yourself," he said, pointedly.

"Oh, I couldn't do that. By the way, I'm going on a concert tour next year in three cities—Shanghai, Beijing and Nanking," Connie said. "It'll be my first time in China."

"Really! You must be very talented to be touring at your age," he said, genuinely interested for the first time. Because she was going to China, or because she now came across as an over-achiever, even though Chinese American?

"I'm just about your age," she said, realizing then that maybe Lisa Mallory had left them alone purposely.

"You could both pass as teenagers!" the American exclaimed.

*

Two months later, she ran into Lisa again. As usual, Lisa began in the middle of her own thoughts. "Did he call?"

"Who? Oh. No, no."

"Well, it's true he's been in China the last three weeks with Bill. They'll be back this weekend."

Connie saw her opportunity. "Are you planning to go to China yourself?"

For the first time, Lisa seemed at a loss for words. She raised her shoulders, than let them drop. Too airily, she said, "You know, there's always Paris. I can't bear not to go to Paris, if I'm to take a trip."

"But you're Chinese. You *have* been to China, you came from China originally, didn't you?"

"I could go to Paris twice a year, I love it so," Lisa said. "And then there's

London, Florence, Venice."

"But—but your business contacts?"

"*My* contacts? Bill, he's the businessman who makes the contacts. Always has. I take care of the New York office, which is a considerable job. We have a staff of eighty-five."

Connie said, "I told Eric I'll be giving a tour in China. I'm taking Chinese lessons right now."

Lisa Mallory laughed. "Save your time. They'll still be disdainful over there. See, *they* don't care," and she waved her hand at the crowd. "Some of them have been born in Buffalo, too! It's the Chinese you can't fool. They know you're not the genuine article—you and I."

Her face was suddenly heightened in color, and she was breathing as if ready to flee from something. "Yes, you heard right. I was born in Buffalo."

"You were!" Connie exclaimed before she could control her amazement.

"Well, what about you?" Lisa retorted. She was actually shaking and trying to hide it by making sudden gestures.

"Westchester."

"But your parents at least were Chinese."

"Well, so were, so are, yours!"

"I was adopted by Americans. My full name is Lisa Warren Mallory."

Incredulous, Connie said, "I'm more Chinese than you!"

"Who isn't?" She laughed, unhappily. "Having Chinese parents makes all the difference. We're worlds apart."

"And all the time I thought . . . never mind what I thought."

"You have it over me. It's written all over you. I could tell even in the dark that night."

"Oh, Lisa," Connie said to comfort her, "none of this matters to anybody except us. Really and truly. They're too busy with their own problems."

"The only time I feel Chinese is when I'm embarrassed I'm not more Chinese—which is a totally Chinese reflex I'd give anything to be rid of!"

"I know what you mean."

"And as for Eric looking down his nose at me, he's knocking himself out to be so American, *but as a secure Chinese!* What's so genuine about that article?"

Both of them struck their heads laughing, but their eyes were not merry.

"Say it again," Connie asked of her, "say it again that my being more Chinese is written all over me."

"Consider it said," Lisa said. "My natural mother happened to be there at the time—I can't help being born in Buffalo."

"I know, I know," Connie said with feeling. "If only you had had some say in the matter."

"It's only Orientals who haunt me!" Lisa stamped her foot. "Only them!"

"I'm so sorry," Connie Sung said, for all of them. "It's all so turned around."

"So I'm made in America, so there!" Lisa Mallory declared, making a sniffing sound, and seemed to be recovering her sangfroid.

Connie felt tired—as if she'd traveled—but a lot had been settled on the way.

DIANA CHANG

Mamala the Surf Rider   MAYUMI ODA
silkscreened print
24" x 36"

Through creating goddesses, I become stronger. Art has been a means for my survival.
Through my creative process I have been creating myself. Goddesses are projections of

Samansabadra   MAYUMI ODA
                        silkscreened print
                            29" x 40"

*myself and who I want to be. Each picture represents a stage of my own development,
the influences I am feeling and the events which are going on around me.*

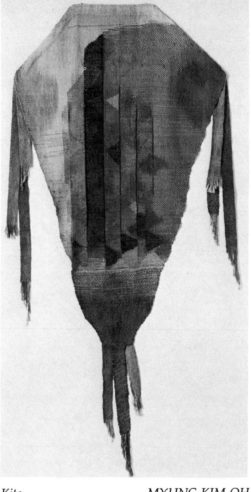

Kite   MYUNG KIM OH
linen, silk, wool, cotton weaving
42" x 58"

Baek-do *and* Kite *are objects (remnants?) of a Korean childhood—kites flown on holidays,* baek-do! *cried during the fever of a family board game—images born of a singular psyche but ones that ultimately address the interplay between personal and cultural memory.*

Baek-do   *linen, cotton, silk weaving*   MYUNG KIM OH
            49" x 58"

Off the loom warp painting, an intrinsic part of both these pieces, allows for discovery during the actual weaving process—so that emerging images enact the very cycle of recovery and erasure by which one comes to understand one's own history and one's place in history.

untitled   *plaster sculpture*   *ALISON KIM*

I continually struggle with the coming out process, whether as a lesbian, as a writer, or as an artist. Being able to name myself I give voice to who I am. My art is the reflection of me—Asian woman.

To Winnie Mandela   BETTY NOBUE KANO
acrylic canvas

As artists, our challenge is to bring humanistic values to an overwhelmingly technological society. It is to give voice to the mute, the meek and the defenseless; it is to nurture the will to live, to inspire hope and to give evidence of the struggle to survive.

Winnie Mandela made a quilt for her husband Nelson's 65th birthday. She has been banned in her native South Africa and he has been imprisoned for nearly 25 years as the leader of the banned African National Congress. The South African police confiscated the quilt because it was GREEN, YELLOW, and BLACK, the colors of the A.N.C.

Carry Me Back to Old Virginny   *whiteware clay*   MASAKO MIYATA
17" x 17" x 12"
photo by Steve Zapton

When I came to the U.S.A. in 1970, I had the intention to blend the concept of Japanese traditional beauty with American ideas toward art. I also have been interested in textiles and quite often drew ideas from old and contemporary fabrics designed in Japan. My

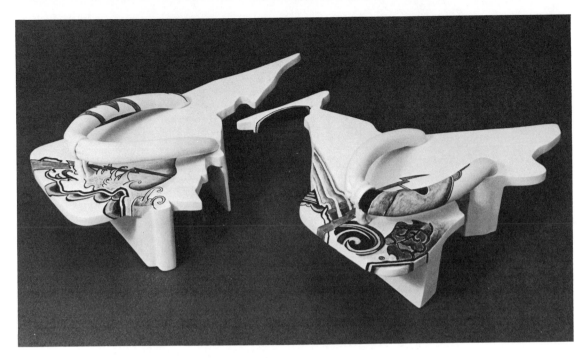

Tatooed Geta With Two States   *whiteware clay*   MASAKO MIYATA
9" x 10" x 4" x 11½"
photo by Steve Zapton

admiration for the elegance of the Japanese traditional wrapping cloth, furoshiki, and
my interest in the beauty which results from the sharp conflict between two or more
incompatible objects materialized in pieces such as [these].

Girl With Vase of Flowers   *acrylic painting*   MINÉ OKUBO
                                 41½" x 52½"

In painting I followed the French Impressionists in their open and pure use of form and color, and I went full circle back to the true vision of a child. Simplicity in the use of form and color returns to the primitive arts and to my ancestral art. With simplicity and beauty as my aim and purpose and by staying with the content of reality and the universal

Cat With Flags   *acrylic painting*   MINÉ OKUBO
                     26" x 34"

timeless and ageless values, I took everything in painting back to the fundamentals and basics. In this discard process I found my own identity and forms to express people and life in a simple, imaginative way.

Drawings from Citizen 13660   *pencil drawings*   MINÉ OKUBO

In the camps, first at Tanforan and then at Topaz in Utah, I had the opportunity to study the human race from the cradle to the grave, and to see what happens to people when reduced to one status and condition. Cameras and photographs were not permitted in the camps, so I recorded everything in sketches, drawings, and paintings. Citizen 13660 began as a special group of drawings to tell the story of camp life for my many friends who faithfully sent letters and packages to let us know we were not forgotten.

These drawings are excerpted from the book Citizen 13660 (University of Washington Press, 1983)

Miné Okubo

Photograph by Clemens Kalischer

MINÉ OKUBO: AN AMERICAN EXPERIENCE

BETTY LADUKE

I learned of artist Miné Okubo through Japanese American poet Lawson Inada. He presented me with an extensive catalog of her drawings and paintings, *Miné Okubo: An American Experience.* The Oakland Art Museum of Oakland, California, published this catalogue in 1972 in conjunction with her major retrospective exhibit. I realized that Okubo and Inada share aspects of an "American Experience" that form a significant bond and focus for their art and writing.

The serene painting reproduced on the catalog cover is Okubo's mother, seated on a bench with a Bible on her lap and a plump cat nestled beside her. A tree-lined path, white frame houses, and a church in the background portray the rural tranquility of Riverside, California, where Okubo was born in 1912 and spent her childhood.

The possibility of an American Dream was shattered for West Coast Japanese Americans when, in 1942 after the outbreak of World War II, the loyalty of second generation *(nisei)* and third generation *(sansei)* Japanese Americans was questioned. One hundred and ten thousand Japanese Americans were evacuated from their homes by the U.S. government into remote relocation camps throughout the country.

Okubo was identified as Number 13,660. In the camp her bitterness turned into a survival philosophy; "I had the opportunity to study the human race from the cradle to the grave and to see what happens to people when reduced to one status and condition." She made her "American Experience" visible in hundreds of pen and ink sketches, charcoal and pastel drawings and watercolor paintings, which told "the story of camp life for my many friends, who faithfully sent letters and packages to let us know we were not forgotten." These powerful images serve as a unique historical documentation of suffering, endurance, and ability to survive with dignity.

I visited Miné Okubo in her small Greenwich Village apartment where she has lived alone for the past 40 years. Her dark brown hair with hardly a touch of grey was pulled back from her smooth, broad face. At age 73 her intense gaze and youthful smile, evident in earlier photographs, had not diminished. An immense accumulation of paintings was stacked along all the walls, the results of long years of prolific production and ongoing commitment to her art. I was delighted when Okubo gradually began to pull out innumerable drawings and paintings from a smaller adjoining room. She generously showed me a view of five decades of her art and her more recent work on the path to "finding my own handwriting." I saw the evolution of the style and content of her work from early figurative realism, through experimental abstract forms to expressionistic landscapes, still life and portrait studies, and concluding with her present acrylic paintings featuring simplified forms in a mood of playful but controlled calm.

Okubo revealed that her mother was a calligrapher, painter, and graduate of the Tokyo Art Institute. After her mother came to the United States and married, her creative endeavors were submerged while she struggled to raise seven children. She always encouraged Okubo to pursue her interest in art. Okubo's father was a "learned man" who first owned a confectionery store, but later worked as a gardener. Okubo recalls her parents as "suffering and always living for their children." "As a child," she says, "I was shy and no one could talk to me," but "among my own brothers, I learned to be a fighter, to have my feet on the ground."

Okubo considers "institutions and routines always a bother for a creative and constructive mind." Nevertheless, she attended the University of California at Berkeley. Her art training included classes in the techniques of fresco and mural painting, useful skills for the subsequent development of her art career. She graduated in 1936 with a Master's degree in art and in 1938 was the winner of the University's highest art honor, the Bertha Taussig Traveling Scholarship, giving her the opportunity to take a freighter (alone) to Europe. There she enjoyed visiting museums, hiking and bicycling, and also produced watercolor paintings about the people and activities she encountered. This experience was a turning point in her art as she began to use brighter colors and more expressionistic brush strokes.

After returning home in 1939 due to the outbreak of World War II, Okubo participated in the Federal Arts Program by creating mosaic and fresco murals for the U.S. Army at Fort Ord, Government Island, Oakland Hospitality House, and Treasure Island, California.

In 1942 Okubo and all the other West Coast Japanese Americans were given three days to condense all their worldly possessions into a few bundles. Her family was split by the evacuation. She and one younger brother were sent to a camp in Topaz, Utah, her sister to Hart Mountain, Wyoming—and an older brother was drafted into the U.S. Army! The forced relocation severed them from their roots, dreams, and aspirations.

In the camp, Okubo began to document the emotional impact of this experience—the depersonalization, restrictions, depression, and shattered dreams. She also documented the many adaptations the detainees made to cope with basic survival, their communal eating, toilet facilities, and mundane work. These scenes are depicted in a series of two hundred pen-and-ink illustrations accompanied by satirical commentary, first published as a book, *Citizen 13660,* in 1946 by Columbia University Press, and more recently by the University of Seattle Press. With a few brief strokes of her pen, she captured the essence of events. The *New York Times Book Review* considered these drawings:

A remarkable objective and vivid art and even humorous account . . . In dramatic and detailed drawings and brief text, she documents the whole episode . . . all that she saw, objectively, yet with a warmth of understanding.

Miné Okubo took her months of life in the concentration camp and made it the material for this amusing, heart-breaking book . . . the mood is never expressed, but the wry pictures and the scanty words make the reader laugh— and if he is an American too—sometimes blush.

Okubo also did hundreds of charcoal and gouache paintings that revealed the psychological impact of camp life. During these years, she tells me, "I hardly slept, I worked mostly all night. To discourage visitors I put a sign up on my door that said 'quarantined.'"

Even from the camp, she maintained her professional connections—by sending work out. She proudly remembers, "Before evacuation, I was winning prizes almost every year from the San Francisco Museum of Art." Later in 1948 she again received the Museum's annual painting prize.

As part of her earlier training, Okubo explained that she had briefly experimented with abstract images. Though she soon abandoned pure abstraction, many of her images of camp life are based on simplified forms with basic rhythmic lines and shapes, often showing children and adults with large, somber facial expressions, small empty hands, and the dismal camp barracks in the background. Her watercolors from this period are more expressionistic. They depict men resting beside their harvested potatoes or camp residents lined up before the communal mess hall. In the catalog essay, *Miné Okubo: An American Experience*, Shirley Sun says of these drawings and paintings:

> The exaggerated heads, the hunched backs, the inward staring eyes all paint for us a psychological and social reality in the profoundest human terms so that no person seeing them can remain untouched. Notwithstanding, the dignity of men, women and children—however diminished—still comes through during this time of moral uncertainties, confusion and contradiction. Always, the human relations are kept intact—no matter how topsy-turvy the world. Indeed the life bond of men, women and children asserts itself more strongly than ever in face of the threat of annihilation.

Trek Magazine was initiated in the camp by Okubo and several friends, including the writer Toshio Mori. Okubo created the cover designs and many of the illustrations appearing in the three issues. The editors of *Fortune Magazine* were impressed by Okubo's illustrations and arranged for her to leave the camp in 1944 (prior to the conclusion of the war), in order to illustrate a feature story about Japan.

She had three days to pack her things. She arrived in New York "with just what I could carry in my hands." Again, Okubo felt as if she was "thrown in the middle of a desert," as she knew no one in New York. Her isolation did not last long. Soon her tiny apartment became a receiving center for many West Coast Japanese Americans relocating to the East after the war.

During the next ten years, Okubo successfully established herself in the commercial art field, working for *Fortune, Time, Life, Saturday Review, The New*

York Times, and *The San Francisco Chronicle,* and illustrating books for leading publishing houses. She painted four murals for the American Lines, a major shipping company. "At first," Okubo said about her work in the commercial art field, "everybody is friendly. Then it becomes establishment, where people are just out for themselves and you're playing a game. I knew all the ropes before I told them all to go to hell." Okubo courageously determined to "go back into painting and dedicate myself to the highest ideals in art." She says, "You can't serve two masters at the same time."

From 1950 to 1952 Okubo returned briefly to the West Coast and the University of California as a lecturer in art, but rejecting a steady teaching routine, she returned to New York. Okubo now realized, "If you're not following the current art trends (abstract expressionism), they think you're really cracked." She abhorred art that glorified "throwing paint and putting titles on it," and "living in a fantasy," and pursued her own inner vision of art based on the "mastery of drawing, color, and craft," and "staying with the subject and reality, but simplifying like the primitives."

In Okubo's paintings of the 1950's and 1960's, the underlying dark fragmented calligraphy which gives structure to her impressionistic portrait, still life and flower forms is overlaid with light pastel tones and occasional deeper accents of pure bright color. For the first time she turns to her Japanese heritage, to Japanese folk traditions, and to her childhood memories for inspiration. Children at play, children juxtaposed to cats, fish and birds are her basic themes. In this "Happy Period," the subject and background are often unified through an interplay of line and shape, like an intricate rhythmic dance step that moves over the entire surface.

Several early major exhibits of Okubo's work include: the Mortimer Levitt Gallery, New York City, 1951, the Image Gallery, Stockbridge, Massachusetts, 1964, and the Oakland Art Museum, California, 1972. Throughout the years she has also participated in many significant group exhibits of paintings and drawings of the Japanese Relocation Camps.

Long years of isolation and rejection followed. Okubo explained to Shirley Sun:

> You either pursue the art business-show business system as a promotion game, or you're on your own, which often means that your works don't sell. I didn't follow any trend or any one . . . My work was not accepted because you are judged by those who play the "game" — the critics and the dealers. Because my paintings are different and don't fit into the ongoing trend, the museums and galleries don't know where to place me. Their doors were closed to me.

"Luckily the people saved me—the little people from whom I borrowed money and the few collectors who helped me with rent. I found that you're better off if you are a nobody. You can't learn until you realize you are nothing."

When I asked her about her personal life, Okubo admitted to being a "universal mother." She has a wide circle of friends that include the neighborhood shopkeepers and their families. She adds, "I am interested in people, but everybody is alone whether they like it or not. I have had many suitors and marriage proposals, but I'd rather be myself, doing what I want to do. I never bothered to get married since woman's role is second, no matter what you think of yourself. Why in the hell should I wash a man's socks?"

Okubo looks back upon the past and says, "Up until 1960, people still had idealism." Since then, due to their "insecurity, fear, and ego, the gates close, and people are locked up in themselves. I'm using painting to prove the McCoy, the truth of life. Subject matter doesn't matter too much. You should never close doors because time always turns something around as nothing has changed since the beginning of time."

The overall surface texture and underlying calligraphy of her earlier work has evolved into larger, bolder, more stylized forms. Her recent paintings (1981-1985) vary in size from 12 by 18 inches to 36 by 48 inches, and include delightful and almost deliberately child-like images such as "Cat with Flags," "Girl with Fish," "Lady, Cat and Lemons" and "Fish and Flag." These ultimate images are representative of what Okubo considers her "long 40-year search for the simple vision we are born with that gets messed up, so I have to go back and find myself again." She admits, "You can't beat the primitives! It's born in them, but I have to arrive at a more intellectualized simplicity."

As a pioneer and a survivor, Okubo has maintained both optimism and humor. "Nothing gets me down," Okubo says. "I can see I'm on the right road, though people think I'm crazy because I'm not on Madison Avenue."

A major event in Okubo's career was her 40-year retrospective exhibit held at the Elizabeth Gallery in New York City in 1985. This unique gallery, also known as the Basement Workshop and Amerasia Creative Arts, was established in 1971 to offer Asian American artists, dancers, writers and actors a place to "create an art and a culture reflective of our experiences and political sensibilities."

Okubo's exhibit contained over 80 examples of her art, including drawings and paintings from the camp experience. The exhibit gave Okubo the opportunity to look back upon her life's work and to affirm for herself that she is indeed "on the right path." She says, almost as if she had been a hermit, "I am barely coming out now, after 40 years of isolation to build myself up; 1986 will be my year for bringing works to the public." Unfortunately, "The research and study took so long that many of my friends who were rooting for me are long gone, but their faith in me has survived."

"Good artists are full of anger," Okubo says. "They see the conditions of our time, the reality, the truth, and how they're up against it." She feels anger makes you fight, but believes that, "If you do your best, you're bound to hit something. The world is all shot to hell, but you still have to go on hope."

As a living repository and documentor of Japanese American history, Miné Okubo is receiving "too many requests" from the younger generation—the *nisei* and *sansei*—for lectures and exhibits of her work. Though pleased by this ongoing recognition, she is also frustrated by "the lack of time to do my own work." Will she once again have to place the "Quarantine" sign on her door?

BETTY LADUKE

CHILDREN ARE COLOR-BLIND

I never painted myself yellow
the way I colored the sun when I was five.
The way I colored whitefolks with the "flesh" crayola.
Yellow pages adults thumbed through for restaurants,
taxis, airlines, plumbers . . .
The color of summer squash, corn, eggyolk, innocence and tapioca.

My children knew before they were taught.
They envisioned rainbows emblazoned over alleyways;
Clouds floating over hilltops like a freedom shroud.
With hands clasped, time dragged them along and they followed.

Wind-flushed cheeks persimmon,
eyes dilated like dark pearls staring out the backseat windows,
they speed through childhood like greyhounds
into the knot of night, hills fanning out,
an ocean ending at an underpass,
a horizon blunted by lorries, skyscrapers,
vision blurring at the brink of poverty.

Dani, my three-year-old, recites the alphabet from
billboards flashing by like pages of a cartoon flipbook,
where above, carpetbaggers patrol the freeways like
Olympic gods hustling their hi-tech neon gospel,
looking down from the fast lane,
dropping Kool dreams, booze dreams, fancy car dreams,
fast foods dreams, sex dreams and no-tomorrow dreams
like eight balls into your easy psychic pocket.

"Only girls with black hair, black eyes can join!"
My eight-year-old was chided at school for excluding a blonde
from her circle. "Only girls with black hair, black eyes
can join!" taunted the little Asian girls, black hair,
black eyes flashing, mirroring, mimicking what they heard
as the message of the medium, the message of the world-at-large:
        "Apartheid, segregation, self-determination!
        Segregation, apartheid, revolution!"
Like a contrapuntal hymn, like a curse that refrains in
a melody trapped.

Sometimes at night I touch the children when they're sleeping
and the coolness of my fingers sends shivers through them that
is a foreshadowing, a guilt imparted.

Dani doesn't paint herself yellow
the way I colored the sun.
The way she dances in its light as I watch from the shadow.
No, she says green is her favorite color.
"It's the color of life!"

GENNY LIM

STANDING IN THE DOORWAY,
I WATCH THE YOUNG CHILD SLEEP

Twenty months out of the womb,
your daughter lies still on the flat plane
of the twin bed, the sheet pulled taut
over her body like a second skin.
With her eyes closed to the dark,
does she remember the curve of your arms,
the slow pace and rhythm of your walk?
Or does she dream
of the swell and curl of the ocean,
drifting with the push of the moon,
the pull of the sun? That night,
you whimpered and clutched
at your pillow. Opening your eyes
to the dead quiet of the house,
you shrank away from the window
where a full moon hung pierced
on an apple tree's thin branches.
Your daughter rubs her cheek with her hand
and I can see our mother folding you
close into the creases of elbow and lap,
resting your head between the hills
of her breasts. Here, in this one shade
of night stretched over the room,
I can almost feel our mother's warm breath
as she leaned forward,
hiding your face
behind a fall of black hair.

SHARON HASHIMOTO

ELEVEN A.M. ON MY DAY OFF, MY SISTER PHONES DESPERATE FOR A BABYSITTER

Sitting in sunlight, the child
I sometimes pretend is my own
fingers the green weave of the rug
while the small shadow of her head falls over
a part of my lap and bent knee. At three,
she could be that younger part of myself, just beginning
to remember how the dusty warmth feels on her back.
"Are you hungry?" I ask. Together we open
the door of the refrigerator. One apple sits
in the vegetable bin but she gives it to me,
repeating her true mother's words "to share."
Turning the round fruit under the faucet,
the afternoon bright in my face, I look down
at a smile in the half moons of her eyes
and for a moment, I'm seven, looking up
at my childless aunt in Hawaii,
her hands and the long knife peeling
the mango I picked off the tree, rubbing my arms
from the stretch on the back porch
to an overhead branch. Plump
with the island's humidity, it tasted tart
like the heavy clatter of rain on a June Sunday.
"Careful," my niece warns as I slice the apple sideways
to show her the star in the middle.
She eats the core but saves the seeds
to plant in the soft earth of my yard.

SHARON HASHIMOTO

LEARNING TO SWIM
for Allan Braaten, 1968-86

In suits bright as birthday balloons
the children float across the pool
without their teacher's hand.
My daughter bobs for bright rings underwater.
The other children laugh.
Pink geraniums and impatiens spill
from redwood planters.
The sky is blue as love.

Allan, if you'd only waited
you could have had this, could have
watched your child swim across a pool,
could have looked into an August sky
and realized that sometimes things
are almost right.

Even in pools, water pulls
at your ankles. Your lungs ache
from learning to breathe.
In your drawing, the darkest feature
was the wave.

The day after your funeral
I wish I could have given you
this sense of water.
I realize why I care so much
that these children learn to swim.

ARLENE NAGANAWA

RED

my shoes are red
a red happy red brighter than the
red i see each month
no rose could ever match
a red as clean
a silken finish
like the sheen
of my shoes
who would think that shoes
a red happy red brighter than the red
i see each month
could make me smile

too bad my feet feel foreign in these shoes
but comfort never couples love

how i love new shoes
and when those shoes are tantalizing red
happier than happy, shinier than a rose
i walk unflinching
towards you
away
and back again

JEAN YAMASAKI TOYAMA

LETTER FROM TURTLE BEACH

Last week
our telephone pole sprouted
orchids. Dad picked 'em and I made leis
for Sunday Swap meet.
Dad and I enjoy going—
We buy bread for 50¢ a loaf,
best of all Dad enjoys
walking, and talking to his old friends.

Today, what a beautiful day.
Dad is poking around outside;
the cabbage got leaves already.
By supper, it'll be big as a head
ready to eat.

Not more to say.
Soon the turtles will be back.
Why don't you come home and help
watch them?

SUSAN K.C. LEE

SEWING WOMAN

I like crack-seed
After I married
I no like.
I like only sewing.
Too busy for eat anything.

Uncle Allen two years older than Uncle Albert
and Uncle Albert one year older than your mother
Your mother two years older than Aunty Alma
Aunty Alma one year older than Tom
and Tom one year older than Boy
and Boy two years older than Uncle Bung Choy

Seven kids I have
I raise them all my own
My husband no give me money
I sew all my kids' clothes
And I try to sell to the neighbors
I sell one dress for one dollar.

I like crack-seed
After married
I no like.
I like only sewing.
Too busy for eat anything.

ALISON KIM

203

PANTOUN FOR CHINESE WOMEN

At present, the phenomena of butchering, drowning and
leaving to die female infants have been very serious.
The People's Daily, Peking, March 3rd, 1983

They say a child with two mouths is no good.
In the slippery wet, a hollow space,
Smooth, gumming, echoing wide for food.
No wonder my man is not here at his place.

In the slippery wet, a hollow space,
A slit narrowly sheathed within its hood.
No wonder my man is not here at his place:
He is digging for the dragon jar of soot.

That slit narrowly sheathed within its hood!
His mother, squatting, coughs by the fire's blaze
While he digs for the dragon jar of soot.
We had saved ashes for a hundred days.

His mother, squatting, coughs by the fire's blaze.
The child kicks against me mewing like a flute.
We had saved ashes for a hundred days,
Knowing, if the time came, that we would.

The child kicks against me crying like a flute
Through its two weak mouths. His mother prays
Knowing when the time comes that we would,
For broken clay is never set in glaze.

Through her two weak mouths his mother prays.
She will not pluck the rooster nor serve its blood,
For broken clay is never set in glaze:
Women are made of river sand and wood.

She will not pluck the rooster nor serve its blood.
My husband frowns, pretending in his haste
Women are made of river sand and wood.
Milk soaks the bedding. I cannot bear the waste.

My husband frowns, pretending in his haste.
Oh, clean the girl, dress her in ashy soot!
Milk soaks our bedding, I cannot bear the waste.
They say a child with two mouths is no good.

SHIRLEY GEOK-LIN LIM

VISITING MALACCA

Someone lives in the old house:
Gold leaf carving adorns the doors.
Black wooden stairs still stand
And wind like arms of slender women
Leading to the upper floors.
It is as I remembered,
But not itself, not empty, clean.

Someone has scrubbed the sand-
Stone squares and turned them red.
The marble yard is stained with rain,
But it has not fallen into ruin.
Weeds have not seeded the roofs nor
Cracked flowered tiles grandfather
Brought, shining in crates from China.

Someone has saved the old house.
It is no longer dark with opium
Or with children running crowded
Through passageways. The well has been capped,
The moon-windows boarded.
Something of China remains,
Although ancestral family is gone.

I dream of the old house.
The dreams leak slowly like sap
Welling from a wound: I am losing
Ability to make myself at home.
Awake, hunting for lost cousins,
I have dreamed of ruined meaning,
And am glad to find none.

SHIRLEY GEOK-LIN LIM

There had been little warning, actually none at all to prepare her for her first encounter with the sea. At breakfast that morning, her son Raza said, "*Ama*, we're going to the seaside today. Jamil and Hameeda are coming with us." She had been turning a *paratha* in the frying pan, an onerous task since she had always fried *parathas* on a flat pan with open sides, and as the familiar aroma of dough cooking in butter filled the air around her, she smiled happily and thought, I've only been here a week and already he wants to show me the sea.

Sakina Bano had never seen the sea. Having lived practically all her life in a town which was a good thousand miles from the nearest shoreline, her experience of the sea was limited to what she had chanced to observe in pictures. One picture, in which greenish-blue waves heaved toward a gray sky, she could recollect clearly; it was from a calendar Raza brought home the year he started college in Lahore. The calendar had hung on a wall of her room for many years only to be removed when the interior of the house was whitewashed for her daughter's wedding, and in the ensuing confusion it was misplaced and never found. The nail on which the calendar hung had stayed in the wall since the painter, too lazy to bother with detailed preparation, had simply painted around the nail and over it; whenever Sakina Bano happened to glance at the forgotten nail she remembered the picture. Also distinct in her memory was a scene from a silly Urdu film she had seen with her cousin's wife Zohra and her nieces Zenab and Amina during a rare visit to Lahore several years ago. For some reason she hadn't been able to put it out of her mind. On a brown and white beach, the actor Waheed Murad, now dead but then affectedly handsome and boyish, pursued the actress Zeba, who skipped awkwardly before him—it isn't at all proper for a woman to be skipping in a public place. Small foam-crested waves lapped up to her, making her *shalwar* stick to her skinny legs, exposing the outline of her thin calves. Why, it was just as bad as baring her legs, for what cover could the wet, gossamer-like fabric of the *shalwar* provide?

The two frolicked by an expanse of water that extended to the horizon and which, even though it was only in a film, had seemed to Sakina Bano frightening in its immensity.

"Will Jamil and his wife have lunch here?" she asked, depositing the dark, glistening *paratha* gently on Raza's plate. She would have to take out a packet of meat from the freezer if she was to give them lunch, she told herself while she poured tea in her son's cup.

"No, I don't think so. I think we'll leave before lunch. We can stop somewhere along the way and have a bite to eat."

"They'll have tea then." She was glad Raza had remembered to pick up a cake at the store the night before (she didn't know why he called it a pound cake), and she would make some rice *kheer*.

If she had anything to do with it, she would avoid long trips and spend most of her time in Raza's apartment cooking his meals and watching him eat. The apartment pleased her. The most she would want to do would be to go out on the lawn once in a while and examine her surroundings.

Bordering each window on the outside, were narrow white shutters; these had reminded her of the stiffened icing on a cake served at her niece Amina's birthday once. And on the face of the building the white paint seemed impervious to the effects of the elements. Discolorations or cracks were visible, and she had indeed craned her neck until it hurt while she scrutinized it.

The apartment building was set against a lawn edged with freshly green, sculptured bushes, evenly thick with grass that looked more like a thick carpet than just grass. Located in a quiet section of town, the apartments overlooked a dark, thickly wooded area, a park, Raza had told her. Although tired and groggy on the evening of her arrival from Pakistan, she had not failed to take note of the surroundings into which she found herself. Her first thought was, 'Where is everybody?' while to her son she said, "How nice everything is."

Looking out the window of his sitting room the next morning, she was gladdened at the thought of her son's good fortune. The morning sky was clear like a pale blue, unwrinkled *dupatta* that has been strung out on a line to dry. Everything looked clean, so clean. Was it not as if an unseen hand had polished the sidewalks and swept the road? They now glistened like new metal. 'Where do people throw their trash?' she wondered when she went down to the lawn again, this time with Raza, and gazed out at the shiny road, the rows and rows of neat houses hedged in by such neat white wooden fences. In hasty answer to her own query, she told herself not to be foolish; this was *Amreeka*. Here trash was in its proper place, hidden from view and no doubt disposed of in an appropriate manner. No blackened banana peels redolent with the odor of neglect here, or rotting orange skins, or worse, excrement and refuse to pollute the surroundings and endanger human habitation.

She had sighed in contentment. Happiness descended upon her tangibly like a heavy blanket affording warmth on a chilly morning. Once again, she thanked her Maker. Was He not good to her son?

"Is the sea far from here?" she asked casually, brushing imaginary crumbs from the edges of her plate. Raza must never feel she didn't value his eagerness to show off his new environment. This was his new world after all. If he wanted to take her to the seaside, then seaside it would be. Certainly she was not about to be fussy and upset him.

"No, *Ama*, not too far. An hour-and-a-half's drive, that's all. Do you feel well?" His eyes crinkled in concern as he put aside the newspaper he had been reading to look at her.

She impatiently waved a hand in the air, secretly pleased at his solicitude. "Yes, yes, I'm fine son. Just a little cough, that's all. Now finish your tea and I'll make you another cup." She knew how much he liked tea. Before she came, he must have had to make it for himself. Such a chore for a man if he must make his own tea.

The subject of the sea didn't come up again until Jamil and his new bride arrived. Jamil, an old college friend of Raza's, angular like him, affable and solicitous, was no stranger to Sakina Bano. But she was meeting his wife Hameeda for the first time. Like herself, the girl was also a newcomer to this country.

"*Khalaji*, the sea's so pretty here, the beaches are so-o-o-o large, nothing like the beaches in Karachi," Hameeda informed Sakina Bano over tea, her young, shrill voice rising and falling excitedly, her lips, dark and fleshy with lipstick, wide open in a little girl's grin. There's wanderlust in her eyes already, Sakina Bano mused, trying to guess her age. Twenty-one or twenty-two. She thought of the girl in Sialkot she and her daughter had been considering for Raza. Was there really a resemblance? Perhaps it was only the youth.

"Well child, for me it will be all the same. I've never been to Karachi. Here, have another slice of cake, you too Jamil, and try the *kheer*."

For some reason Sakina Bano couldn't fathom, sitting next to the young girl whose excitement at the prospect of a visit to the seaside was as undisguised as a child's preoccupation with a new toy, she was suddenly reminded of the actress Zeba. The image of waves lapping on her legs and swishing about her nearly bare calves rose in Sakina Bano's mind again. Like the arrival of an unexpected visitor, a strange question crossed her mind: were Hameeda's legs also skinny like Zeba's?

Drowned in the clamor for the *kheer* which had proven to be a great hit and had been consumed with such rapidity she wished she had made more, the question lost itself.

"*Khalaji*, you must tell Hameeda how you make this," Jamil was saying, and Hameeda hastily interjected, "I think you used a lot of milk."

"Have more," Sakina Bano said.

Tea didn't last long. Within an hour they were on their way to the sea, all of them in Raza's car. Jamil sat in the front with his friend, and Sakina Bano and Hameeda sat in the back, an unfortunate arrangement, Sakina Bano discovered after they had driven for what seemed to her like an hour. It wasn't Hameeda's persistent prattle that vexed her, she realized, it was her perfume. So pungent she could feel it wafting into her nostrils, it irritated the insides of her nose, and then traveled down her throat like the sour after-taste of an over-ripe orange. But her discomfort was short-lived; soon she became drowsy and idled into sleep.

*

To be sure she had heard stories of people who swam in the ocean. She wasn't so foolish as to presume that swimming was undertaken fully clothed. After all, many times as a child she had seen young boys and men from her village swim, dressed in nothing but loincloths as they jumped into the muddy waters of the canal that irrigated their fields. But what was this?

As soon as Raza parked the car in a large, compound-like area fenced in by tall walls of wire mesh, and when her dizziness subsided, Sakina Bano glanced out of the window on her left. Her attention was snagged by what she thought was a naked woman. Certain that she was still a little dazed from the long drive, her vision subsequently befogged, Sakina Bano thought nothing of what she had seen. Then the naked figure moved closer. Disbelief gave way to the sudden, awful realization that the figure was indeed real and if not altogether naked, very nearly so.

A thin strip of colored cloth shaped like a flimsy brassiere loosely held the woman's breasts, or rather a part of her breasts; and below, beneath the level of her belly button, no, even lower that that, Sakina Bano observed in horror, was something that reminded her of the loincloths the men and youths in her village wore when they swam or worked on a construction site in the summer.

The girl was pretty, such fine features, hair that shone like a handful of gold thread, and she was young too, not much older than Hameeda perhaps. But the paleness of her skin was marred by irregular red blotches that seemed in dire need of a cooling balm. No one with such redness should be without a covering in the sun, Sakina Bano offered in silent rebuke.

The woman opened the door of her car, which was parked alongside Raza's, and as she leaned over to retrieve something from the interior of her car, Sakina Bano gasped. When the young female lowered her body, her breasts were not only nearly all bared, but stood in imminent danger of spilling out of their meager coverage. O God! Is there no shame here? Sakina Bano's cheeks burned. Hastily she glanced away. In the very next instant she stole a glimpse at her son from the corners of her eyes, anxiously wondering if he too were experiencing something of what she was going through; no, she noted with a mixture of surprise and relief, he and Jamil were taking things out from the trunk of their car. They did not show any signs of discomfort. Did she see a fleeting look of curiosity on Hameeda's face? There was something else, too, she couldn't quite decipher.

Relieved that her male companions were oblivious to the disturbing view of the woman's breasts, Sakina Bano sighed sadly. She shook her head, adjusted her white, chiffon *dupatta* over her head, and slowly eased her person out of her son's car.

The taste of the sea was upon her lips in an instant. Mingled with an occasional but strong whiff of Hameeda's perfume, the smell of fish filled her nostrils and quickly settled in her nose as if to stay there forever.

Milling around were countless groups of scantily clad people, men, women, and children, coming and going in all directions. Is all of *Amreeka* here? she asked herself uneasily. Feeling guilty for having judged Zeba's contrived imprudence on film a little too harshly, she tightened her *dupatta* about her and wondered why her son had chosen to bring her to this place. Did he not know his mother? She was an old woman, and the mother of a son, but she would not surrender to anger or derision and make her son uncomfortable. His poise and confidence were hers too, were they not? Certainly he had brought her to the sea for a purpose. She must not appear ungrateful or intolerant.

While Raza and Jamil walked on casually and without any show of awkwardness, laughing and talking as though they might be in their sitting room rather than a place crowded with people in a state of disconcerting undress, she and Hameeda followed closely behind. Her head swam as she turned her eyes from the glare of the sun and attempted to examine the perturbing nakedness around her.

Sakina Bano's memories of nakedness where short and limited, extending to the time when she bathed her younger brother and sister under the water pump in the courtyard of her father's house, followed by the period in which she bathed her own three children until they were old enough to do it themselves. Of her own nakedness she carried an incomplete image; she had always bathed sitting down, on a low wooden stool.

Once, and that too shortly before his stroke, she came upon her husband getting out of his *dhoti* in their bedroom. Standing absently near the foot of his bed as if waiting for something or someone, the *dhoti* a crumpled heap about his ankles, he lifted his face to look at her blankly when she entered, but made no attempt to move or cover himself. Not only did she have to hand him his pajamas, she also had to assist him as he struggled to pull up first one leg and then the other. A week later he suffered a stroke, in another week he was gone. It had been nearly ten years since he died. But for some reason the image of a naked disoriented man in the middle of a room clung to her mind like permanent discolorations on a well-worn copper pot.

And there was the unforgettable sharp and unsullied picture of her mother's body laid out on a rectangular slab of cracked, yellowed wood for a pre-burial bath, her skin, ash-brown, laced with a thousand wrinkles, soft, like wet, rained-on mud.

But nothing could have prepared her for this. Nakedness, like all things in nature, has a purpose, she firmly told herself as the four of them trudged toward the water.

The July sun on this day was not as hot as the July sun in Sialkot, but a certain oily humidity had begun to attach itself to her face and hands. Lifting a corner of her white *dupatta*, she wiped her face with it. Poor Hameeda, no doubt she too longed to divest herself of the *shalwar* and *qamis* she was wearing and don a swimming suit so she could join the rest of the women on the beach, be more like them. But could she swim?

They continued onward, and after some initial plodding through hot, moist sand, Sakina Bano became sure-footed; instead of having to drag her feet through the weighty volume of over-heated sand, she was now able to tread over it with relative ease. They were receiving stares already, a few vaguely curious, others unguardedly inquisitive.

Where the bodies ended she saw the ocean began, stretching to the horizon in the distance. The picture she had carried in her head of the boyish actor Waheed Murad running after Zeba on a sandy Karachi beach quickly diminished and faded away. The immensity of the sea on film was reduced to a mere blue splash of color, its place usurped by a vastness she could scarce hold within the frame of her vision; a window opened in her head, she drew in the wonder of the sea as it touched the hem of the heavens and, despite the heat, Sakina Bano shivered involuntarily. God's touch is upon the world, she silently whispered to herself.

Again and again, as she had made preparations for the journey across what she liked to refer to as the 'seven seas,' she had been told *Amreeka* was so large that many Pakistans could fit into it. The very idea of Pakistan fitting into anything else was cause for bewilderment, and the analogy left her at once befuddled and awed. But had she expected this?

The bodies sprawled before her on the sand and exposed to the sun's unyielding rays seemed unmindful of what the ocean might have to say about God's touch upon the world. Assuming supine positions, flat either on their backs or their bellies, the people on the beach reminded Sakina Bano of whole red chilies spread on a rag discolored from overuse, and left in the sun to dry and crackle. As sweat began to form in tiny droplets across her forehead and around her mouth, the unhappy thought presented itself to her that she was among people who had indeed lost their sanity.

In summer, one's first thought is to put as much distance as possible between oneself and the sun. Every effort is made to stay indoors; curtains are drawn and jalousies unfurled in order to shut out the fire the sun exudes. In the uneasy silence of a torrid June or July afternoon, even stray dogs seek shade under a tree or behind a bush, curling up into fitful slumber as the sun beats its fervid path across the sky.

Sakina Bano couldn't understand why these men and women wished to scorch their bodies, and why, if they were here by the shore of an ocean which seemed to reach up to God, they didn't at least gaze wide-eyed at the wonder which lay at their feet. Why did they choose instead to shut their eyes and merely wallow in the heat. Their skins had rebelled, the red and darkly-pink blotches spoke for themselves. Perhaps this is a ritual they must, of necessity, follow, she mused. Perhaps they yearn to be brown as we yearn to be white.

She felt an ache insidiously putter behind her eyes. The sun always gave her a headache, even in winter, the only season when sunshine evoked pleasing sensations, when one could look forward to its briskness, its sharp touch. The heat from the sand under the *dari* on which she and Hameeda now sat seeped through the coarse fabric after a while and hugged her thighs; as people in varying shades of pink, white and red skin ran or walked past them, particles of sand flew in the air and landed on her clothes, her hands, her face. Soon she felt sand in her mouth, scraping between her teeth like the remains of *chalia*, heavy on her tongue.

Ignoring the sand in her mouth and the hot-water-bottle effect of the sand beneath her thighs, Sakina Bano shifted her attention first toward a woman on her left, and then to the man on her right whose stomach fell broadly in loose folds (like dough left out overnight); he lay supine and still, his face shielded by a straw hat. Puzzled by the glitter on their nakedness, she peered closely and with intense concentration—she had to observe if she were to learn anything. The truth came to her like a flash of sudden light in a dark room: both the man and the woman had smeared their bodies with some kind of oil! Just then she remembered the oversized cucumbers she had encountered on her first trip to the Stop and Shop; shiny and slippery, one fell from her hands as she handled them, and she exclaimed in disbelief, "They've been greased!" How amused Raza had been at her reaction.

It's really very simple, Sakina Bano finally decided, sighing again, these people wish to be fried in the sun. But why? Not wishing to appear ignorant, she kept her mouth shut, although if she had addressed the query to Hameeda, she was sure she would not have received a satisfactory reply. The girl was a newcomer like herself. In addition, she was too young to know the answers to questions which warranted profound thought preceded by profound scrutiny. She didn't look very comfortable either; perhaps the heat was getting to her, too.

Raza and Jamil, both in swimming trunks, appeared totally at ease as they ran to the water and back, occasionally wading in a wave that gently slapped the beach and sometimes disappearing altogether for a second or two under a high wave. Then Sakina Bano couldn't tell where they were. They certainly seemed to be having a good time.

She and Hameeda must be the only women on the beach fully clothed, she reflected, quite a ridiculous sight if one were being viewed from the vantage point of those who were stretched out on the sand. And while Sakina Bano grappled with this disturbing thought, she saw the other woman approaching.

Attired in a *sari* and accompanied by a short, dark man (who had to be her son for he undoubtedly had her nose and her forehead) and an equally short, dark woman, both of whom wore swimming suits (the girl's as brief as that of the woman Sakina Bano had seen earlier in the parking lot), she looked no older than herself. Clutching the front folds of her *sari* as if afraid a sudden wind from the ocean might pull them out unfurling the *sari*, leaving her exposed, she tread upon the sand with a fiercely precarious step, looking only ahead, her eyes shielded with one small, flat palm.

This is how I must appear to the others, Sakina Bano ruminated. Suddenly, she felt a great sadness clutching at her chest and rising into her throat like a sigh as she watched the woman in the *sari* begin to make herself comfortable on a large, multi-colored towel thrown on the sand by her son and his wife; those two hurriedly dashed off in the direction of the water. Why are they in such haste? Sakina Bano wondered.

Her knees drawn up, one arm tensely wrapped around them, the woman appeared to be watching her son and her daughter-in-law. But could Sakina Bano really be sure? The woman's hand against her forehead concealed her eyes. As she continued to observe the woman's slight figure around which the green and orange cotton *sari* had been carelessly draped, she wondered what part of India she might be from. Perhaps the south, which meant she spoke no Hindi, which also meant a conversation would not be at all possible.

Sakina Bano's attention returned to Hameeda who had not said a word all this time. Like a break-through during muddled thought, it suddenly occurred to Sakina Bano that there was a distinct possibility Hameeda would be swimming if it weren't for her. In deference to her older companion she was probably foregoing the chance to swim. Will Raza's wife also wear a scant swimming suit and bare her body in the presence of strange men? The question disturbed her; she tried to shrug it aside. But it wouldn't go away. Stubbornly it returned, not alone this time but accompanied by the picture of a young woman who vaguely resembled the actress Zeba and who was clothed, partially, in a swimming suit much like the ones Sakina Bano saw about her. Running behind her was a man, not Waheed Murad, but alas, her own son, her Raza. Was she dreaming, had the sun weakened her brain? Such foolishness. Sakina Bano saw that Hameeda was staring ahead, like the woman on the towel, her eyes squinted because of the glare. Frozen on her full, red lips was a hesitant smile.

Once again Sakina Bano sought her son's figure among the throng near the water's edge. At first the brightness of the sun blinded her and she couldn't see where he was. She strained her eyes, shielding them from the sun with a hand on her forehead. And finally she spotted him. He and Jamil were talking to some people. A dark man and a dark girl. The son and daughter-in-law of the woman in the *sari*. Were they acquaintances then, perhaps friends? The four of them laughed like old friends, the girl standing so close to Raza he must surely be able to see her half-naked breasts. The poor boy!

They had begun to walk toward where she and Hameeda were seated. Raza was going to introduce his friends to his mother. How was she to conceal her discomfort at the woman's mode of dress?

"*Ama*, I want you to meet Ajit and Kamla. Ajit works at Ethan Allen with me. Kamla wants you to come to their house for dinner next Sunday."

Both Ajit and Kamla lifted their hands and said "*Namaste*," and she nodded and smiled. What does one say in answer to *namaste*, anyway?

Hameeda was also introduced. Kamla made a joke about "the shy new bride," Hameeda showed her pretty teeth in a smile, and then Kamla said, "You have to come, Auntie." Sakina Bano wondered why Raza appeared so comfortable in the presence of a woman who was nearly all naked. Even her loincloth was flimsy. Granted it wasn't as bad as some of the others she had been seeing around her, but it was flimsy nonetheless.

"Yes, it's very nice of you to invite us. It's up to Raza. He's usually so busy. But if he is free . . ."

"Of course I'm free next Sunday. We'd love to come, Kamla."

Kamla said, "Good! I'll introduce you and Auntie to my mother-in-law after a swim. Coming?" She laid a hand on Raza's arm and Sakina Bano glanced away, just in time to catch Hameeda's smile of surprise. Well, one's son can become a stranger too, even a good son like Raza.

"Sure. *Yar*, Ajit, are you and Kamla planning to go to the late show?"

"Yes we are. You? Do you have tickets?" Ajit wasn't a bad looking boy. But he didn't measure up to Raza. No, Raza's nose was straight and to the point, his forehead wide and his eyes well-illuminated. But he had changed somehow; she felt she was distanced from him. A son is always a son, she thought and smiled and nodded again as Ajit and Kamla uttered their *Namaste's* and returned to the water with Raza and Jamil.

"*Khalaji*, why don't we wet our feet before we go?" Hameeda suddenly asked her.

"Wet our feet?"

"Yes, *Khala*. Just dip our feet in sea water. Come on. You're not afraid of the water, are you?"

"No, child." She wasn't afraid. Her mind was playing tricks with her, filling her head with thoughts that had no place there. A change was welcome. "Yes, why not?" she said, as if speaking to herself. When she attempted to get up she found that her joints had stiffened painfully. "Here, girl, give me your hand." She extended an arm toward Hameeda. Why not, especially since they had come so far and she had suffered the heat for what had seemed like a very long time.

Hameeda had rolled up her *shalwar* almost to the level of her knees. How pretty her legs are, the skin hairless and shiny, like a baby's, and not skinny at all, Sakina Bano mused in surprise, and how quick she is to show them.

She must do the same, she realized. Otherwise Hameeda would think she was afraid. She pulled up one leg of her *shalwar* tentatively, tucked it at the waist with one swift movement of her right hand, then looked about her sheepishly. Hameeda was laughing.

"The other one too, *Khala!*"

Who would want to look at her aged and scrawny legs? And her husband was not around to'glare at her in remonstration. Gingerly the other leg of the *shalwar* was also lifted and tucked in. How funny her legs looked, the hair on them all gray now and curly, the calves limp. Now both women giggled like schoolgirls. And Raza would be amused, he would think she was having a good time, Sakina Bano told herself.

Raza and Jamil burst into laughter when they saw the women approach. They waved. Sakina Bano waved back.

Holding the front folds of her *shalwar* protectively, Sakina Bano strode toward the water. As she went past the other woman in the *sari* she smiled at her. The woman gave her a startled look, and then, dropping the hand with which she had been shielding her eyes from the sun, she let her arm fall away from her knees, and following Sakina Bano with her gaze, she returned her smile.

"Wait for me," Sakina Bano called to Hameeda in a loud, happy voice, "wait, girl."

TAHIRA NAQVI

I received a letter from my ex-husband. My almost late ex-husband because
he says he's dying. Not that it'll affect me at all since I'm hard as iron. Imagine
a house burning, everything turns to ashes. The fire escape alone remains
standing. That's me. He's always envied me this quality because he himself is
sensitive. That's why he's dying before his time. It's not his kidneys, lungs,
liver, that's killing him. It's his heart. It palpitates so. He feels everything. Felt
it when I said six years ago, "All right go!" He didn't mind the parting. But
there's a standard way of doing these things. Tears and pleading on my part,
firm refusal on his. Instead I took the initiative away from him as if I were the
man. And it's not as though I'm an American woman born and bred. Not that
he knows anything about American women or any other for that matter because
he's a decent man.

And it's this tendency to forget I'm a woman that brought down all our
misfortunes upon us. A tendency he detected in me even when he was living
in my father's house as the orphan nephew who had to be fed and clothed and
educated. Being a decent man he's grateful, though it was all done out of a
sense of duty, not affection. He sensed that. A nuisance, a poor relation. He
was only ten and I was sixteen when he was orphaned. Suddenly they both
died in an accident, his parents, sitting together in a horse-drawn *tonga* on a
stormy winter night in Lahore. The truck driver said how could he see the *tonga*
when there wasn't even a lantern dangling from it? That wasn't true because
they found the shattered lantern by the three bodies. The *tongawallah* died too.
Four if you count the horse which had to be shot later. What chance does a
tonga have against a truck?

. . . a question he asked himself throughout the period of our marriage—
a rhetorical question of course, because he always knew the answer. But he
was fatalistic, so he agreed to marry me. Now they all tell him he never should
have, but how could he have said no? Consider the scene. My father lay on his
death bed. I lay on the shelf. He pretended not to see. But then from his death
bed my father begged. She's twenty-five, he called out. The anguish in that cry.
In all decency then, the offer had to be made. How was he to know that my
father would survive another ten years and run through his fortune himself?
Or that when he brought me down from shelf to bed he'd turn the other way.
Dark, shapeless and hairy. He slept for years on his left side and dreamt of

buffaloes.

Still, he was young then. He came to America with such high hopes thinking that the streets were paved with gold. He discovered that the street in Brooklyn where we lived was riddled with bullets instead. He's sure to this day those were bullet holes. So he stayed in the studio. About the size of a servant's quarter at home, without a bathroom, rats, roaches, flies, even mosquitoes, everything the lower classes there are used to. Plus neighbors worse than ever he'd imagined, junkies all, he was sure. While I, having nothing to fear from bullets, lost no time, jumped on a subway to seek my fortune, got off at a station chosen at random. There I stood astonished. Naturally. Because Jackson Heights in New York City is like the smell of sandalwood coming from an apple tree. My senses whirled even faster than the *saris* on high-heeled *chappals.* Oiled plaits swung like pendulums against bare midriffs. Gold earrings tinkled, glass bangles jingled. Netted beards and saffron turbans. Hindi, Urdu, Punjabi, Bengali, English, too, in thick accents. And of course the smell of sandalwood. Then suddenly the spinning stopped and in my head I clearly heard a whirring sound.

And imagine his amazement when peeping anxiously through the window (where in his waking hours he kept constant watch with the blinds drawn down, of course) he saw me come home that same evening. I was lugging a sewing machine which I proceeded to open as soon as I entered. Without a word of explanation I sat down cross-legged (a common tailor sitting by a roadside sewing *shalwars* for laborers immediately came to his sensitive mind) and started sewing *sari* petticoats. He paced the floor for months exclaiming tragically, "A Master's in Persian poetry from Punjab University is sewing *sari* petticoats!" I could not see the tragedy for the dollar bills which Sardarji of Sari Mahal paid me regularly. But the green of the dollar bills which I flaunted at him so shamelessly made him so bilious he had to leave the country, went back to Lahore. There, he writes, it's all patronage and he's discovered he isn't a landowner's son. We're first cousins he reminds me in the next sentence. That's a relationship which can never be severed. Americanized as I am, that's surely something I still understand. The doctor's bills, he repeats . . .

Two thousand four hundred *rupees,* two thousand—I drum my fingers on my mahogany desk and look out of the picture window. It's not all that much he's asking. He doesn't know how my view's improved since I bought out Sardarji. I can see every one of the tall ships which will pass by today on the East River on their way to Miss Liberty to celebrate her centenary. I've waited all week for this moment. But now it's here all I can hear is hooves and wheels clattering down cobbled streets, the *tonga* and the truck. How I love that bit!

The stroke of genius I can't resist! Perhaps I shouldn't, but my weakness is still poetry. So I give in, take out my cheque book. Besides, suppose he's really dying. It's true about the first cousin anyway. And, as he points out, two thousand four hundred *rupees* at twelve *rupees* to the dollar equals only two hundred dollars. I pick up my pen then put it down immediately. He's not dying, it's a lie! The *rupee* is seventeen to the dollar in the black market. Over my dead body.

"Come and see," calls out my neighbor from her balcony.

I step out. It is indeed a fantastic sight, the East River. It's filled with *tongas*.

I go in and take out my calculator. At seventeen to the dollar two thousand four hundred *rupees* equal . . .

TALAT ABBASI

Last evening my husband told me that he was tired of seeing me looking so washed out and sick. He said, when I come back from the office, the least I can expect is a smiling face. You don't even give me that. It's bad enough that the house is in a mess, but you don't even seem to have time to entertain my friends properly when they come home. They must be wondering what sort of a wife I have. I tell you, I'm tired of all this. And he walked out of the room, slamming the door behind him.

My baby looked up and went back to her toy. My darling, I told her, my *rani beti*, do you like the toy, do you like it baby? Next time I'll get you a big doll that will open and close its eyes just like you. I nuzzled her and she gurgled with pleasure.

What I say doesn't even affect you, groaned my husband, returning to the room. Look at you, your face unwashed, your hair uncombed, lying on the bed like that. That's not what I married you for. For heaven's sake, get up and prepare something, my friends are coming home for tea. I said, today? He mimicked, yes, today, today. Is the *Maharani* too busy to look after them? I got up and went to the kitchen. O God, where to begin? The dishes had to be washed, the dinner to be made, also snacks for his friends. I put the potatoes to boil, best to make some *aloo sabji* and use the rest of them for *tikkies.* Then I took out the *sooji* to make *halwa.* That should be enough for them. Why did they have to come today? Even I was tired after a day at the office. The dishes were so dirty. I didn't expect my mother-in-law to wash them, but she could have soaked them in water at least. I suppose I should be thankful she remembered to fill the buckets before the water finished. Please God, I prayed, don't let the electricity go off too, these power cuts will be the death of me. I put the *dal* in the pressure cooker and began the dishes. How could I smile? What was there to smile about?

The bus back home had been so crowded. More so than usual, because the previous bus was held up by some college boys who were protesting about the irregular service. I could hardly get in and once I got in I couldn't move. It was horrible. I don't understand these men. Even if you are sitting they edge closer and closer to you and you can't do a thing. When the bus reached my stop I couldn't get out because I was stuck in the crowd and by the time I reached the door, the bus had started moving again. I told the driver to stop and he said something rude, but did. The air, how fresh it was, and the slight breeze against my face, so cleansing. I walked home slowly. This is the only time I ever get to myself. Sometimes I wished that I didn't know typing so that I didn't have to work, but if I didn't work we couldn't make ends meet. In my husband's matrimonial advertisement his family had insisted that they wanted a working girl, so I suppose it wouldn't be fair at this point to say that I just couldn't cope. When I was working before marriage, Ma would pack me a lunch of soft *parathas* with *sabji*. And when I came back she would make me a cup of hot tea and ask me how her *rani beti* was. Then she would talk to me and give me all the day's gossip—how lazy the *jamardani* was—how Mrs. Sharma next door had a fight with her husband. I always had a good laugh about Mrs. Sharma's fights, she had such a loud voice that very often we could hear her in the house. I wondered what she fought about. Sometimes I wish that I could fight, but I don't know how to, so whenever I'm upset I just go to the bathroom and cry instead. They all think that nothing bothers me. Let them. I long for Ma to come here and stay with me, but when I last wrote to her and asked her to do so she was very angry. Beti, she wrote, now you are a married woman and you must understand that a mother does not stay with her daughters, it is not the right thing to do. I miss her so much. No one talks to me here. Oh, they do in one sense, but not like Ma.

My mother-in-law called me, and I went to her room where she was lying down. She is always lying down. What are you doing, she asked me. She always wants to know what I am doing, whether I am in the kitchen or in the bathroom. Cooking, I said. Do you want any help, she asked as she did every day. No, *Mataji*, you rest, I replied as I did every day and returned to the kitchen. I remember once when I had said that I did need some help (some people were coming over for dinner that day) she never let me live it down. She kept telling the guests, the child is still young, she just cannot cope with the housework. She smiled gently as she said this and the guests all looked pityingly at me. Later my husband reproached me for letting her take on so much of my work. I felt so guilty.

The potatoes were ready. I kept half of them for the *sabji* and began to mash the other half for the *tikkies*. Vegetables were so expensive these days, not to mention essentials like sugar. One needs another emergency to get our country out of this mess, my husband had said as he cast his vote. But with the new government, prices have gone up still further. Once economy meant buying a *saree* or two less, now we have to cut down on things like fruits and sugar. Household stuff is almost impossible to buy. At the time of my marriage my parents gave me a refrigerator and a T.V. We would never have been able to buy them on our own. In the beginning my family was against giving the T.V., but my husband's side insisted, and as they were not taking any cash, my parents said that they might as well. Still, it was all so expensive, they spent about 50,000 *rupees* on the wedding and even then people said that they could have married me off in better style, considering that there were just my sister and I. Now my husband has taken out a policy for our daughter so that when it matures in another twenty years, we will have one *lakh rupees* for the marriage expenses. The price of gold has gone up so much. My parents gave me three sets of jewelry. I doubt if I can give my daughter even two. God knows how we'll ever have money to build a house after that. And house rents are soaring too, our tiny two-bedroom house costs us 1,500 *rupees* and that is supposed to be cheap! No wonder people are corrupt. How else can they build such huge houses in a city like this? That way my husband isn't bad—he doesn't take bribes, but when he sees other people doing it, he gets mad and takes it out on me.

I put the oil on the gas and began frying the *tikkies*. They should be here any minute. Oh, God, time for baby's milk. I put the milk to heat and got the bottle ready. Is everything ready? asked my husband from the next room. Almost, I replied. He never entered the kitchen. On principle. He can't even heat a glass of milk. That's a woman's job, he said when I once asked him to heat the milk for Baby while I was engaged in some other work. Once, when I was ill and my mother-in-law away, there was no one to look after the house. What chaos. My husband lived for three whole days on bread, butter and cheese, while I, in bed, was given the same. I had no alternative but to get well and stagger about the house, cleaning up the place and washing the dishes which had mounted alarmingly. During those two days he used twelve mugs, six plates, seven glasses, four knives, eight spoons and two forks—all of which awaited me. Also two trousers, two shirts, four banyans, one pair of *pyjama kurta* and three handkerchiefs. Thank God you're all right, he sighed when he heard me in the kitchen that evening. It is the nearest he has come to paying me a compliment—if you can call it one.

Well, the *tikkies* were ready. Just a few minutes for the *halwa*. I quickly gave Baby her bottle, went back to the kitchen and heard my husband yell that they had come. For heaven's sake, get dressed, he said, coming into the kitchen. You should have finished everything by now. Once you get stuck in the kitchen, you get stuck. Learn to be systematic. I rushed to the bedroom and feverishly washed my face and combed my hair. Should I change my *saree* or not . . . might as well, or he'd say something again. I changed and went to the drawing room with a smile.

Namaste, Bhabiji, Namaste, his friends said, what wonderful smells coming from the kitchen. Oh, it's nothing, I murmured, what will you have, tea or coffee? Please don't bother, they said. No bother at all, I replied, you must have something. Oh, well, said one, I'll have tea, the other said he would have coffee, but not to bother about anything else, no formality please. No, no, not at all, I said and went to the kitchen. I put one vessel for the tea and another for the coffee. Why couldn't they have asked for the same thing? Sometimes I felt glad that I was working, it provided some variety to this life of cooking and washing and cleaning. In the morning I get up at 5 a.m., make tea for everyone, milk for Baby, then get breakfast ready for the family. Sometimes my husband wants *parathas,* sometimes toast and eggs, sometimes he gets this craving for *dosas.* Then I pack our lunches for the office, make the beds and rush to catch the bus to work. No time to talk to Baby or cuddle her.

I took the tea and coffee to the drawing room. Thank you, thank you, they said, perfect weather for hot drinks. I looked out of the window. It was raining . . . I hadn't even known. Yes, perfect weather for tea and *pakodas,* they exclaimed. Good idea, excellent idea, beamed my husband, let us have some *pakodas.* Ah, this is what you would call doing poetic justice to the weather. So I went to the kitchen to do poetic justice to the weather. When they were ready I put the *pakodas, tikkies* and *halwa* on the tray and took it to them. Wonderful, wonderful, they said. What a feast you have laid out for us, you really shouldn't have bothered. No bother, no bother at all, I said. So, they enquired, how is your office? Fine, I smiled. It wasn't. Not now. In the beginning, when I started working, it was all so interesting. I met new people, got a salary, felt independent. But people are so strange. One day I happened to talk to one of my colleagues longer than I usually do. He was telling me about a book he was reading and I got so caught up in what he was saying that I hardly realized how time passed. That evening the girl who sits next to me said, so you had a nice chat did you? Yes, I replied, and then the way she was looking at me made me go red. The next day when he lent me the book I noticed another of my colleagues (male) looking meaningfully at me. Now whenever by chance I happen to talk to him everyone in the office watches and I feel so wretched. The men, especially, gossip so much. At lunchtime they sit among themselves and giggle. They seem to know everything—who is talking to whom, who is wearing what and who the boss favours . . . everything. They never seem to discuss books or music . . . and I miss both. We get bored *yar,* they say, we don't know what to do on weekends. Oh, how I long to be bored. Or just lie in bed with a book and listen to music. That's my idea of heaven.

It's nice to be independent, said my husband's friend, women like you will change the face of this country. Very nice *pakodas*, very nice indeed. Thank you, you're very kind, I murmured. We don't feel like leaving, he added as he settled more comfortably into his chair. Stay for dinner, said my husband at once, then we can all relax and *gup-shup*. That will be too much of a bother for your wife, said his friend. No problem, no problem, said my husband heartily. What is there? The food is ready, there is no such formality in this house. They all looked at me. Of course, I said, it's no bother. I excused myself and went to the kitchen. Would there be enough food for them? I felt like flinging the *dal* and *sabji* into their faces and was shocked at the force of the feeling. My husband followed me into the kitchen. Will the food be enough for them? I replied, it had better be. He hissed, what is the matter with you, stop acting difficult. I said, stop breathing down my neck. You invited them, not I. My husband said, this is the limit, I don't understand you. Is this the time to make a scene? Why don't you make another *sabji* and some *khir?* Because there is no other *sabji* and no milk for *khir*, I replied. We stared into each other's faces. I should have expected this, said my husband. Even my friends are not welcome in this house. If you are not prepared to look after them, you should have warned me earlier. This last-minute hysteria I will not stand for. I sank back against the sink. I said, then go and get the milk and *sabji*. Furious, he replied, how do you expect me to go; then who will look after them? I said, that's your problem. We don't have a servant. My husband said, you're always creating problems, this is what comes of being unsystematic. I reminded him, but you told me not to buy more vegetables and milk than was absolutely necessary because of the prices going up. This made him even angrier. What is the matter, can I help you, said my husband's friend, walking into the kitchen. I said, no, no, please. I can manage. I wondered what he would do if I had said yes, please help. The thought made me smile and my husband, seeing my face, gave a sigh of relief and ushered his friend out of the kitchen.

For dinner there were *puris, aloo, dal, karelas,* and mangoes with the cream that I had been collecting for the week's butter. I was so tired by the end of it that I could hardly eat. Then I put Baby to sleep and gave them all coffee. They finished the coffee, and said, *chalo, chalo,* let us go for a movie. Now? I asked. Of course, they replied. If we rush we can get tickets for the night show, *chalo,* let us go. Let us, agreed my husband, these impromptu decisions are always so enjoyable, one shouldn't always plan. I said, I have to wash the dishes. They replied, oh, do that tomorrow, you mustn't always work so hard. I said, but I have to go to the office tomorrow, and I'm tired. My husband replied, don't make a fuss, you are not the only one who has to go to office, even I have to go. That is the trouble with you. You don't know how to enjoy yourself. And *Mataji* will look after the baby. Don't make *her* an excuse now. *Chalo, chalo,* let us hurry.

I put the dishes in the sink, and then we rushed. The tickets were not available so we bought them in black—ten *rupees* each. In spite of that, we were just four rows away from the screen. As the hero and heroine sang their first song to each other I fell asleep. A deep sleep. My husband woke me up when it was over. They were all amused. Even here she sleeps, said my husband indulgently.

We reached our colony at 1 a.m., just managed to get the night service bus back home. I slept in the bus, too. As we walked back home from the bus stop, my husband's mood expanded. What a night, what a night, he exclaimed. He stopped and looked up at the heavens,

> *Palace-roof of cloudless nights!*
> *Paradise of golden lights!*
> *Deep, immeasurable, vast . . .*

he quoted dreamily. I leaned sleepily against his arm and he looked at me with something akin to pain. Sleep, always sleep, he said. Why can't you rise above such purely physical reactions? You lack soul.

When we reached home, I made the beds and sank into mine with a groan of satisfaction. Heaven. The trouble with you, said my husband, is that your whole attitude to work is wrong. You'll never get tired if you change your attitude to work. Learn from Khalil Gibran, and he quoted:

> *Always you have been told that work is a curse, and*
> *labor a misfortune.*
> *But I say to you that when you work you fulfill a part*
> *of earth's further dream, assigned to you when that dream*
> *was born,*
> *And in keeping yourself with labour you are in truth*
> *loving life,*
> *And to love life through labour is to be intimate with*
> *life's innermost secret.*

That is poetry, philosophy, truth, mused my husband. So were the *pakodas,* I sighed and slept.

ANJANA APPACHANA

Glossary:

RANI BETI: a term of endearment
ALOO SABJI: a vegetable preparation made out of potatoes
TIKKIES: cutlets
SOOJI: ream of wheat
HALWA: a sweet preparation
DAL: lentils
PARATHAS: a wheat preparation
SABJI: vegetables
JAMARDANI: sweeperess
EMERGENCY: the state of Emergency declared by Mrs. Gandhi
NAMASTE: a greeting with folded hands
BHABIJI: a term used to address one's sister-in-law
PAKODAS: another elaborate preparation
KHIR: milk pudding
CHALO: let us go
YAR: friend
GUP-SHUP: gossip

It has fallen into place finally. Yes, finally.

I was four then, but some memories are still vivid, etched in my mind, like the red bougainvilleas by my grandparents' house. The colours, everywhere the colours, outside, the garden, inside, bursting forth from vases in every room. My mother's embroidery all over the house, brilliant hues of red and gold and green, like the *sarees* she wore. Memories of fog and fireflies, and Ponni in her purple frock . . . her lice . . . my lice. Smell of firewood drifting from the bathroom to the kitchen, mingling with the smell of meat curry. Yes, meat curry and my tantrum, the Queen of all Tantrums.

My mother and I were living with her parents. More than a year, she tells me now. My father, a distant but beloved figure, was away. He was always away, she says. We hardly saw him those years. Papa. My Papa. Who tossed me up in the air, again, and again, made me fly. Who, in his green uniform and maroon beret, was the handsomest man in the world. Who took me for walks and told me the names of all the different flowers and trees. From whom I learned at age two, to recognize and say *Pottilocus* with aplomb. To whom I was always waving goodbye. For my father was in the army.

Where we lived, it was always raining, and I remember the sound of the rain that night as my mother told me my bedtime story. She alternated between the *Ramayana* and children's stories. That night it was Peter Rabbit's turn. Mother Rabbit cautioned her babies not to wander into Mr. McGregor's garden. Remember the end of your father, she says, Mr. McGregor put him in a pie. At this point my mother began to laugh. I asked, why are you laughing? Because, she replied, they made Papa Rabbit into a pie. What is a pie, I asked. (I did not know English then.) My mother struggled to find an Indian equivalent. At last she said, meat curry, my *Rani*. Mr. McGregor made Papa Rabbit into meat curry and ate him up. And so Mama Rabbit doesn't want her babies to wander into his garden. She began laughing again.

Meat curry? Papa Rabbit cut up into little pieces? Brown bits of Papa Rabbit floating in thick gravy, gone forever? Leaving them behind, never to return? I caught hold of my mother's *saree* with one hand and began pounding her thighs with the other. Tears coursed down my cheeks as I screamed, don't laugh, don't laugh, don't laugh. But she couldn't stop and I threw myself on the floor, screaming and kicking my legs in a fury of anger and anguish. What's the matter with you? asked my mother, trying to raise me, but I resisted and screamed louder. She picked me up and dumped me on the bed. Quiet, she said, quiet. Papa, I screamed, *my* Papa. If someone made *him* into meat curry and ate him, would you laugh, would you laugh? My mother's expression changed and she wiped my tears. No one will do that, she said. I shouted, will you laugh *then*, will you laugh *then*? She hugged me. I quieted down, but stiffened as I felt her body shaking with laughter. I pushed her away, and screaming again, threw myself on the floor.

My tantrum lasted an hour. My grandfather smacked my bottom and I kicked him, my grandmother cajoled me with sweets and I threw them, my mother tried to kiss me and I spurned her. It was one of my few tantrums on my father's behalf and left them all exhausted. When it was finally over, I sat quietly hiccupping on the floor and my mother apologised to me for having laughed. Looking suspiciously at her face, I saw no trace of amusement there and accepted her apology. Forgiven, she went through our nightly ritual of telling me how much she loved me—more than she loved my father, more than she loved my grandparents, more than she loved even God whom she knew so well.

Yes, my mother knew God. They were in constant touch. When I lied she would look into my eyes, then declare, you're lying. Broken, I would say, you know? And she would reply, God told me. God told her everything. When I spoke the truth, He told her it was the truth. I was sure my mother was conspiring with the gods in my grandparents' room, which had all their photographs and images. Were they all in league with her—Lord Rama, Lord Krishna, Lord Shiva, Lord Venkateshwara, Goddess Parvati, Goddess Saraswati, Goddess Lakshmi? I suspected it was Lord Rama who told my mother, for it was him she prayed to, his stories she told me every night. Or maybe it was Rama's devotee, Lord Hanuman. The more I pondered, the surer I was that it was Hanuman. Hanuman was a mischief maker, had created wonderful trouble against Rama's enemy, Ravana, raided his orchards, burnt his kingdom. How I laughed when my mother told me about his escapades, how I adored him for his loyalty to Rama. When we prayed to Hanuman on Tuesdays at the little temple outside our house, I placed extra hibiscus flowers at his feet in the hope that he would refrain from carrying tales to my mother. To no avail. My only friend, four-year-old Bina, refused to believe me when I told her of my mother's relationship with God. A box of matches tucked into her pinafore, she urged me to come with her to the end of the driveway where we could, one by one, burn them all. My hands itched with desire but my mother had once caught us at this activity and sternly forbidden it. God will tell her, I whispered to Bina. No He won't, she said, and taking my hand led me to the end of the curving driveway. The house was out of sight. We spent ten blissful minutes taking turns striking the matches against the box, watching them burst into flame and throwing them on the ground where they slowly burned out. Then, hand in hand, we walked back to the house and sat in the veranda. Soon my mother emerged with milk and cake. So, she said, placing them on the table, you have been playing with matches again? Bina's mouth fell open. I shook my head dumbly. Look into my eyes, my mother commanded, and gazing deep into them, said, God tells me you're lying. Don't do it again. She left, and Bina, wide-eyed, said, it's true. Yes, I replied, triumph struggling with frustration, it's true.

I loved my mother passionately, obsessively, jealously. I was well behaved only so long as no one made overtures to her, or to me. She was careful not to show anyone affection in my presence. On the rare occasions she slipped—kissed a sister, hugged a friend—the house resounded with my screams. Fond gestures that came my way were met with immediate, unequivocal rejection. My mother warned as many people as she could, but there were always those who didn't know, and suffered. One such woman, after a singularly unpleasant rejection of her advances, said of me, she has all her family's arrogance and nothing of their beauty. This was promptly conveyed to my mother who tells me how it made her seethe, all the more because she knew it was indefensible. Yes, I had none of the family's beauty, was actually almost ugly, and quite oblivious of the fact. Flat nose, huge nostrils, practically no eyebrows, a wide forehead, ears that stuck out and an expression of such pugnacity that most people kept their distance. Next to my parents I looked an anomaly, for they were both exceptionally good-looking. I was a late child, born after ten years of their marriage. During my mother's pregnancy, everyone predicted that I would be a beauty. Then I was born and they perceived that I was not, was in fact quite the opposite. But, says my mother, they were all quite polite about it, said you were a healthy child.

How I loved her. Every night and every morning she told me how much she loved me, a ritual I never tired of. And if an ugly child could be said to bloom, at each such declaration of her love, I blossomed. Her bedtime stories filled me with delight for they were mostly about mothers and children and she would demonstrate how much the mother loved the child by kissing and cuddling me. It was my mother who made all my dresses and sweaters, and when people complimented me on what I wore, I acknowledged the compliments unsmilingly. They were only giving my mother her due, and I would only smile for her. Why was I so insatiable? She could not have possibly given me more than she did. But I wanted more, more, more. When the dishes were cleared after our meals, I would insist that my plate be placed over hers. Once, as I suspiciously watched the plates being stacked, my grandfather's plate was placed over my mother's. It could not be borne, and neither, says my mother, could the tantrum that followed. On the days she washed her hair, I found the separation unbearable and waited outside the bathroom to ascertain that she came out. When I could no longer contain myself I would shout through the keyhole, Ma, call me your *Rani*, and she would respond, my *Rani*, my own *Rani*. Ma, call me your darling. Darling, my own darling. *Properly*, Ma, *properly*. *My* darling, *my Rani*. And then the endearments would become briefer and briefer as my mother lathered her hair, mixed the hot water from the big drum with the cold water in the bucket. I heard the sounds of water being poured, and waited. Then at last, *Rani*, I've finished, and I knew the worst was over.

We wrote to my father every day. My mother filled pages to which I added a few lines in exactly the way she did, the same round squiggles, the same periodic dots. And every day the postman delivered my father's letter. My mother gave me the envelope and read the letter over and over. Once when she had torn up my father's envelope, I had a prolonged tantrum.

I liked my grandparents. I had been made to understand that my mother was to them what I was to my mother and father. It did not seem possible though, for they had grey hair and wrinkles, belched and snored, smelled of snuff and incense, had eight other children and never told my mother stories or cuddled her. They didn't even want her on their laps. Once I insisted my mother sit on her mother's lap. My mother did, very gingerly, my grandmother groaned softly, and then they looked pleadingly at me. No, their relationship made no sense. My grandfather was delighted with this tableau, pinched my cheeks and said that I wasn't so bad after all.

And Ponni, the servant girl, three times my age, Ponni of the purple frock, Ponni with the lice. I passionately desired the frock, got instead the lice. Ponni, my companion, playmate, instructor. While my mother told me her nightly tales of the *Ramayana* and Red Riding Hood, Ponni informed me that newly married couples *had* to sleep together without clothes. My newly married aunt came to visit with her husband, and, in a roomful of chattering, excited relatives, I shook an admonishing finger at her. I said, I know what you have done. Oh, Ponni, Ponni, they sent you away, I never got to wear your purple frock and the delousing was painful.

And like the rain the people descended. Everyone wanted to visit my grandparents. They ate up all my cake, took my mother away from me, filled the house with talk. In the summer, which was the wedding season, it was worse—a torrent of daughters, sons, grandchildren from far-off cities, many related to us—all came to our town, and all came home. They brought with them cards, wedding cards, printed in gold, with Lord Ganesh or Goddess Lakshmi at the top, also in gold, with the promise of more glitter, more colour.

And one dark evening when the hills could not be seen for the fog and the fireflies were dancing beneath the big tree, he came. A distant cousin of my mother, it was his first trip in years to our little town. I had never seen anyone so tall, with eyes that danced and laughed and were the colour of ash, brown hair that glinted when the light touched it. After dinner we sat in the drawing room and I stared unblinkingly at him. He fished in his pocket, took out a wedding invitation card and tossed it on the table. For you, he told me, I want you to come for my wedding. I picked up the card and ran my finger over it. The gold print left gold dust on my finger tip. Nice. To my mind all worthwhile wedding cards did that. My mother murmured, she's not a very friendly child. He raised his eyebrows and surveyed me with his laughing eyes. Will you come for my wedding? I nodded. I would go. All those colours, beautiful women, and, best of all, the bride, like a big doll, as quiet, and exquisite in red and gold. I sat at Uncle-Grey-Eyes' feet and removed my socks. I said, I have red feet, and put them up for him to view. He expressed his pleasure, while my mother looked at me in shock. After showing him my red feet I somersaulted five times and told him none of my friends can do that. He shook his head in admiration. My mother tells me, you made me feel such a fool. I wouldn't let him leave. I showed him all the sweaters my mother had knitted for me and sang two songs that Ponni had taught me. Finally, protesting, I was taken to bed by my grandmother.

After that I remember him coming often, and always, with a wedding card for me. On mornings when wedding music drifted up to our house from the *samaj* at the hill below, I imagined it was his wedding and urged my mother to take me. But I was told that it was still a long time away. Often in the evenings, he, my mother and I would go for walks up and down the hills. They talked a lot, my mother and he, and I remember her so often, laughing. He even made me giggle—no mean achievement. Green misty green hills, my mother's *saree* a brilliant yellow, he tall in grey beside her, I, rolling down the hill.

I wish I could remember more. How badly I want to, for there must have been more. Or was there? I cannot remember and this, I cannot ask her. They have filled in most of the other details of those days, all but this. But then, why should they, they didn't know, he bore no relevance to anyone but the two of us. What was he like, I wonder. Gentle, ruthless, humourous? Wicked, tender, scheming? Innocent? Handsome? I don't remember.

Because, after that, I only recall *that* day, a day filled with sunshine, when our garden was a riot of roses and the bougainvilleas ablaze. He had come visiting again, was having coffee inside with my mother. My grandfather was asleep upstairs and my grandmother and I were in the garden, admiring the flowers. We walked up and down the driveway, talking amicably. Love for my mother filled me, could not be contained. I told my grandmother, big-big eyes she has. Yes, she nodded. I said, long-long hair. True, she agreed, true. I said, she's *my* mother, patting my chest with my hand. Yes, said my grandmother, cutting a red rose. *Only* my mother, I said. Unable to express more, I ran towards the house to show her how I felt.

They were in the drawing room, she on the sofa, he on the chair opposite the room and there was a terrible stillness in the air. He was looking at her and she at him and I was filled with such terror that I cried out her name aloud. They started. I shrieked, go, you go. He looked at me uncomprehendingly. I jumped up and down on the carpet, my fists clenched, panting, you go, go, go, go. He got up and came towards me. I lowered my head, charged and butted him hard below his knee. I heard him take in his breath and felt my mother's fingers grasping my shoulders, as I lowered my head again. I didn't stop screaming till he left, escorted outside by my flustered, apologetic grandmother and sleepy, irritable grandfather.

Spoiled, awful child, my grandfather told my mother when they came in. No manners, no sense of propriety. My mother, pale in her red *saree*, said nothing. I glowered at him. My grandmother shook her head reprovingly. She said, such an unpredictable child. She should mix more with children her age. My grandfather bent down and told me, bad girl, waking me up with your screaming. Furiously, I replied, *you* bad boy, you snore and wake *me*. My mother said, shhh.

I remember him coming just once more, and when I saw him in the driveway I began screaming like a person possessed. He stopped, turned and walked away. I trailed my mother with renewed persistence, refused to go anywhere without her, did not allow her to go anywhere without me. My mother's daily bedtime stories became abstracted.

Then, suddenly, there were those endless days without her. My grandmother told me that she had fever and that the doctor was making her all right. I was inconsolable. I wandered from room to room, looked for her in the bathroom, in the kitchen, under the beds and in the cupboards, finally shutting myself in her wardrobe, smelling her among her *sarees*, her talcum powder smell. My grandmother found me there much later, holding her petticoat against my face. She tells me that she couldn't bear it, burst into tears and asked my grandfather to send a cable to my father.

And my father came. My grandmother says, you held on to him and did not let go of him that entire evening. You didn't even let him get up to eat or go to the bathroom. Your poor, patient father. That night his unfamiliar body occupied the bed I shared with my mother and I cried for her again.

And my mother came. It was just five days, you know, she tells me. The reunion was ecstatic, if dramatic. How you women wept, my grandfather says, shaking his head. You, your mother, your grandmother. All weeping. But at least this time you didn't have your famous tantrum. And, says my father, I had my posting orders by then, there would be no more separations for us. I ask, but what happened, what *was* this illness? We are sitting in the veranda in my grandparents' house, it is the summer holiday and once again, the garden is bursting with colour. Nervous breakdown, says my grandfather. What, I exclaim. Nothing serious, he says. Must be running in the family, your grandmother had one too. Lucky for you that your mother was back in just five days. My grandmother kisses her hand and places it on my cheek, saying, she was back only because of you. She couldn't live without you. I say, oh Ma, how lonely those years must have been for you. Very, she answers, very.

Must be running in the family, he said. Well, either that or the tantrum. At thirty-six you couldn't have opted for the tantrum, could you, Ma. At twenty-five, neither can I. Too old for tantrums, too old. And I managed not to have the other, came back here instead, the memory returned, they filled in the rest and the dust slowly settled. Yes, finally.

There is a long silence and then my mother smiles and tells me, that night when the three of us were finally together, you put your arms around your father's legs, reached up and kissed his bottom. You said, Papa, they didn't make you into meat curry.

ANJANA APPACHANA

PICTURE BRIDE. Cathy Song, foreword by Richard Hugo, Yale University Press, 92A Yale Station, New Haven, CT 06520, 1983, 85 pages, $10.95 cloth, $4.95 paper.

Cathy Song, a writer living in Honolulu, Hawaii, received sudden, and some would say glorious, visibility, with the appearance of her first book of poems. Picture Bride is the 1983 winning manuscript in the Yale Series of Younger Poets Competition, perhaps one of the most prestigious literary prizes in the nation. Selected from among 625 entries by Richard Hugo, Picture Bride joins the company of other first books also published in the series, including books by previous Yale Younger Poets such as Adrienne Rich, W. S. Merwin, John Ashbery, and Muriel Rukeyser.

Song, a graduate of Wellesley College with an M.A. in Creative Writing from Boston University in 1981, is a relative unknown in the poetry world, although of late her poems have been appearing in small press journals and regional periodicals such as The Greenfield Review and Hawaii Review. Her first book, however, composed of 31 poems divided into 5 sections, shows a strong talent with a fully achieved style and recognizable voice. Its publication celebrates the full-blown emergence of a major figure on the Asian American literary scene.

In an interview in the Honolulu Star-Bulletin, 31 March 1983, Song expressed concern that her work may be seen as leaning too heavily on the Asian American theme. While she notes "it is a way of exploring the past," she adds, "I'll have to try not to write about the Asian American theme." Song's unease with Asian American materials is interesting, for it indicates her sensitivity to the possibilities of restrictiveness inherent in the fixed exploration of ethnocentric experiences. Nonetheless, her first book clearly attempts an ethnic identity, although it is uncertain whether the attempt was initiated by the poet or advised by her editors. Song had first called her book "From the White Place," after the title of a love poem dedicated to Georgia O'Keeffe, a favorite painter and perhaps a strong aesthetic influence; however, between winning the prize and its publication, the book's title was changed, reflecting a reordering of thematic emphasis.

The title poem which opens the collection is not among the strongest pieces in the book, but it does serve to underline the autobiographical, portrait-like, and not, incidentally, regional and ethnic thrust of the work. "Picture Bride" is an autobiographical piece on the poet's Korean grandmother who came to Hawaii to marry a stranger, thirteen years older than she, and it very neatly cues the reader to the major motifs in the book: the family, the Hawaiian rural landscape, the juxtaposition (if not actual conflict) of immigrant and New World cultures, and underlying these surface explorations, the tug of suggested tensions, chiefly sexual and aesthetic, in the image of the grandmother "politely" undressing herself in the dry hot wind blown from the burning cane fields and in the imaginative transformation of a room in a sugar mill camp to luminosity from the wings of moths / migrating out of the cane stalks.

The volume is indeed a heavily familial document; even where it is obvious that Song is not so much drawing upon direct autobiographical experience as framing observations and emotions in an invented fiction, kinship is a primary element in her work. Thus, in the final poem, "The Seamstress," the narrator/character maps her world by locating and observing her kin, her *ninety-two-year-old father* and her three other unmarried sisters. It is *a world of miniatures*, yet an attitude of approval halos the seamstress' (the alter-ego of the isolated craftsman) narrow interior life, almost as if the poet were suggesting that her domestic limitations and reassurances are analogous to discipline and achievement of the artist: *I work best in a difficult light. / The world for me is the piece of cloth / I have at the moment beneath my fingers.* There is a parallel irony accompanying the quiet heroism of the life described, for the poet tells us at the same time that such narrowness of experience and focus occur in *a lean-to of a room . . . an entire / wall without windows* and that the seamstress' dedication has lead to a spinal deformity, *the silhouette of a coat hanger.* The closed world of secure kinship and craft has its price, the unconsummated sexuality of the four sisters and their ultimate ignominious end. The poem's triumph lies in its fusing of irony and praise, so that the final resonance is in the paradox of the seamstress' fate, which is both pitiful and admirable.

Over two-thirds of the poems treat in some way family relationships; often they are recognizably autobiographical, first person, female. As the sequence of poems unfolds the reader begins to fill in the density of lives in intersecting histories and places: daughter/mother, daughter/ father, sister/brother, grandchild/grandmother, granddaughter/grandfather, and so on. These poems are family history, family album, testimony to the continuing strength of generational ties, and generally to the fructifying communion of kin with kin. It is little wonder then that a minor theme is that of the desire for children, of conception, and of child-bearing. Even in the poems where the poet appears to explore the larger world beyond the family (aptly enough, when the poems move beyond the Hawaiian environs to the Mainland and Europe), her escape is only momentary and she finally, gracefully, and almost gratefully, returns to the arms of her family.

"Blue and White Lines After O'Keeffe" demonstrates this emotional and experiential pattern. A microcosm of the collection, containing in its ambitious structure all five section titles of the book, the poem moves in geographical space, covering New York, New Mexico, Maui, Andalusia, and Wisconsin. The narrator is a young artist whose travels are the fiction that forms the occasion for the poet to evoke the five landscapes, ranging from *this skull hotel* with *an infantry of roaches* to *the back-bent hills / hold(ing) olive fields.* Her descriptions are vivid, particularistic, displaying her skills at metaphoric accuracy and dazzlement. The poem, however, comes to the point only in the last section when the narrator/artist abandons her geographical psychological flight to return to the mother whom for years she had *despised.* The mother, like the seamstress, inhabits a *constricted, shrinking* world and the artist must crawl *out from under your wide skirts* in order to discover *my own autonomy.* So far, we have a rather conventional formulation of the smothering mother and the artist as rebellious child. The poem, however, concludes with a reconciliation, in fact, with a recapitulation on the part of the artist / *I have come to rest at your feet /* who now accepts that her internal artistic motivations are embedded in, indeed, indistinguishable from the relationship with her mother: *When I stretch a canvas / to paint the clouds, / it is your spine that declares itself.*

Song's concentration on family portraits, history, and psychology just misses being claustrophobic, for together with the celebration of the ties that nurture is the contrary stubborn hymn to the self, the inner assertion which squints at symbiosis, and which dourly and in multiple aching associations waits the escape of the self from the mother. "The Youngest Daughter" and "The White Porch" are eminently successful expressions of this countertheme; in the first, the daughter dutifully washing her elderly mother, is *not to be trusted* and imagines her escape as in a sudden breeze, *a thousand cranes curtain the window.* In the second poem, the daughter is again trapped in domestic duties with the mother, in whose presence she wears her hair braided. The mother wears a gold ring and sleeps in *tight blankets.* At night, released from the mother's supervision, the daughter lets her hair down *like a measure of wealth* for her lover. The poem's imagery is wonderfully organic, beginning with the daughter washing her hair, following her through the restraints of housework and the intricacies of mother/daughter relationship, suggested in the mother's grabbing of her braid and in the strands caught in the gold ring, and ending with the lover smuggled in through cloth, hair, and hands.

Song's greatest strength lies in this marvellous organic nature of her imagery and in the complete fusion of form, image, occasion, and emotion. Every poem is marked by this naturalness of form, based unpretentiously on phrasal pauses or the breath of a line, by an unforced storyline or ease of observation; almost every poem has a sudden eruption of metaphor which startles, teases, illuminates.

At the same time, the collection sometimes is in danger of falling into predictable mannerisms, often mannerisms associated with Asian American culture. In her desire to present an Asian American culture, Song understandably reaches for the sensations, the tastes, smells, sounds, colors particular to that ethnic experience; some of her most forceful, because original, images come from this reaching out to Asian American particulars. For example, *The children are the dumplings / set afloat. . . . Wrap the children / in wonton skins, bright quilted bundles. . . .* But in this stylistic venture Song sometimes becomes too dependent on linguistic conventions which appear like a nervous tic throughout the poems: jade, sour plums, Mah-Jongg. In "Tribe," the girl has dumpling cheeks and tofu skin, the sister is *like a little Buddha.* One almost sees the creative writing instructor breathing over the poet's shoulder, urging her to write concretely about the particulars of her ethnic background, and although one can also imagine that it may be possible to write about jade, tofu and buddhas so that they illuminate Asian American experiences, Song's repeated use of these Asian cultural fragments is strained, mechanical, and unconvincing. Compare these decorative metaphors with the image of the mother and the aunts *in pedal pushers and poodle cuts, / carrying the blue washed eggs* in "Easter: Wahiawa, 1959," for genuine imaginative surprise and pleasure. Song writes most deeply when she gives up her concern with surface ethnic-coloristic effects and concentrates on the details of her world, her vision, in whose singularity we can all recognize ourselves.

Picture Bride shows us a true poet, but whether Song will choose to nourish her poetry on ethnic fare or to reach out to the undifferentiating totality of the life of the work still remains to be seen.

Shirley Geok-lin Lim

ASIAN-AMERICAN LITERATURE: AN INTRODUCTION TO THE WRITINGS & THEIR SOCIAL CONTEXT. Elaine H. Kim, Temple University Press, Broad & Oxford Streets, Philadelphia, PA 19122, 1982, 364 pages, $34.95 cloth, $12.95 paper.

In the "Preface," Elaine Kim acknowledges the ground-breaking nature of her book, *the first attempt to integrate the Asian American literary voice in one book-length study,* but modestly presents it as *a beginning, a conversational gambit.* This is the only occasion in her exhaustive, meticulously documented, and sensitive study where she is less than accurate.

Kim examines creative literature written in English by Asian Americans from four different national groups—Chinese, Japanese, Koreans, and Filipinos—chiefly from the point of view of the social history of Asians in the United States. Elucidating the socio-cultural contexts, she traces the evolution of Asian American identity as expressed in the autobiographies, fiction, drama, and poetry of the various ethnic minorities. As such, her book is an important contribution to the growing scholarship on ethnicity, cultural pluralism, and minority literature in the United States.

In the area of Asian American literature, however, Kim's book will long remain an indispensable source. The first of its kind in scope, it is, as the *Library Journal* pointed out, the only title on this subject currently in print. On its own merits it may well remain the first in choice of texts on the background to Asian American literature. It is difficult to imagine how Kim's study as an introduction to Asian American literature can be improved.

Her range is thorough. Beginning with an analysis of images of Asians in Anglo American literature, she covers writing by early Asian immigrant writers such as Lin Yutang, Younghill Kang, and Carlos Bulosan. She then progresses to examine the work of second-generation Asian Americans, before mining the individual contemporary ethnic scene. There are chapters on portraits of Chinatown, on the Japanese American family, and on the 1970's and '80's search for a new self-image, aptly titled "Chinatown Cowboys and Warrior Women." The study ends with a chapter on Asian American poetry and the new directions these poets are taking in discovering their political and social realities.

Her work is both chronologically schematized as well as ethnically differentiated and serendipitously thematized. She deals with extensive and massive materials. Her "Notes" testify to a copious industriousness capable of unifying and synthesizing enormous readings in history, sociology, economics, psychology, political science, as well as in literature. Reading the "Notes" is itself almost as satisfying as reading her carefully written, closely argued, and densely documented text. One learns in her notes about the different approaches of writers of Eurasian ancestry; about a little known writer's (Louis Chu's) biography; or the meaning of Okada's title, *No-no Boy: A "no-no boy" was a person who answered "no" to the two critical questions on the loyalty questionnaire, thereby refusing to serve in the American armed forces and refusing to foreswear allegiance to Japan and pledge loyalty to the United States.* In short, Kim wears her learning gracefully and unpretentiously.

There is no doubt as to the research and information to be found in the book. In her text, literary criticism is grounded in solid familiarity with the social and historical contexts. There is never a sense of disciplines juxtaposed together. Instead her discussions of the literature and her evaluations of achieved style and final work rise naturally and spontaneously from her socio-cultural, materialist explanations. While there is nothing of Marxist polemics in her arguments, her critical approach is based on the best of the sociology of literature theories. There is an entire avoidance of theoretical cant; instead Kim offers a readable gestalt of social history illuminating and in turn illuminated by the writings of Americans of Asian descent. There are plenty of summaries of novels, short stories, plays, even non-fiction works and poems for those readers new to the field. There is also insightful interpretation of characters, themes, and choice of forms and styles for the student of literature. She quotes liberally and forcefully from the works. The overall effect is to make her readers want to get to the works themselves, for her analyses are so lucid

and compelling that they uncover and communicate the wealth of experience from which the literature springs.

Nor is she afraid of evaluating the literary quality of the work. Tactfully weaving in socio-political discussions on racism, stereotyping, sexism, the internment of Japanese Americans during World War II, the Vietnam War, the Third World movement, she is nonetheless anchored in the literary culture. While sympathetically elucidating Frank Chin's themes of Chinese American masculinity, for example, she does not evade the central judgment that his basic contempt for his characters, his misogyny and alienation result in incomplete portrayals and an uneven achievement. Similarly, while taking into account Asian American women's support for their men, she is able to demonstrate the issues of sexism, within the ethnic community as well as outside, which are surfacing in recent feminist writing from this group.

Since its publication in 1982, *Asian American Literature* has received much deserved praise from scholars, teachers and the writers themselves. Maxine Hong Kingston called Kim a pioneer in producing *this excellent work of scholarship.* Kim has indeed mapped out a vast territory, made it coherent, and given it permanent significance in her study. But her book is not merely a pioneering feat, it is a substantive body of scholarship which will dominate the area for decades.

Shirley Geok-lin Lim

OBASAN. *Joy Kogawa*, David R. Godine, 306 Dartmouth St., Boston, MA 02116, 1981, 250 pages, $14.95 cloth.

Obasan is a novel with historical and social documentation of the persecutions of Japanese Canadians after the attack on Pearl Harbor in 1941. Although Canadian citizens, thousands of *Niseis* (first generation Japanese Canadians) and their families on the West Coast were stripped of their rights and possessions and sent to concentration camps. Joy Kogawa takes this ugly scar on Canadian history, and transforms it into an anguished novel in which narrative forms approach the poetic in their power to express and move.

Using the first-person point of view, Kogawa frames the child Naomi's sensitive and fragmented experiences in the adult Naomi's intelligent, insistent probing for the truth. At five, Naomi says goodbye to her mother who is visiting her aged mother in Japan. The eruption of hostilities between Japan and the Western Allies lead to the permanent loss of her childhood home, separation from her father, and her mother's disappearance. Shielded by the submissive silence of her *Nisei* elders, Naomi's life is a series of mystifications that block her emotionally. Only later as a thirty-six-year-old woman does Naomi unravel the reasons for, and significances of, her childhood traumas.

The novel's progressive disclosures of the historical facts behind the internment of Japanese Canadians and its vivid re-creation of their displacement and material and spiritual sufferings make up a damning indictment of Canadian racism and political oppression. Its power, however, lies not merely in this reminder of national shame, but also in its personal animus of the wounded self. Kogawa's poetic images and penetrating prose express a primeval scream of lost love, rage and anguish rising from a life-long suppression of emotion.

The trope of silence, individual and collaborative, rules the fiction. Some families, she tells us, *disappear from the earth without a whimper.* Obasan, Naomi's Japanese aunt, symbolizes those forces of silence which, although well-intentioned, collaborate with the oppressors in their victim's fate. *The language of her grief is silence. She has learned it well, its idioms, its nuances. Over the years, silence within her small body has grown large and powerful.*

Naomi is the theater for the conflict between destructive silence and liberating truth. She is drawn between Japanese Obasan and Canadian Aunt Emily who has documented the injustices of the internment and who continues to protest the past. *It's all recorded,* Aunt Emily tells her, and sends a package of family and political records to help her discover the truth. The difference between Obasan and Aunt Emily is not only the difference between two individuals or cultures; it is the tension from which all writing comes: the tension between the inert and incommunicable and the necessity to speak out, to reach across gaps, to signify.

Naomi discovers that her mother, caught in the Hiroshima holocaust, died after much suffering from radiation sickness. Because she had requested the children not be informed of her situation, Naomi has spent her life emotionally numb, abandoned to ignorance. *SILENT MOTHER, YOU DO NOT SPEAK OR WRITE,* the adult/child narrator accuses. It is her mother's protective silence that ironically has lead to Naomi's psychological alienation. *Our wordlessness was our mutual destruction,* Naomi asserts, even as she is healed finally by the breaking of silence.

Obasan is a technically masterful novel in its seamless weavings of past and present, its structuring of juxtaposed fragments of scenes, characters, and memories. But this technical tour-de-force is all in the service of the deepest psychological and social themes. Kogawa has produced a complex fiction whose totality encompasses political and individual realities, and whose impact resonates like that of strong poetry.

Shirley Geok-lin Lim

DANGEROUS MUSIC. *Jessica Hagedorn,* Momo's Press, 45 Sheridan St., San Francisco, CA 94103, 1975, 52 pages, $3.50 paper.

Reading Hagedorn's poems is to be swept into her pulsating, highly original, often quirky point of view and there is no mistaking her voice for any other poet. She weaves her own world, drawing upon jargon, brand names, TV personalities and the commercial hype bombarding the immigrant to our shores:

. . . the paranoia/that raised me/and cristina/
with her wonderful breasts/stunning the world/
in her saks fifth avenue/brassiere
or . . . and here we are,/cathedrals in our thighs/
banana trees for breasts/and history, all mixed up/
saxophones in our voices/when we scream/
the love of rhythms/inherent/when we dance

Included are prose selections chronicling the aspirations and eventual disappointments of Pearl and Bong Bong (Antonio Gargazulio-Duarte) in their attempts to make it in America. Pearl fails to achieve her goal as dance performer; Bong Bong never accepts the life of computer programmer held up to him as the ultimate salvation. Both are swept into the maelstrom of day-to-day living, buying this and that to subsist like everyone else. They remain strangers in a strange land, doomed to alienation in a mixed-up society whose mores they cannot begin to understand. Violence, deprivation, cruelty, loneliness and indifference greet them, whether in San Francisco or on New York City streets.

Filipino by heritage, her poems discuss Manila, her origins:

where the sun is scarlet/like a beautiful slut/
. . . the nuns with headdresses/like wings of doves/
n beating you/into holy submission/
with tales of purgatory/. . . the presidents wife/
dictates martial law/
with her thighs

This is the tough, street-smart, seen-it-all voice of a survivor. She has an unerring ear for the phony and a discerning mind, listing for America all the traps and materialistic junk held up as necessities of life. The rhythm of her poems, insistent and hypnotic as jungle drums, beats an indelible message into my brain.

The book lives up to its title: these poems sear and smolder. It is a siren call of poetic music that deserves a wide audience.

Momo's Press is to be commended for the attractive format with a handsome layout, design, and cover.

Jessica Saiki

WHAT MATISSE IS AFTER. *Diana Chang,* Contact II Publications, Box 451 Bowling Green, New York, NY 10004, 1984, 41 pages, $4.00 paper.

What Matisse Is After is poetry with an economy of language as elegantly inclusive as the line and motion rendered by the French master himself. To read these poems exploring paradoxical perception is to breathe in the rhythmic interplay of word, image, idea, feeling. Each synthesizes one into the other, simulating change which, like the lines of Matisse, are a *departure / toward returning / in the teeth of our dying.*

Natural, human, and aesthetic experience are mutually transposed in "As Green Comes." Generated by breath/spirit the appearance of poems is analogous to both the pubescent breasts of girls and nature's budding. Significantly, in "A Double Pursuit," the painter signs not the perishable canvas but ephemeral air, the spirit's mode. Light/energy are synecdochic of spirit infusing meaning. Many poems emit a phosphorescent glow. In "Wonder" personified light reflects itself enabling us to see objects. Through light a person becomes *extraordinary.*

Physical reality is afforded its due when the poet declares in "Most Satisfied by Snow," *Matter / matters / I,too, / flowering.* Combining colloquial language with a synaesthetic image, Chang writes, *The democratic inner eye / But melts its shores about the room.* The poet in "Abstract Kingdom: Picture Gallery," reinforces subjective perception by which *Portraiture's estate commences / individual geography.*

Chang's unique perception of an elusive inner-self coupled with a more accessible outer-self whimsically emerges in "A Dialogue With My Own Temperament." A more mysterious manifestation looms in "The Divorced" where, surrealistically, she gazes at a man on a roof across from her bedroom. Her inner poet, Miss Lee, who *passes out calling cards / busy and shy with her need,* emerges from her rational self, compelling both selves to *cross a gulf of death* in order to join with the stranger. Only when the speaker assimilates the inner/outer, the ominous/rational, is she able to achieve wholeness.

This inverse psychological perspective has a spiritual/material counterpart which permeates her imagery. Her aunt in "On Seeing My Great Aunt In A Funeral Parlor" becomes matter transposed into a *winter bride / Her wedding bed the earth.* The *aunt receives the spade* and *The trees are human veins.*

Experience in these poems is threaded by a thin but persistent threat of horrific disintegration. The poet uses language which characteristically changes from concrete to metaphysical as in "Friday Night" where the speaker matter-of-factly arrives at her house to be hurled into an abyss as she *opens the dark.* Kinetically transformed she and a scampering cat merge to *clamber* into the safety of lamplight.

Reflective of Matisse's compositions entitled *Jazz,* "An Alphabet" interprets paradoxical experience in colors. White, which *strikes / jazz of presence* is an apt symbol of being; it awaits fulfillment while simultaneously reflecting the spectrum. Jazz is a music of counterpoint. Terror surfaces as the persona warns *prepare . . . / The pull of black / is home.*

Horror is transcended with wit and humor in "Ah Yes Wisdom" when the speaker, who studies Kierkegaard in the bathroom, piquantly dismisses what *was strenuous at thirty.* Then a montage of imagery shifts the tone as time encroaches like *someone's afternoon . . . falling through the clock.* At the apex of slaughter, when the moon *mugs and slays her,* wisdom, heightened by the sweep of enjambment, opens: *Loveliness is more than enough / where / now / (oh yes) / is joy.*

Language, image, syntax, and theme are indivisible in "The Coast," a metaphor of tangible realities. The speaker's inner voice is a male surfcaster. Minimal punctuation and enjambment allow the poem to create itself, paralleling the full sweep of surf, suggesting the inclusive arc of self, and the materialization of spirit. Similar to Matisse's preoccupation, Chang understands it is individual perception that gives the senses an awakening in consciousness, singing *alive / wild.* In "A Poet," she identifies rummaging the disordered mind with the creative process, finally unveiling herself, *a heavenly body / radiant / in a world of masked men.*

Although Diana Chang uses ethnic referents, she moves outside the boundaries of ethnicity. In "On Gibson Lane, Sagaponack" she speaks of her Chinese strangeness in an Anglo culture. Yet, she and a blond girl share the experience of riding *along the same edge* of being; each mysteriously evolving, then returning to self.

In "Twelve-Year-Olds," the room which is a *tunnel* is given motion by the dance of blossoming pre-adolescents. As mantises, they are both prophets and insects groping with *tuxedo-elegance,* as if *praying* against a backdrop of *centuries of jungles.* *What Matisse Is After* opens and closes in perfect symmetry. A surge of green transposing into growing bodies of girls, like Matisse's women effortlessly filling space, returns as nature's disordered dance. Energy languorously evolving, convoluting the animistic and human, instinc-

tively flourishes.

Janice Bishop

IN THE CITY OF CONTRADICTIONS. Fay Chiang, Sunbury Press, Box 274, Jerome Ave. Station, Bronx, NY 10468, 1979, 62 pages, $3.00 paper.

DREAMS IN HARRISON RAILROAD PARK. Nellie Wong, Kelsey St. Press, PO Box 9235, Berkeley, CA 94709, First Printing: 1977, 45 pages, $6.00 paper.

CAMP NOTES AND OTHER POEMS. Mitsuye Yamada, Shameless Hussy Press, Box 424, San Lorenzo, CA 94580, 1976, 45 pages, $4.45 paper.

As a first generation Chinese American, Fay Chiang is caught in the contradiction between an image of the American (as white middle class) and the experience of being an American who does not fit that image. In "Chinatown" she talks about the invisibility of Asians in the predominant vision of America:

american tv sold mickey mouse and donald ducks
      to little alice and jerrys and run spot run
            in the suburbias of white picket fences
                  and automobiles
and american society sold cheap labor and self hatred
      to little chins and wongs and run dog run
            in the ghettos of railroad flats
                  and dead end streets

This exclusion extends to all minorities and people in marginal positions, such as women or the working-class poor. Chiang's poems embrace a range of roles and experiences of women. She writes of women who are mothers ("Defense of Seasons,"

"Mother of My Soul"), women who are part of men's fantasies ("Choreopoem"), women who leave home for freedom and truth ("A Woman Speaks"), women who are strong as well as women who are victims. She also identifies with and gives a voice to the disabled or homeless inhabitants of the city: *Hodusai-san costumed as a blind man / fumbled through the crowd with his monkey / perched and cracking peanuts / for the poor lost souls . . .* ("Chants"). She takes on the voice of a street bum trying to borrow change in "10$," or talks with a *starving nun on a dollar's credit* ("Images").

Chiang's style conveys the flexibility and range of her vision. Her lines never lie solidly against a margin, but continually shift, expressing her sense of life as movement. Nor are her forms or genres static. "Transactions," for example, is a mini-play. Here also are prose pieces, found letters, journal entries, and poems that have been performed in varied mediums, such as "Choreopoem." Her poem, "New York City" contains snatches of speech, newspaper headlines, dialogue, and prose sections.

As this range and diversity of form suggests a web of opposition, contrast, and paradox on the technical level, *In the City of Contradictions* also confronts these issues on a thematic level. The opening and title poem locates New York City as the focus of these contrary forces. Here, beauty co-exists with sordidness, destruction with regeneration. Chiang's personal struggles with issues of gender, race, and class become universal themes of the fight for freedom. The city itself becomes a metaphor for this struggle:

we are among the survivors
we, with our hands tool foundations

in our songs, dreams and dances,
our myths, legends, symbols,
our systems of work

These lines echo the cadences of Allen Ginsberg and affirm Chiang's inheritance as a seer and a prophet. Her poems take on the tone of a revolutionary spirit. She feels the movement and experiences the life of the city as directed force: *there is a popular spirit and movement / growing and pushing / rearranging the order of things / that nothing can hold back* ("Chinatown"). Sustaining this image is a commitment to the concrete in action and in detail. She refuses to allow her ideals to remain in the abstract, but works actively to express them in her poetry and in projects such as the Basement Workshop, a center for the development of Asian American culture.

In one of the last pieces in the book, "Home," Chiang describes returning to the city and to her mother's house after a pastoral outing. Her return is treated without ceremony but a meal awaits:

I hear the voices the moments and remember the daily gatherings at meal time, rituals, the leaving, coming back in our family . . . I am full, eating steamed rice.

Home, finally, is where we perform the rituals of living and struggle. In defining a place out of placelessness, Ms. Chiang's poems enact the empowering transformation they envision.

Place and placing are also issues in Nellie Wong's *Dreams in Harrison Railroad Park*. And naming is one way of locating oneself. In an early poem in the book, Wong expresses the importance of this connection between identity and place in "How A Girl Got Her Chinese Name." In this poem, the young child, Nellie, is given a Chinese name by her schoolteacher: *Nah Lei / which means* where *or* which place. Her parents rename her *Lai Oy, Beautiful Love,* which could also mean **Lost pocket** / *depending on the heart / of a conversation. Between these names,* the poet says, *I never knew I would ever get lost.* As the syntax suggests, the coming of age, of *realizing one's name,* ironically involves the danger of misplacement, the loss of one's identity. These, then, are poems about losing and finding oneself.

Part of this process of maturity is the discovery of sexuality. In "Like the Old Woman Suggested" the young girl *stays under the covers / imagines her skin is cream. / It is her toy, / her itching, her temporary relief.* And with this discovery comes an awareness of her own role as a woman in society and the codes of commodity in which that role is packaged: *Once her skin becomes cream, / she will be ready for market.* Against these codes, writing about her experiences as a woman is an act of exposure that Wong confronts with ambivalence.

In "Woman in Print" the speaker observes a woman wearing a print dress in a coffee shop. This woman, who is *always coatless,* is seen walking by construction sites where *construction men watch,* and, the speaker assumes, *she descends their darkened stairs.* The speaker maintains an ambivalent attitude toward the woman, identifying with her (*I am a woman*), while denying any connection with her exposed sexuality (*I wear a coat*).

Learning to throw off the obscure covering of the coat / the role / the mask, and to break down these barriers of self-alienation, is the direction in which Wong's poems move. From "Woman in Print" she turns to "Loose Women, You Say?," a poem in which she challenges this labelling of women who exult in life. Another poem challenges the stereotypical roles of race. In "Not From the Food," the speaker organizes dinner and a tour for office friends, *gulped wine, holding my nose / masked, playing oriental, / inscrutable, wise . . . I recall that time / and I want to puke / not from the food, my friend, / not from the food.* In this role / mask / stereotyped image, she recognizes her complicity in perpetuating the racism which she now rejects. Reclaiming the personal and the individual from the stereotypical is also a theme in "Magazine Poem for Father's Day," a poem made up of cliches taken from advertisements. It ends: *This not for you, my father / who sold mustard greens from a truck / in your shorts somewhere, / your knees I laughed and loved.* What a commercial image of America excludes—the experiences and images of other cultures and classes—poetry can recover, and it is this act of recovering the immaterial from the commercial, the personal from the stereotypical, that characterizes Wong's work.

"Picnic," the last poem in the book, completes this movement towards self-recovery. Its lush description of a New Year's feast can be read as a rewriting of "Not From the Food":

Together we celebrate Tiger's Year
We fast on chicken, mushrooms and the monk's dish,
Pregnant with its cellophane noodles and fine black hair . . .

Our laughter is perfumed with incense
that the spirits dish.

This meal, shared with parents, is an exchange between generations. The engaged sharing is a sharp contrast to the alienated role-playing of "Not From the Food." The poem here expresses an acceptance of an inheritance: *The chrysanthemums bend their heads. / I gather fresh lichee and leave my mother and father / my only silk coverlet.* As Wong makes wholeness out of self-affirmation in her poems, the dialogue between daughter and parents engages that between reader and author, creating a bridge that crosses boundaries between generations and cultures, loss and replacement.

Mitsuye Yamada was born in Japan and raised in Seattle until World War II, when her family was evacuated to a relocation camp in Idaho. These poems are an ironic comment on the idea of relocation as an experience of misplacement, or placelessness.

As a young girl growing up in this environment, Yamada struggles for a new identity after hers has been appropriated and misnamed by racial prejudice. In *Camp Notes,* she forges an identity out of the very incongruity of her position. Thus, in "Relocation: Minidoka, Idaho," *white / majorette boots / tassels from Montgomery Ward* exist alongside barbed wires and are as real. Only the jarring juxtaposition informs us that the experience is of a different kind. Or, in "The Watchtower," the poet passes the rec. hall in which a band plays and *Tired teenagers / leaning on each other / swayed without struggle,* and she reflects that *This is what we did with our days. / We loved and lived / just like people.*

As a poet, Yamada works to reclaim not only her identity, but her experience, by resisting false names. Thus, in "Desert Storms," she writes
This was not
im
prison
ment.
This was
re
location.

For, however it is labelled, prejudice cannot be contained or placed elsewhere, as the speaker discovers in "Cincinnati" when she leaves the camp and embraces the anonymity of a *real City / where . . . no one knew me,* only to have her privacy brutally violated when *one / hissing voice . . . said / dirty jap / warm spittle on my right cheek.* The poem ends with the painful realization, *Everyone knew me.*

Only when she identifies with another victim of prejudice, as with the black man in "Thirty Years Under" who says, *there is nothing more humiliating . . . than being spat on . . . like a dog,* can she release the pain and the anger suppressed for so long. If at times her poems have the pointed jab of political pronouncements, it is because they carry the conviction that poetry is a powerful vehicle for the relocation of vision, that can release an individual through identification with another perspective. As she points out in "Thirty Years Under," the refusal to accept one's own experience is a refusal of one's own identity: *I had packed up / my wounds in a cast / iron box . . . and traveled blind / for thirty years.* Expressing that experience so that someone else can identify with it is a way of unlocking in order to re-see.

Poetry, then, can be a powerful reflection as well as a release. In "Mirror, Mirror" when her son, troubled by his image says, *Trouble is I'm American on the inside / and Oriental on the outside,* the poet offers him another vision of himself: *No Doug / Turn that outside in / THIS is what American looks like.* It is this re-seeing which allows one to make a place between *Here* where the *neighbor boys called out / MIT SUYE CHOP SUEY,* and *There* where the Japanese children call out *American no ojo-o san / doko ni iku-u . . . Girl from American / where are you going?* These are poems of courageous seeing, naming, and placing.

Marian Yee

THOUSAND PIECES OF GOLD. *Ruthanne Lum McCunn,* Design Enterprises of San Francisco, PO Box 14695, San Francisco, CA 94114, 1985, 308 pages, $10.95 cloth, $5.95 paper.

Thousand Pieces of Gold is a fast-reading, highly descriptive, yet memorable biographical novel. It is the story of Lalu Nathoy, a Chinese American pioneer woman, her struggles through a childhood of poverty in China, and her subsequent life as a slave and free woman in America.

Lalu is introduced as a child already making unorthodox decisions concerning her survival. To do field work and avoid being sold by her family, Lalu had her feet unbound, although it caused her much pain and her friends ostracized her. Lalu found great satisfaction in doing men's work and in exercising some control over her life.

After being sold and a torturous voyage to North America in the cramped, dark hold of a ship, Lalu and the reader realize that her position is not unique. In fact, the reader may begin to compare Lalu's situation with that of pre-Civil War black slaves. Lalu finds herself among many Chinese women and children being prepared for auction; they are washed, stripped and sold. The city is San Francisco; the time the early 1870's.

If not for any other reason, *Thousand Pieces of Gold* is worth reading because it is a fine history book. It helps to fill in the gaps, putting the contributions and sufferings of Chinese women in perspective with the greater volume and confusion of American frontier history. It also prompts us to ask: What happened to all the Chinese women who came to America during those early years?

Lalu matures, prospers and maintains a long-term relationship with a man she eventually marries, but she never resolves the conflict between her loneliness for things Chinese and her need and love of western life. She even declines having children, believing they would suffer being half white and half Chinese. Lalu tried to explain her loneliness to her husband by telling him about a performing monkey that once visited her village:

The man divide the audience in two and give each side one end of a rope to hold. Then the monkey walk carefully back and forth between the two sides. At each end, he stop a little bit, but he cannot stay, and so he walk again until he so tired, he fall.

I think even now many Asian Americans can empathize with Lalu's situation, regardless of how well adjusted and sophisticated many of us feel.

The novel is divided into seven chronologically ordered parts, each dealing with a distinctive phase or event in Lalu's life. As a bonus, each part begins with an old black-and-white photo depicting either Lalu, a place she lived, or a Chinese woman of her time. The combination of history and old photos in this novel is especially personal, somewhat like peeking into your grandmother's family album. Throughout, McCunn gives the reader little details, little gems from Lalu's life: gold buttons, red underwear, an old Durham tobacco tin, little keys to Lalu's personality—making her seem more like a relative someone forgot to tell us about than an historical figure.

The research McCunn did for this novel is evident on every page, yet like the subtle accent she has given Lalu, it is not overwhelming. McCunn shows us how this strong woman reacts to spreading anti-Chinese sentiment, registration laws for Chinese laborers, and the gold rush, but she never overshadows the history or romanticizes. She gives us a frank look at a practical woman whose most valuable resources are her courage and decision-making skills.

Margo P. Harder

WINGS OF STONE. *Linda Ty-Casper,* Readers International, 8 Strathway Gardens, London, NW3 4NY, Great Britain, 1986, 170 pages, $16.95 cloth.

The place is Manila during the waning days of the Marcos regime. The hero, a Filipino expatriate named Johnny Manalo, has chosen this time to return to his home country after an absence of 13 years. The years in Boston, where he works in radiation therapy, have left him prosperous but full of *doubts rotting inside.* A graduate of MIT, he has married an American woman he does not love in order to legalize his status in the United States. The trip itself is almost a whim: the *idea of coming home,* he says, had simply *occurred to him.* When his plane lands in Manila, he panics, realizing for the first time that *he had taken the trip not to go anywhere, not even home—he had brought no homecoming presents, no* **pasalubongs**—*but simply to take off, to be free of the earth for the duration of the flight. Having touched down in Manila, he was ready to fly back on his open-ended return ticket.*

The reunion with his father, a doctor, is polite but revives painful memories. His father, whom he remembers as *a man with fierce passions, unwavering in the face of reasonable appeals,* now looks *as if everything he wanted to say had been said and there was no one, any more, that he wanted to meet: someone, as painlessly as possible, using up what was left to him of mortal time.* His mother has died, and the house where he grew up and where his father saw his patients now smells of *damp old wood.* His bed, *narrower than he remembered,* releases an odor of *dust and the wings of dead moths,* and the whole place makes him think of *decayed inheritance and children born to other people.*

Meanwhile, social and political realities intrude. We are in the period just before the February 1986 election that toppled Ferdinand Marcos from power, when political forces of both the Right and the Left were gearing up for a massive confrontation. There is also increasing polarization between the social classes. Walking the streets, Johnny describes as *a kind of violation* the *juxtaposition of ragged clothes and fashion jeans, of bodies bent under loads carried all day and those springing high and erect like wheat panicles, of need that survived on selling gum by the stick and of means that allowed the purchase of the same cosmetics sold on Boston's wealthy Newbury Street.* This polarization is reflected in Johnny's own family: his father dreams of opening a clinic in a squatter area, while his only brother, Martin, has allied himself with the corrupt regime, serving as errand boy for a shady business tycoon with ties to the government.

Shortly after his arrival, Johnny becomes the reluctant witness to terrible crimes: a nine-year-old boy, the son of a squatter who has dared to protest the government's squatter relocation program, disappears after Johnny sends him to get a taxi and is found a few days later, brutally murdered. A young member of the fledgling opposition is mysteriously shot while riding in the car of one of Martin's friends, and Martin takes charge of the cover-up. These crimes call out for resolution, but none is forthcoming. Johnny's initial reaction to the nine-year-old boy's death is shockingly callous: looking into the boy's coffin at the funeral, *remorse did not come since he knew nothing in particular about Rio.* Although he despises his brother—*Who was Martin anyway but someone who lost and gained by mere handfuls, small of vision and with oddly parcelled dreams*—he does nothing when, after the second murder, Martin informs him: *I told the driver to dump the body behind the trees, then take Sylvia on to Hidden Valley. Not to stop till he got there and not to tell anyone. He can be trusted. Come on. They're waiting for us. It's still a birthday party. Leticia wants it to last as long as possible.*

The most shocking murder is reserved for the end of the book. A "self-ordained priest" who has ministered to the residents of one of Manila's shantytowns is gunned down before Johnny's eyes by a local official whom the priest has inadvertently angered. Standing over the body, Johnny's self-doubt is such that he feels *nothing princely or even clear and true about*

himself. He could not act—and to say anything was to lie. He could only stand there like a bird with wings of stone, attempting to fly.

Ty-Casper's book is certainly gloomy, but there is more to the novel than just a collection of outrages. Mysteries abound: what were the real circumstances surrounding Johnny's birth, and was it he or Martin who was born to a poor, nameless woman in his father's clinic? Will Johnny forsake his American wife for the glamorous socialite, Sylvia Mendez, who makes *powerful rhythms and blunt melodies surge through him, forcing him to shiver where he stood?* Like the plot of a convoluted Filipino movie, there is almost too much here for one novel to handle.

But one cannot fault the quality of the writing. Ty-Casper is a wonderful stylist, and her novel is nothing if not engrossing. Her Manila is an old city, rank with decay. Its churches are *so dark, so old*, that even the light in them seems to be *falling apart.* There is an aura of sadness about the houses, dimly lit with low-wattage bulbs that *burned like a candle going out*, and the gardens with their old trees, the *spreading acacias*, the large **macopas**, *too old to be shaped by the wind or turned by the sun any longer.* In Ty-Casper's Manila, plants and people grow rampant, *stirring with the furtiveness of new life swarming.* This fecundity sometimes brings alarming visions, as when Johnny looks up at the branches covering the sky and sees what appear to be *pieces of flesh impaled on the branches by birds, entrails and eyes where insects might have laid their eggs*, or when, experiencing the incredible congestion of Manila's streets, Johnny thinks of *Goya's monstrous mouths stuffed with human bodies, the faces decaying in full view, corpses standing up to firing* *squads: everywhere the coarse imprint of death's celebrations.*

Ty-Casper strives for some powerful effects, and if at times she seems to be stretching, it is probably because hindsight has given us a different, more optimistic view of the future of the Philippines. Manila today is under a different government, and if Ty-Casper were writing today, knowing now what we know about the bloodless revolution that toppled Ferdinand Marcos from power, she might have written a different book. But *Wings of Stone* is still powerful material. One has the feeling that her description of some of Manila's most disturbing aspects will be around for a good while longer.

Marianne Villanueva

BEYOND MANZANAR: VIEWS OF ASIAN AMERICAN WOMANHOOD. *Jeanne Wakatsuki Houston*, Capra Press, Box 2068, Santa Barbara, CA 93120, 1985, 65 pages, $7.50 paper.

An attractive paperback of unusual format, *Beyond Manzanar* is precisely one half of this back-to-back book by a husband-and-wife writing team; the other sixty-five pages, entitled *One Can Think About Life After the Fish is in the Canoe*, form an essay collection by James D. Houston. His essays focus on geographical place as inspiration and sustenance; hers focus on the psychological space of a Japanese American woman and particularly on the customs and behavior that differentiate her from Caucasian women.

As *Farewell to Manzanar* gave most readers their first inside view of the Japanese American internment experience, so *Beyond Manzanar* continues the task of explaining Japanese ways to non-Asians, focusing specifically on the roles of Japanese women that Americans find most fascinating: the geisha, the picture bride, and the *submissive, docile, self-sacrificing, artlessly perfect wife*. It also delineates, in some poignant detail, the author's own position of bi-cultural role-playing, vacillating from 'Good Morning America,' and 'Ms. Confidence' to a *soft and submissive oriental maid.*

Though some readers may find Wakatsuki's tone overly apologetic and accommodating, the greatest contribution these essays make to our understanding of women is their clear and forthright explanation of the core of strength underlying the traditional Japanese woman's softness. For example, Wakatsuki demonstrates that her mother regarded such household chores as washing the family clothes on her knees beside the bathtub not as menial and degrading but as a part of a proud and important role, motherhood. *She never confused her tasks with who she was.* In other words, her mother's identity, her personhood, was not diminished by the household labor she performed, but instead her work took on lustre, gained dignity, from the role in which it plays a part. In the Wakatsuki family, her father had all the bluster and swagger, but her mother provided the emotional support. The *forms in their relationship, the rituals of their roles* seemed to affirm his power over her, but in reality, as he, nearing death, acknowledged to his wife, *You've always been the strong one.*

Influenced by her Japanese mother's Old World example but growing up in the New World, Jeanne Wakatsuki Houston finds herself between worlds. In the early days of her marriage, she laid out her husband's underwear and socks sporadically: *On the days when I felt I should be a good Japanese wife, I did it. On other days, when I felt American and assertive, I did not.* She makes a positive assertion about her between-world condition that is less persuasive than she intends: *Because I am culturally neither pure Japanese nor pure American does not mean I am less of a person. It means I have been enriched with the heritage of both.* This conclusion lacks conviction, for her tone when explaining Japanese ways has been apologetic and sometimes almost incredulous and embarrassed rather than proud. The pain of alienation and self-rejection seems too easily swept aside and buried.

When she compares her parents' marriage to a sailboat depending *on the natural element of wind* and her own to a jet airliner dependent on *modern technology*, she is again unconvincing and even inaccurate, for the ways of the good Japanese wife, like her mother, are learned ways, no more *natural* (in fact, perhaps less) than the ways of the modern American woman; both are conditioned from childhood to behave in the manner considered proper and desirable in their society.

As guarded as Wakatsuki Houston is about her personal reactions to her ethnicity, however, she is amazingly frank about her sexual preference: revealing that her taste in men was developed by the images of male beauty found in Hollywood movies —all Caucasian images. Simply and directly, she writes of sentiments that have explosive ramifications: *Of course, no one was like my father. He was so powerful. The only men who might possess some of that power were those whose control and dominance over his life diminished his. Those would be the men who interested me.*

The book picks up pace as it gains distance from the purely personal. In the last two chapters, taken from her forthcoming novel, *Picture Bride*, the characters seem well drawn, the dialogue convincing, the situation interesting. *Picture Bride* promises to be a very good book.

Beyond Manzanar is guarded, though often charming, as personal revelation, and extremely useful as a guide to intercultural understanding. It is written simply, directly, not always penetrating, but interesting.

Amy Ling

WITH SILK WINGS: ASIAN AMERICAN WOMEN AT WORK. *Elaine H. Kim with Janice Otani,* Asian Women United of California, 3538 Telegraph Ave., Oakland, CA 94609, 1983, 138 pages, $10.95 paper.

When I first heard of *With Silk Wings: Asian American Women at Work*, I was naive enough to think that it would reflect some of my experiences as an Asian American woman working in this country and some of the experiences of my mother or of other Asian American working women I have known. I should have guessed that it would be just another picture book filled with success stories of the already stereotyped model minority. As a book that aims to educate Asian American girls and women on their "career opportunities" and on the Asian American women's work situation, it fails to accurately portray the struggles and realities faced by most Asian

American working women in this country. In trying to provide positive role models, it has only succeeded in delivering yet another model of assimilation based on the line, "work hard and you'll make it."

The first half of the book consists of detailed profiles of twelve Asian American women in various professions. Although many of these women are admirable individuals who have worked hard to become doctors, lawyers, playwrights, architects, filmmakers, etc., one cannot help but notice a general success pattern in this section of women working hard, going to college, and becoming professionals. Granted, we would all prefer to have meaningful and decent paying work, but these select women are the exceptions to the majority of clerical workers, domestics, seamstresses and sales clerks that make up more than 80% of Asian American women workers. By encouraging Asian American girls to aspire towards the professions without stating why the percentage of Asian American women professionals is so low ignores the reality that many girls from working class and poor families cannot afford a college education and will most likely end up working in the low paying, "minimum" skill job category typically filled by Third World women in this country. Showing only those women who have succeeded without analyzing why they are the exceptions does not help Asian American women to understand their career options or the reasons behind their limited opportunities as workers.

In a book on Asian American women and work, one might also expect the contents to reflect the experiences of Asian women as Asians and as women on the job. But the book, continuing on a superficial view of its subject, devotes the next section to blurbs about 40 Asian American women in non-traditional occupations talking briefly about their job responsibilities, one or two interesting aspects of their job, how they stumbled into their line of work, or just how much they like it. There is little or no mention of racism, sexism, or sexual harassment on their jobs. The authors certainly do not include any political perspective on the U.S. economic structure and Asian American women's role within this hierarchy. Their advertising/promotional approach to women's non-traditional work leaves us feeling that these women's stories have yet to be told.

In addition to the less than informative main sections, we also have the pleasure of reading brief summaries of Asian American women's history and their current situation written with a textbook mentality. We are told who came, when they came, where they stayed, what they did, and of events that occurred such as discriminatory legislation. These fragments of history left unconnected fail to tell the real history of Asian American women and their families. Asian American women are shown standing in the shadow of Asian American men and without voices of their own.

As for the book's theme of the non-traditional Asian American woman, we see photos throughout of women hanging onto the arms of their boyfriends or husbands, saying such independent things as, "I don't know what I would do without so and so!" The authors made a point of showing how these Asian American women still know how to be "women" even though they have "careers" of their own.

While reading *With Silk Wings,* I had images of houses in the suburbs with two car garages. It was a nightmare of assimilationist attitudes that was poorly written and reflected very little of my experience as a Chinese American immigrant and lesbian or of the experiences of other Asian American women workers that I know.

As the only book published on Asian American women and work, some people may find it useful or, at least, better than none, but let's utilize educational grants and Asian American women's time to produce writings that fully analyze, and therefore can hope to grasp the reality of our lives as workers.

Kit Quan

THIS BRIDGE CALLED MY BACK: WRITINGS BY RADICAL WOMEN OF COLOR. Edited by Cherríe Moraga, Gloria Anzaldua, Kitchen Table: Women of Color Press, PO Box 908, Latham, NY 12110, Second Edition 1983, 261 pages, $9.95 paper.

The reissue of *This Bridge Called My Back* by a press staffed by and devoted to writings by women of color, signals that this anthology of writings by radical women of color is becoming a contemporary classic. When it was published by Persephone Press (which has ceased operation) in 1981, *Bridge* marked a real turning point: it was one of the first collections of writings by and on Third World women in the U.S. who weren't middle-class or necessarily straight—Afro Americans, Asian Americans, Latinas, Native Americans. And it was much more. From piece to piece, the collection has an intensity of emotion—rage, grief, tenderness—a clarity of perception, and a toughness without bitterness or macho, that leaps out of the pages. *Bridge* is voices—voices long silenced by multiple and interwoven kinds of oppression against color, class, sexual preference, and radical politics. *Bridge* explodes with voices outside the academically-oriented, white middle-class women's movement of the seventies. Part of its power comes from naming sources of oppression as not only the institutions of class and heterosexual power, but also the collaboration, if unintentional, of white women in maintaining those institutions.

Looking back from the point of view of the late eighties, *Bridge* seems prophetic. Most of its essays, poems and dialogues, written in the late seventies, have the raw energy of first-generation politics. The positions defined around such issues as separatism, ethnic identification with men, women-identified solidarity, and relationships to mothers, mentors and lovers, have come to be dominant questions of the eighties. As the myth of a monolithic feminism crumbled and non-academic cultural pluralism began to inform the discussion of feminist issues, the considered base and hard-fought clarity of a position such as Audre Lorde's about academic tokenism, Barbara Smith's on the double oppression of gay women of color, or Mitsuye Yamada's on the invisibility of Asian American women, have become bottom-line stances for articulating difference. *Bridge,* throughout the eighties, has been bridging the ignorance and complacency of white women about the *differences* of women of color that may not, and must not, be subsumed under one feminist umbrella.

Speaking as a white, midlife, sometimes academic single mother, I want to make clear that I can't speak of what *Bridge* has meant to, say, a Latina lesbian over the last decade—how it offered recognition, community, empowerment, sisterly voices. I can, however, speak to the audience of white middle-class women who may feel we're on the outside looking in, with *Bridge*. *Bridge* forces us to deny the comfort of that distance by naming hard issues about white feminism's contribution to the oppression of women of color and its denial of difference that renders women of color invisible: Audre Lorde, for example, points out that white feminists can attend the conference at which she's been asked to be the Black token because women of color are minding their houses and children. In a now-famous and all-too-prophetic essay, "The Master's Tools Will Never Dismantle the Master's House," Lorde rejects the *tolerance of differences* that she finds characteristic of white middle-class feminism and argues for understanding difference as *that raw and powerful connection from which our personal power (as Black women, as lesbians) is forged*. At a time when we, as white femists, may have normalized discourses of oppression and neutralized their original energy, *Bridge* still has a lot to say about the relationship of racism and heterosexism, about hierarchy and domination, about privilege or the lack of it.

I want to focus on contributions by Asian American women to *Bridge*. There's a strange thing: while Asian Americans are visible throughout the collection— Nellie Wong and Mitsuye Yamada have two pieces each, Barbara Noda, Merle Woo, and Genny Lim have one each—they don't seem as strongly represented as Afro American or Latina women. For example in the last section, "The Vision," there are no contributions by Asian American women, which suggests something about the anthology's priorities as a manifesto. And there's a different tone to much of the writing by Asian American women represented—more considered, reflective, critical of the legacy of anti-Asian bigotry and of their own invisibility—but not so angry, not so accusatory, as most other contributions and rarely outspoken about sexual identification. There's a wall of pain and anger behind those voices, but it has been, at least in the late seventies, filtered through social conventions that inhibited self-trust. The Asian American women's dialogue and understanding, above all with their mothers, is apparent in order to legitimize their own voices. But protection of their jobs, children, status, prevents a pure, clear rage about oppression. My sense is that, by 1987, there's more empowerment, more naming of issues—and a lot more voices. *Bridge* is a powerful and persuasive book of continuing value, but where Asian American women are concerned, it points to the need for a collection exclusively on Asian American women. The myth of invisibility and accommodation, of cheerful, unquestioning upward mobility, needs, once and for all, to be laid to rest by a wide spectrum of Asian American women as they connect the power and intelligence of their voices to a legacy that is at once of exceptional culture and of the experience of profound, distorted oppression.

Julia Watson

CROSSING THE PENINSULA AND OTHER POEMS. *Shirley Lim*, Heineman Educational Books (Asia), Ltd., Singapore, 1980, 100 pages, $5.00 paper.

NO MAN'S GROVE. *Shirley Lim*, Department of English Language and Literature, National University of Singapore, 1985, 94 pages, $5.00 paper.

ANOTHER COUNTRY AND OTHER STORIES. *Shirley Lim*, Times Books International, Singapore, 1982, 152 pages, $7.00 paper.

Shirley Lim's poetry and fiction express unspoken feelings, giving voice to the silent. Hers is a personal poetry that transcends the merely personal of a confessional. Her poems urge us to affirmation as she orchestrates a complex of identity, a multi-cultural self-exploration of roots and wide branching. This rich exploration is tempered with a straightforward honesty that admits no sentimentality and speaks with self-confidence.

Her poetic landscape is wide: poems of love and its erosion, of women's sexuality, of being parent and child, of country lost and country found—sonnet, epigram, villanelle, haiku—forms both free and traditional. Her sensibility is feminist in the broadest sense, that is, concerned with the lives of women. She is out to paint women whole. Chinese Malaysian, American wife, mother, teacher, writer—multiple, fragmented identities crowd through her works.

In one poem from *Crossing the Peninsula*, the poet speaks from under the skin of a crocodile, projecting the greatest moment of the animal's fear at, paradoxically, the second when she is about to pounce on an unsuspecting swimmer. She touches on the paradox of moving time, and calls our attention to suicide as the death of one who is healthy:

> . . . *blood*
> *Ruby fresh, lungs uncorroded*
> . . . *tight, unblemished heart*
> *All these he kept as if to start*
> *Someplace anew.*

Her interest in probing the paradox of the feminine leads to some of the best poems in this volume. She writes of the many faces of women worn in daily life, among the coiffured heads shopping at the supermarket, *I am an elegant starling coxcombing the alleys,* or at home, *In the deep enclosing heart of a household.* She tracks feelings likely to disintegrate under less skilled transcription.

Lim's chronicle of female life takes on a special dimension as she meditates on her own life as a double transplant, a Chinese Malaysian born in Malaysia and educated there until 24 when she started a new life as an American teacher and writer. The poems in *Crossing the Peninsula* won the Commonwealth Prize in 1980. She was the first Asian and woman to be a winner. Approximately ten percent of the eighty-eight poems directly refer to Malaysia, but the physical/cultural voyage which the poet describes also is a metaphor for loss and renewal, as well as a record of her own wrenching split. "Adam's Grief" is chiefly about exile, about the loss of native country. It identifies that pain peculiar to all separation, an experience particularly difficult for women.

In Lim's hand the foreign is not strange. Many of her poems set in Asia send out shocks of recognition, reminding us how unexpectedly well we can connect and understand. These poems are enriched by the texture of social history and non-western geography that informs them. "The Dulang Washer" is a portrait, in lines of subtle alliteration and assonance, which draws our sympathy:

The dulang-washer, squinting like a witch
Squats with rag-wrapped head and begging bowl.
The sun mocks her with false gold.
Still she bows her head acquiescently.

Not much of a leap is required to see her as a sister to the bag ladies on American streets. For them, as for the dulang-washer, there is *The monotonous rhythm of search / And discarding . . .* There will be *no glamour of departure*, but rather *the shift / From landscape to landscape a meager drift.*

In the title poem of the collection, the poet relives *monsoon / Climate*, in Malaysia, *the migrating season / When nets and boats come home to shelter.* Strong in Wordsworthian reverberation and limpid lines, this poem is a metaphor for universal yearning:

We dream like grey gulls blown inland
Or as one-eyed ships, blown, espying
The bright-shelled peninsula.

The second volume, *No Man's Grove*, chronicles the effects of a decision to *walk between water and land.* This is a decision not to turn her imagination from one country to the other, but rather to live imaginatively in both the new and the old. The poetry of the title section recognizes this decision, and avoids the dilemma recounted in the final poem, "Identity No Longer," where the speaker who would become a *citizen of the world* is *caught short* as *the line for the exit shuffles off.* The poems in the final section will not be caught short; instead, they press the truth that country is important.

Lim takes us into the tragedies of Chinese history, the aesthetics that have painted the Chinese landscape, and those of the Great World Amusement Park of Malacca. At these scenes we *gape till we are filled*, and take in both the idiom and the outlook of the underclass in the country of return:

Master he dead
Kneeled from brain fever,
Cooked in new-day sun,
Waiting at the bar.

We hear the Pidgin accents of those who accept their fate:

Tidak apa got no power
To change it. What the hurry
Sun come up again. No matter
Just take it easy.

The poet is making a journey both outward and inward, a journey to origins of country, family, and self. A return to the missionary school where *simple natives / believe in / breastless women stuffed with God*, believe that *What's sacred must be possessed / Beneath white vestal dress.* Visiting the grave of her father, she pays ritual respect to one *who did not live for my returning.*

The reader has been chosen to participate in the poet's return. Simply but forcefully, *I've made you my reader.* We read *flickering snake tongues in the poet's eyes* and *The mess of guts spilling over / The neat formica countertop.* The poems in this first section, called "Burning Ground," deal with sexual drive, birth and women. We are drawn into the August heat of desire in six quatrains that reflect the blending of the full and half rhyme that Lim favors. We are saturated with summer as it flows into stirrings that drive the poet . . . *to the open empty page.* In "Summer Bugs," an insect ensemble burrows, sucks, mates and teases the nature-aroused poet until she sinks *like a potted plant* before the surrounding fecundity.

The poet's canvas is filled with women's experiences reflected in the titles: "On Hearing a Woman Poet Read," "I Look for Women," "Woman and Vase," "Working Woman," and "A Dream of Duty." This last ironically catalogs the life of a woman who knows her duty to

a clean house with shaken
rugs, oiled picture frames.
The woman moves among
glossy plants and tiles,
child and husband dusted.
Free of strange desires
here is my life, she says.

In dexterous conclusion the poet reveals that this woman, so sure about surfaces, has lost her self in these duties and is a visitor in her own house.

One poem from the "No Man's Grove" grouping perhaps best combines the poet's anguish at the treatment of women, and her Asian background. "Pantoun for Chinese Women" has an elemental chant-like magic. The form itself is a blending of East and West, having been borrowed from Southeast Asia by Victor Hugo and other French poets. In this act of empathy with the women of China, the poet laments the ultimate injustice to the female sex—female infanticide.

The vital thread that weaves through Lim's poems is the mother-daughter tie, for this poet a troubled one. In "Mother," the mature daughter looks hard at her now old mother. *Toothless, sag-skinned / Coconut round and brown with scar . . . ungainly now, unstrung.* This poem prepares us for the longest selection, "The Windscreen's Speckled View," a sequence of five poems saved for the end of the volume. Here the poet mourns both her mother and their unhappy relationship. We feel the guilt as the daughter says, *I have never loved you enough.* She struggles in vain to keep the image of her mother, but *You are receding into fiction so fast,* and, further, *You are changed into the sign of your defeat.* In the fifth and last of the sequence, the final poem of the volume, the speaker is back in suburban U.S.A., *She looks at herself between deaths,* and thinks of

Mother, smoking in final blaze.
The crematorium follows the speaker home
from Malaysia, and These Asiatic reveries
disturb some wavering sense:

. . . as apparitions, crossing
between unwashed windscreen
and some suburban park.

Published between the two volumes of poetry is a collection of short stories. Watching one writer at work in two distinct genres has its own special interest—vision, theme, background are recognizable, but the resulting product of new rules and goals is, of course, a new world. Some of the earlier pieces are closer to memoir and autobiographical sketch, having charm in their own right, but not the depth of the rich and full stories which characterize the volume. "Mr. Tang's Girls," a story which won the *Asiaweek* short story competition in 1982, may be the very best. For an American reader, the unveiling of Chinese Malaysian society is an enticement.

Mr. Tang has, after all, two wives and two sets of children. He commutes to the home of Number Two and his four daughters every Saturday for a weekend of rest and peace in the arms of quiet, pliant wife Number Two. All of Mr. Tang's needs seem to be met, but he comes into sharp conflict with his eldest, an emotional 15-year-old bursting into womanhood, taking no pains to hide her metamorphosis or her increased needs for attention from repose-seeking Daddy. The unexpected ending is violent but earned.

The pervasive atmosphere of the female: painted toe nails, hair in curlers, fashion magazines, long legs in short skirts, subdued giggles, and the wife's soft accessible at-your-service sexuality are in stark contrast to Mr. Tang's authority, his aura of proprietorship. Lim challenges patriarchy in this subtly crafted tale. What disturbs Mr. Tang is not just his eldest daughter's increasing awareness of herself as a woman, but rather the unspoken threats this poses to him—her youth as a sign of his age, his own sexual arousal that he must keep repressed, and, most of all, her slipping out from the obligations and charms of young Chinese daughterhood. In this story we see the same authorial control that Lim's poetry suggests: no wasted words, careful modeling of character, just enough setting to make you comfortable in a new place, and a keen sense of balance between plot and character.

As we see in another strong story, Lim uses symbols respectfully, with just enough emphasis to prod you beyond the immediate. "Keng Hua," a well-groomed piece, is the story of a lonely Malaysian school teacher approaching her thirty-sixth birthday, and her ambivalent relationship with a colleague, an American ex-priest who drinks too much. Pungent racial, sexual and feminist hostilities run underground as the heroine, tempted but threatened by the clumsy, bulky white man and jealous yet scornful of her well-married friend, faces and fails in a moment of opportunity symbolized by the blossoming of her Keng Hua plant—a rare bloom said to bring good luck to those who know how to take advantage of it.

Another Country is a volume that visits many places where women live. These stories profile the lives of Chinese/Malaysian women of varying ages and social classes. Several are told from the fresh point of view of the child, or by women looking back at their lives through the lenses of childhood. The opening story, despite the title "All My Uncles," is about the women of the family, and is told by a child cared for by busy, indifferent aunts after her mother has abandoned her. This eagle-eyed little girl takes us into a traditional Chinese/Malaysian household where the families of four brothers live in separate apartments but share a common kitchen. The women gather there to prepare food and gossip, and listening, the young narrator is initiated into family history and legend.

Shirley Lim's poetry and stories take us home. Their journeys are interior travels extending the experience of being female. These poems and stories return us to ourselves:

All we can know with least destruction
Is self in the little while here.

Phyllis Edelson

SUMMITS MOVE WITH THE TIDE. Mei-mei Berssenbrugge, The Greenfield Review Press, Greenfield Center, NY 12833, 1974/82, 68 pages, $4.00 paper.

THE HEAT BIRD. Mei-mei Berssenbrugge, Burning Deck Press, 71 Elmgrove, Providence, RI 02906, 1983, 62 pages, $4.00 paper.

To enter Berssenbrugge country one must suspend presumptions about language, ethnicity, time, space, and poetry. Hers is a sublime, elusive, idiosyncratic world—*something that can only be seen/in infinite slender sections.* One cannot clamor for quick understanding. Given the poet's education at Reed College and Columbia University (where she received her MFA) her un-pretentious, spontaneous style is all the more unusual.

Summits Move with the Tide, her second book, is a handsome edition of thirty-two poems and a play which explores the human spirit, the unconscious, and cultural heritage.

"Fish and Swimmers and Lonely Birds Sweep Past Us" captures an angle of love, "Spaces are Death" illuminates death-in-life, and a tribute is paid to New Mexico in "Los Sangres De Cristos, N.M.," "Hopi Basketweaver Song," and other poems with much the same reverence as is found in Georgia O'Keeffe's paintings.

But Berssenbrugge's elusiveness comes across as indecision in the play, "One, Two Cups." Its impact may well depend on stage interpretation. (This play does however contain some of her few written recollections of China, where she was born in 1947.)

The poet's treatment of death showcases her combination of optimism and disen-chantment. In "Poor Mouse," she writes: *I hear a vibration fading away / but I never hear the thing striking.* In "In Bhaudanath," she comforts: *if your shining / amber skull / fills with liquid / you know / it is clean / water / from the mountains.*

The physical end isn't the only death. She writes in "The Old Know by Midsummer": *I want to see my death / remembering my birth, my first love / and my second, without ever / healing to any death / When gods separated men from women / for being too perfect / they doubly separated us / I want to be the man and the woman / and the child and the elder.* And other deaths include living with a diminished past (scars over old wounds), accepting limiting identities as sex or age, stasis, and perfection—a veneer on life.

Berssenbrugge writes in shifting imagery or metaphor rather than static fact. She addresses this tendency in "Ricochet off Water" from her fourth book **The Heat Bird:** *These days I'm suspecting grief over you is / a metaphor for grief in me. I used to think I / made a metaphor out of every fact to screen / you. Then I suspected there actually were facts, or / it was advantageous to imagine there were, but / now I draw from actual longing a longing locus / where any dry leaf clatters against the windowpane / in a web.* As the poem progresses, the poet lapses into metaphor.

The Heat Bird consists of four sections, each a grouping of brief narrative prose stanzas: "Pack Rat Sieve" sifts through experience, from a time when the narrator lived in Alaska; "Farolita" is a play on both color and light, and about a woman's identity: *Open the door / Light falls like a collar point on the blond floor boards / She crosses this point, and light falls on her / and it falls on her as she goes out / but it is different light.* Berssenbrugge is more openly biographical in this work: *The Eurasian at the party would not speak to her . . . Mei-mei, you've walked in that garden before.* "Ricochet off Water" examines the relationships between things in an internal landscape: *There is no shape to the space, but there is weight / Everything is within it or within the wheel rim / of its track.* And the title poem, "The Heat Bird," deals with the nuclear threat, ending with the line: *If a bright clearing will form suddenly, we will / already know of it.* For all the topic's grimness, Berssenbrugge injects humor: *A critic objects to their 'misterian' qualities / I look it up and don't find it, which must relate / to the mysteries in religions.*

Berssenbrugge demands much of the reader. One delves into an inner, wordless place in answer.

Shalin Hai-Jew

CRUELTY. Ai, Houghton Mifflin Company, 1 Beacon Street, Boston, MA 02108, 1973, 46 pages, $2.95 paper.

KILLING FLOOR. Ai, Houghton Mifflin Company, 1979, 49 pages, $3.95 paper.

SIN. Ai, Houghton Mifflin Company, 1986, 80 pages, $5.95 paper.

In her first collection of forty-six poems, Ai addresses the violent human psyche in its many manifestations: child abuse, rape, prostitution, suicide, murder, and other forms of cruelty. This poet willfully and eloquently deals with taboo subjects. Her obsession with violence never lapses into melodrama, self-indulgence or condescension.

Sexuality is one door through which the soul is glimpsed. In "Cruelty": *Drinking ice water hasn't, / nor having the bedsprings snap fingers / to help us keep rhythm. / I've never once felt anything / that might get close. Can't you see? The thing I want most is hard, / running toward my own teeth / and it bites back.* From "Woman": *The blood, halved and thinned, rolls down my legs, / cupping each foot in a red stirrup / and I am riding that invisible horse, / the same one my mother rode. / It's hungry, it has to be fed, / the last man couldn't, can you?* Relations between women and men are unsatisfactory, but basic. In "Why Can't I Leave You?," the speaker assails, *I know we can't give each other any more / or any less than what we have. / There is safety in that, so much / that I can never get past the packing, / the begging you to please, if I can't make you happy, / come close between my thighs / and let me laugh for you from my second mouth.* In "1931," a man realizes his companion will *follow, always behind or ahead of me, / never at my side. We don't mix, even in bed,* says "Woman to Man."

Ai's titles reveal the futility of such relationships: "The Estranged," "Disregard," "The Rivals," "Possessions," "Recapture," and "One Man Down." This antagonism between the sexes comes out in encounters between prostitutes and clients also. The "Tired Old Whore" brags, *I'll be the only whore within fifty miles / who can claim she did something with her hands / that didn't get a man hard.*

Murder is erotic and refined in "Cuba, 1962": *Juanita, dead in the morning like this. / I raise the machete— / what I take from the earth, I give back— / and cut off her feet. / I lift the body and carry it to the wagon, / where I load the cane to sell in the village. / Whoever tastes my woman in his candy, his cake, / tastes something sweeter than this sugar* cane; / it is grief. / If you eat too much of it, you want more, / you can never get enough.

Ai has matured in *Killing Floor*, a Lamont Poetry Selection of the Academy of American Poets. In these two dozen poems, she has transferred her talents to illuminating history with the voices of the people who made or witnessed it. Time is transcended and obliterated until the events are as vivid and impassioned as when they occurred. We see that the present is guided as much by human violence and folly as the past. Ai writes: *I step over— / —the years fly up in my face like a fine gray dust.*

The most stunning historical poem of this collection is "The Gilded Man," about the 1561 expedition of Lope de Aguirre: *Vera Cruz. Listen. My heart is speaking. / I am the fishes, the five loaves. / The women, the men I killed simply ate me. / There is no dying, only living in death. / I was their salvation. / I am absolved by their hunger.*

Familial discord frequently appears in poems, like "Lesson, Lesson," "The Expectant Father," "Father and Son," and "Sleep Like a Hammer." "The Kid" murders his whole family at age 14. Morbidity is no deterrent. "The Mortician's Twelve Year Old Son" indulges in necrophilia, while a woman buries her dead man in "Ice."

Ai acknowledges the influence of two late Japanese writers: Yukio Mishima in "Nothing But Color" and Yasunari Kawabata in "Talking to His Reflection in a Shallow Pond." With Mishima, she shares a fascination with violence, an erotic sensibility, and the non-acceptance of death-as-end (reincarnation, continuance of souls); with Kawabata, she shares a meditation on beauty; and with both, she shares a sparseness of language and skilled repetition of imagery.

Every seven years, Ai has managed to come out with a strong book of evocative poetry. And so it is with *Sin*, a collection of twenty poems that reflect our new age of cynicism. *The Twentieth Century is there, / wearing a necklace of grenades / that glitters against its black skin. / I stare, see the pins / have all been pulled.*

The poem "Elegy" is a lament for all wars, in the voice of a Twentieth Century soldier. "They Shall Not Pass" deals with the Spanish Civil War. "The Journalist" and "The Detective" are two indirect casualties of the Vietnam War. "Kristallnacht" revolves around the November 9, 1938 night of anti-Jew violence in Germany, and the persona of an accused murderer of some twenty-eight black children in Georgia speaks in "The Good Shepherd: Atlanta, 1981." In "Blue Suede Shoes," the person of Joe McCarthy says: *I'm an American. / I shall not want. / There's nothing that doesn't belong to me,* and in "The Testimony of J. Robert Oppenheimer," the poet says: *Like a bed we make and remake at whim, / the truth is always changing, / always shaped by the latest / collective urge to destroy.*

"Immortality" tells of a chance meeting between a man and woman in the Great War, and their later association: *And just like that, we parted. / Then one day you found me hoeing potatoes. / **Let me help,** you said, / and handed me a child / with bright red hair like yours. / I married you.*

One of Ai's rare serene poems, "The Man with the Saxophone," may reveal something of the poet's ambition: *If only I could / turn myself into a bird / like the shaman I was meant to be, / . . . for that moment, / I'm the unencumbered bird of my imagination, / rising only to fall back / toward concrete.*

One can imagine this poet's use of imagination to be shaman (conduit) to the many voices travelling through her. She hands us black flowers that bloom.

Shalin Hai-Jew

DWARF BAMBOO. *Marilyn Chin*, The Greenfield Review Press, R.D. 1, Box 80, Greenfield Center, NY 12833, 1987, 84 pages, $8.95 paper.

Chin's collection of forty-three poems is, for me, quintessentially Chinese American. Her works draw knowledgeably from Chinese history, literature, Buddhism, philosophy, language, *and* Americana.

This poetry is meant to be read aloud. From "Ode to Anger": *Soak in a hot bath; / arrange my futuristic hair, / then, the futon & the cushioned tatami . . . / And here you come— / a cricket's dance in the woods— / in a fog-colored zoot suit.* The humor is wry, tongue-in-cheek. In "The Narrow Roads of Oku": *My name is Buddha, Buddha Grosemon, / My personal name is Gozo, / But too many grrrs are bad for the throat.* In "The Cricket": *I am sad for the cricket, / Sadder for the late First Century B.C. Tibetans / Who tried to get rid of it.*

Chin addresses the deep connection Chinese Americans have with exploring their heritage in "Child," and in "Exile's Letter," hints at the potential for corruption and loss of culture: *And behind that briared fence / the boys are watching, even now, / the white boys,* as in "Repulse Bay": *The rain over Hong Kong falls / Over all of us, Li Ching, though / This postcard will tell you nothing / About the country I have lost—.*

Chin writes eloquently about love, as in "Unrequited Love": *She shall always sit this way, her back toward you, / her shoulders bare, / her silk kimono in manifolds around her waist—blue as the changeless sea. / You sit prostrate before her, bruise your forehead, / chant the Dharmas.*

Chin deals politics with a light touch, as in "Beauty, my Sisters, is not Regalia": *The virtue of America / Is that she has no direction. / The problem with Imperial Japan was that / She knew too well / Her direction. / And China's direction / I think / Today / October 30, 1980 / Is good.*

This writer has a knack for the apt description. In "Grandmother Poems (Hard Jade)," she writes: *Mother was the cross / mulish woman, who scrubbed her house bald. / Her floor, her child / must be clean, clean to impress. / Now the soap still sticks to the ceiling / of my mouth. . . .* In "First Lessons," *I learned **goodness** before I learned my name. / I learned the strokes, their order, but never the message: / that the good shall never rise from their knees is my river-to-cross.*

In "Art is What Humans Leave Behind, Roberto":

My love, this is no philosophical problem.
This is not a meditation on existence.
This is the goddam truth about my existence,
and I don't think I'm very fond of it . . .
Emancipation never comes. It winds, unwinds,
but never comes . . .

In these poems Chin has forged a place for herself.

Shalin Hai-Jew

ANGEL ISLAND PRISONER 1922. Helen Chetin, New Seed Press, PO Box 9488, Berkeley, CA, 1982, 24 pages, $7 paper.

In fourth grade we studied the American pioneers who left family and friends to travel a long way to seek a better life in a new place. *Angel Island Prisoner 1922* is the story of pioneers too, pioneer women from China who leave their homes and pets and make a long voyage to immigrate to a distant land.

Wai Ching is a young girl who is both sad and happy to be coming with her mother and baby brother to live in San Francisco where her father owns a store. She is sad to leave her grandmother in China, but she is also excited about being with her father again. When they are stopped at Angel Island, Wai Ching doesn't know if the "white demons" will allow them to immigrate at all. There they will wait with other women for the decision from the American immigration officers.

The women are scared, worried and confused. Wai Ching is afraid too but, like many other pioneer women, she has courage and is strong. She makes a good friend her own age and learns to tell stories from a grandmother she meets. She learns also how the women help each other and keep their dignity during their long wait.

The book cover is bright and appealing. I loved that it is in both English and Chinese so I could practice reading Chinese characters. I liked also the way the author used many Chinese words to describe people and places, like *Gum San* for Gold Mountain and *fan-gwai* for foreign demons. The pictures are nice and appear right on the page where the writing is so you can't miss them!

Wai Ching is also a poet and this was one way she used her long waiting time. She wrote a poem on the wall to help other women who came after her to Angel Island. Here is part of it:

I sailed away on a giant fish
to the land of Golden Mountain.
My mother and I came with only dreams
to the island in the mist.
We wait like lost birds
in the white demon's cage . . .

Will all these "lost birds" ever leave Angel Island and be able to join their families in San Francisco? You will have to read it yourself to find out!

Michelle Yokoyama   Age 11

CONTRIBUTOR NOTES AND INDEX

*NOTE: These contributor notes serve as an **index**. The genre, title, and page number of each contributor's work are noted in **bold face** at the end of their entry.*

TALAT ABBASI is from Pakistan and has lived in the U.S.A. for over eleven years. Her stories have been published in *Ascent* (University of Illinois), *Feminist Studies* (University of Maryland), and *Short Story International Seedling Series*. **Prose:** *Sari Petticoats,* **218.**

SIU WAI ANDERSON was born in Hong Kong, then was adopted and raised by an Anglo family in the U.S.A. She attended Stanford University (CA) and received a B.A. degree in Writing from Vermont College (Montpelier). In the late 1970's she joined the Asian community in San Francisco. There for the first time she found an important link to her heritage and identity as an Asian American. Currently she is a book reviewer for *The Asian American Resource Workshop Newsletter* and an Editorial Assistant at Little, Brown in Boston. **Prose:** *Autumn Gardening,* **54.**

ANJANA APPACHANA is an M.F.A. candidate at Pennsylvania State University (University Park). She has been published in *The Illustrated Weekly* and *Imprint* (India), *Room of One's Own, The Webster Review,* and *Sojourner*. She graduated from Delhi University and did post-graduate work in New Delhi. **Prose:** *To Rise Above,* **221,** *My Only Gods,* **228.**

TOMIE ARAI is a third-generation Japanese American living in New York City. She has coordinated Third World community mural projects since the 1970's and works in printmaking, graphic design, illustration, and painting. Her work has been exhibited widely and she has been awarded an Artists Fellowship by the Printmaking Workshop in New York City. **Art:** *Self Portrait,* **65,** *Portrait of a Japanese Girl,* **66,** *Rice Eaters,* **67,** *Garden,* **68,** *Chinese Family,* **69.**

MEI-MEI BERSSENBRUGGE is Chinese American and lives in New Mexico. She was born in Beijing and grew up in Massachusetts. Her books include *The Heat Bird* (Burning Deck Press, 1983) and *Empathy* (1987). **Poetry:** *Duration of Water,* **147,** *Chronicle,* **148.**

SUJATA BHATT was born in India and emigrated to the U.S.A. in 1968. She has an M.F.A. from the Writer's Workshop of the University of Iowa (Ames). Her first book, *Brunizem,* was released in 1988 (Carcanet Press). Her work has appeared in *The Painted Bride Quarterly, Calyx, The Iowa Journal of Literary Studies,* and *Yellow Silk*. **Poetry:** *Go to Ahmedabad,* **25,** *Muliebrity,* **28.**

JANICE BISHOP is a poet, a performer of poetry with Viveca Lindfors and Players, and a frequent guest on radio poetry broadcasts. She holds a Master of Liberal Arts and an English Masters in Medieval Studies from the University of New York at Stony Brook. **Review:** *What Matisse Is After* by Diana Chang, **241.**

VIRGINIA R. CERENIO is a second-generation Filipino American. Her poems and short stories have been published in *Breaking Silence* (Greenfield Review Press), *Without Names* (Kearny Street Workshop Press), *East Wind Magazine, Bridge Magazine, Berkeley Fiction Review, Asian Journal,* and *Liwanad*. **Poetry:** *Family Photos: Black and White: 1960,* **77.**

DIANA CHANG teaches Creative Writing at Barnard College (New York). She is the author of six novels and is a poet and a painter. Her poetry and short stories have been published in numerous magazines and anthologies. Her second volume of poetry is *What Mattisse is After* (Contact II Press, 1984). She identifies herself as an American writer whose background is mostly Chinese. **Poetry:** *On Being in the Midwest*, **123**, *On The Fly*, **124. Prose:** *The Oriental Contingent*, **171.**

MARILYN CHIN was born in Hong Kong and raised in Portland, Oregon. She is a recipient of a National Endowment for the Arts Writers Fellowship for Poetry, the Stegner Fellowship in Creative Writing (Stanford University), and the Mary Roberts Rinehart Prize. She lives in San Francisco. Her first book of poetry, *Dwarf Bamboo* (Greenfield Review Press, 1987), was nominated for the Bay Area Book Reviewer's Award. She received her M.F.A. from the University of Iowa Writer's Workshop. **Poetry:** *We Are Americans Now, We Live in the Tundra*, **17.**

CHITRA DIVAKARUNI is originally from India and immigrated to the U.S.A in 1977. She completed her Ph.D. at the University of California, Berkeley in 1987. Her book, *Waiting for Rain*, is being published by Writers Workshop Press (Calcutta, India). She also has had work published in *Nexus* and *The Berkeley Poets Coop Magazine*. **Poetry:** *At Muktinath*, **29.**

PHYLLIS EDELSON chairs the Department of English/Communications at Pace University, White Plains, New York. She is the book review editor of *Antipodes*, a journal of Australian literature and criticism. **Review:** *Crossing the Peninsula and Other Poems, No Man's Grove, Another Country and Other Stories* by Shirley Lim, **255.**

MEI MEI EVANS has lived in Alaska for twelve years. She is currently at work on a novel entitled *Felix Creek*. She was born and raised in Philadelphia by a Shanghai Buddhist mother and a Philadelphia Quaker father. She is a writer, housebuilder, fisherperson. **Prose:** *Gussuk*, **150.**

LYNNE YAMAGUCHI FLETCHER has deep roots in both Kyoto, Japan and the Arizona desert. A founding editor of *Hayden's Ferry Review*, she currently freelances in southeastern Massachusetts. Her poems and translations have been published in *The Greenfield Review* and *Colorado Review*. **Poetry:** *After Delivering Your Lunch*, **119**, *Higashiyama Crematorium . . .*, **120**, *The Way April Leads to Autumn*, **122.**

JESSICA HAGEDORN was born and raised in the Philippines. She is the author of *Dangerous Music* and *Pet Food & Tropical Apparitions* (Momo's Press). Her theatrical pieces have been produced extensively, most notably by Joseph Papp at New York City's renowned Public Theater. She lives in New York City and is at work on her novel, *Dogeaters*. **Poetry:** *The Song of Bullets*, **144.**

SHALIN HAI-JEW received her B.A. and M.A. degrees from the University of Washington (Seattle). Her manuscript, "Looking for the Catalyst," was a 1985 Wesleyan Press finalist in the "New Poets Series." She works for a social service agency in Kent, Washington. **Poetry:** *Father's Belt*, **91. Reviews:** *Summits Move With the Tide, The Heat Bird* by Mei-mei Bersssenbrugge, **259.** *Cruelty, Killing Floor, Sin* by Ai, **260.** *Dwarf Bamboo* by Marilyn Chin, **262.**

MARGO P. HARDER is an Amerasian and a native Seattle resident. She grew up participating in the activities of the Seattle Filipino community and is a director of an ESL program. She received a B.A. in Communication Disorders from the University of Washington (Seattle). **Review: *Thousand Pieces of Gold* by Ruthanne Lum McCunn, 247.**

SHARON HASHIMOTO's poetry has been published in *The Seattle Review, Poetry Seattle, Gathering Ground: New Writing and Art by Northwest Women of Color* (Seal Press), and other periodicals and anthologies. She lives in Seattle (WA). **Poetry: *Standing in the Doorway . . .*, 198, *Eleven A.M . . .*, 199.**

LORI KAYO HATTA is a second-generation Japanese American born in Honolulu who grew up in New York City. She received her Bachelor's degree from Stanford University and is currently studying filmmaking at the University of California, Los Angeles. She has been a staff member of *East Wind*, a semiannual publication of politics and culture of Asians in the U.S.A. **Art: Obachan *Hatta, Kailua-Kona Fields,* 62, Obachan *Hatta, Kaimalino Housing,* 63, Obachan *Matano, Honolulu,* 64.**

ROSE FURUYA HAWKINS was born in 1944 in the war-time relocation camp in Poston, Arizona. She is an English teacher at Allan Hancock College (CA) and a consultant for the South Coast Writing Project at the University of California, Santa Barbara. She co-authored the textbook *Thinking on Paper* (Holt, Rinehart and Winston). **Poetry: Excerpts from *Proud Upon an Alien Shore,* 21.**

JUDY HIRAMOTO was born in Japan and raised in Honolulu, Hawaii. She received her Bachelor's degree from Antioch University (OH) and studied at the San Francisco Art Institute (CA). Her work has been exhibited widely, and she is the recipient of the 1986 Creative Arts Award from the Japanese American Citizen's League. **Art: *Cactus Heart,* 136, *Fool's Play,* 137, *Desert,* 138, *Piano Solo,* 139.**

BETTY NOBUE KANO was born in Japan in 1944 and moved to the U.S.A. in 1949. She studied Fine Arts and Painting at San Francisco State University and received her M.F.A. from the University of California, Berkeley. Her work has been widely exhibited and reviewed including *"Saludo al Pueblo"* (Managua, Nicaragua) and "South Africa State of Emergency" (*Galeria de La Raza*, San Francisco, CA). **Art: *To Winnie Mandela,* 183.**

ALISON KIM is a Chinese Korean born in Hawaii and raised in California. She is a Virgo with a Scorpio moon and Virgo rising, an activist, a lesbian, a writer, and an artist. **Art: untitled, 182. Poetry: *Sewing Woman,* 203.**

MYUNG MI KIM was born in Korea and moved to the U.S.A. when she was nine. She received her M.F.A. from the University of Iowa Writer's Workshop in 1986. She has taught English as a Second Language, translated, tutored, and is the director of Student Support Services, Luther College (IA). Her poetry has been published in *Ironwood, Antioch Review, How(ever),* and *Pavement*. **Poetry: *Into Such Assembly,* 18, *A Rose of Sharon,* 20.**

TINA KOYAMA received her M.A. and B.A. from the University of Washington (Seattle). She has been published in numerous anthologies and periodicals including: *Willow Springs, The Seattle Review, Poet and Critic, Contact II,* and *Breaking Silence: An Anthology of Asian American Poets* (Greenfield Review Press). She is the recipient of the 1983 Oberg Award for Poetry. **Poetry: *Currents,* 128, *Downtown Seattle in the Fog,* 129.**

BETTY LADUKE is Professor of Art at Southern Oregon State College (Ashland) and an artist. She initiated courses on "Women and Art" and "Multi-Cultural Arts." She is the author of *Compañeras: Women, Art and Social Change in Latin America* (City Lights, 1986). **Interview: *Miné Okubo: An American Experience*, 189.**

CAROLYN LAU was born in Hawaii and educated in China and California. She teaches poetry and movement to bi-lingual Chinese and Southeast Asian immigrant children. She has been published in numerous anthologies including *California Quarterly* and *Hawaii Review* and in literary collections in China. **Poetry: Zhoukoudian *Bride's Harvest*, 126.**

SUSAN K.C. LEE is a third-generation Chinese American born and raised in Hawaii. She received her B.A. from the University of Oregon (Eugene) where she is a Creative Writing Teaching Fellow and the recipient of the 1987 Graduate Award in Poetry. **Prose: *A Letter for Dar*, 92. Poetry: *Letter from Turtle Beach*, 202.**

GENNY LIM is author of the play "Paper Angels" (it aired on PBS's American Playhouse, 1985) and co-author of *Island: Poetry and History of Chinese Immigrants on Angel Island, 1910-1940*. Her first book of poetry, *Winter Place*, will be published by Kearny Street Workshop Press, Fall 1988. **Poetry: *Children are Color-blind*, 196.**

SHIRLEY GEOK-LIN LIM received the 1980 Commonwealth Poetry Prize for her first book of poems, *Crossing the Peninsula* (Heineman Educational Books, 1980). Book publications also include *Another Country* (Times Books International, 1982), *No Man's Grove* (National University of Singapore, 1985), and forthcoming, *Modern Secrets, New and Selected Poems* (Dangaroo Press, London). Her criticism has been published in *Asia, Asiaweek, Kunapipi, Contact II,* and *MELUS*, among others. Her work is also included in the anthology *The Third Woman*. **Prose: *Native Daughter*, 109. Poetry: *Pantoun for Chinese Women*, 204, *Visiting Malacca*, 206. Reviews: *Picture Bride* by Cathy Song, 235, *Asian-American Literature: An Introduction to the Writings & Their Social Context* by Elaine H. Kim, 238, *Obasan* by Joy Kogawa, 239.**

AMY LING was born in Beijing and came to the U.S.A. at age six. She has a Ph.D. in Comparative Literature from New York University. She has published numerous scholarly articles, a chapbook of poetry and paintings, *Chinamerican Reflections*, and is at work on a book, *Between Worlds, Women Writers of Chinese Ancestry*. She teaches in the English Department at Georgetown University in Washington, D.C. **Review: *Beyond Manzanar: Views of Asian American Womanhood* by Jeanne Wakatsuki Houston, 250.**

VALERIE MATSUMOTO recently completed her Ph.D. in History at Stanford University (CA). Her dissertation was a study of three generations in a Japanese American farming community in central California. She teaches at the University of Arizona (Tucson). **Prose: *Two Deserts*, 45.**

CAROL MATSUYOSHI is *Sansei* (third-generation Japanese American) from Waimea, Hawaii now living in Portland, Oregon. She has been working with clay since 1976 and enjoys hand building because of its spontaneity and speed. She is also involved in Asian programming on community radio in the Portland (OR) area. **Art: *Fish Jumping*, 140.**

YONG SOON MIN emigrated from South Korea at the age of seven and grew up in California where she received her B.A. and M.F.A. from the University of California,

Berkeley. In 1981 she moved to New York City for a residency at the Whitney Museum and reconnected with the Asian community of artists. Since then she has become concerned and involved with the growing Korean community. **Art:** ***Back of the Bus, 1953, 70, American Friend, 71, Echoes of Gold Mountain, 72, Whirl War, 73.***

MASAKO MIYATA was born in Japan and came to the U.S.A. in 1970 where she received her B.F.A. from the School of the Art Institute of Chicago and was a recipient of the James Nelson Raymond Foreign Travelling Fellowship Award. She received her M.F.A. from Pennsylvania State University and is currently an Associate Professor in Ceramics at James Madison University (VA). Her work has been exhibited widely and is in the following permanent collections: Museum of Modern Art (Milan, Italy), Museum of Rhode Island School of Design, and the Erie Museum (Erie, PA). **Art:** ***Carry Me Back to Old Virginny, 184, Tatooed Geta with Two States, 185.***

KYOKO MORI was born in Japan and has lived in the Midwest for the past decade. Her work has been published in *The Northwest Review, Sun Dog, The Beloit Poetry Journal, The Denver Quarterly, South Florida Poetry Review,* and *The Graham House Review.* Her first collection of stories, *The First Cicada,* is seeking a publisher. **Prose:** ***Yellow Mittens and Early Violets, 31.* Poetry: *Heat In October, 82.***

ARLENE NAGANAWA is Japanese American and has lived all her life in the Northwest. She received her B.A. from the University of Washington (Seattle) and teaches high school in Renton (WA). **Poetry:** ***Learning to Swim, 200.***

TAHIRA NAQVI is originally from Pakistan and currently lives in Connecticut. She has M.A. degrees from Punjab University (Pakistan) and Western Connecticut State University where she teaches English. Her work has been published in *The Wooster Review, Bridge Magazine, The Journal of South Asian Literature,* and *Translation.* An anthology she translated, *The Life and Works of Saadat Hassan Manto: Another Lonely Voice,* was published in 1985 in Pakistan. **Prose:** ***Paths Upon Water, 207.***

FAE MYENNE NG is a Creative Writing Fellow at The Mary Ingraham Bunting Institute of Radcliffe College (Cambridge, MA). Her fiction has been published in *The Pushcart Prize XII, The American Voice, The Crescent Review,* and *City Lights Review.* **Prose:** ***Last Night, 165.***

MAYUMI ODA was born in Japan and received her Art degree from Tokyo University of Fine Arts. She has lived in New York and Cambridge and now makes her home in northern California on San Francisco Zen Center land. Greatly influenced by the study of Buddhism, her goddess prints have been shown extensively in the U.S.A. and Japan at noted galleries and museums. **Art:** ***Mamala the Surf Rider, 178, Samansabadra, 179.***

MYUNG KIM OH left Korea at nineteen and received her B.F.A. and M.F.A. degrees from Kent State University (OH). Her work has been exhibited at the Cleveland Art Museum, Aromant Gallery (TN), and the Mary Cassat Mansion Invitational Show. She is the recipient of the Kathryn Wellman Award by the Philadelphia Handweaver's Guild. **Art:** ***Kite, 180, Baek-do, 181.***

MINÉ OKUBO was born in California of Japanese parentage. She received her B.A. and M.A. degrees from the University of California, Berkeley. During World War II she was interned in the Tanforan Assembly Center (CA) and the Topaz Relocation Camp in Utah. Her book *Citizen 13660* (Columbia University Press, 1946) documents her camp experience. She is well known in the U.S.A. and abroad. In 1972 the Oakland Museum of Art held a retrospective exhibit of her work. In 1985 the Catherine Gallery in New York City held a 40-year retrospective. **Art:** *Girl With Vase of Flowers,* **186,** *Cat with Flags,* **187,** *Drawings from Citizen 13660,* **188.**

SONG-JOOK PARK was born and educated in Pusan, Korea and has published six collections of poems and one book of essays. She is a member of the Korean Modern Poets Association and lives in Pusan with her husband and two sons. Translated by **HYUN-JAE YEE SALLEE** who has been published in *Permafrost, Florida Review, Blue Unicorn, Antigonishi Review,* and *Image.* She has been translating Korean literature into English for a number of years; in 1983 she won the Annual Translation Award in Korea. **Poetry:** *On Such A Day,* **130.**

MYRNA PEÑA REYES was born and raised in the Philippines, and her poetry has been published in the U.S.A. and the Philippines. She holds an M.F.A. in Creative Writing from the University of Oregon (Eugene). **Poetry:** *San Juan,* **142,** *Toads Mate and Father Cleans the Pool,* **143.**

KIT QUAN emigrated from Hong Kong to San Francisco when she was eight. She has worked as a grocery clerk and delivery truck driver as well as at a feminist bookstore. She resigned from the feminist bookstore collective due to unresolvable conflicts of class, race, and power issues in the group. **Review:** *With Silk Wings: Asian American Women at Work* by Elaine H. Kim with Janice Otani, **251.**

JESSICA SAIKI is author of *Once, A Lotus Garden,* a collection of short stories set in Hawaii where she grew up. It won the 1986 Minnesota Voices Project and was selected by Publishers Weekly as one of the best books published in 1987. **Review:** *Dangerous Music* by Jessica Hagedorn, **241.**

STEPHANIE SUGIOKA is Japanese American. She has an M.A. in Chinese Literature from the University of Wisconsin (Madison). Her work has been published in *The Beloit Poetry Review* and *The Little Magazine.* She works as a freelance editor and a medical editor. **Poetry:** *Legacy,* **88.**

JEAN YAMASAKI TOYAMA was born and raised in Hawaii and teaches French at the University of Hawaii (Honolulu). Her poetry has been published in *Creative Moment, Mele, Bridge, Hawaii Review,* and *Bamboo Ridge.* Translations of her work are published in *La Prensa Literaria* (Nicaragua), *Cormoran y delfin* (Argentina), and *Minas Gerais* (Peru). **Poetry:** *Red,* **201.**

YOSHIKO UCHIDA was born in California. During World War II she and her family were relocated, first to a horse stall at Tanforan Race Track and then to the barracks at Topaz (the bleak concentration camp in the Utah desert). She received a Master's degree from Smith College (Northampton, MA) and has more than twenty-five titles published. These include: *Picture Bride* (Northland Press, 1987), *Journey to Topaz* (an ALA Notable Book), and *Desert Exile* (University of Washington Press). **Prose:** *Tears of Autumn,* **39.**

MARIANNE VILLANUEVA is from Manila (Philippines) where she received her B.A.

from Ateneo University. She received her M.A. in English from Stanford University (CA). Her publications include: *The Journal of Philippine Studies* (Manila), *Panorama* (the Sunday magazine of the Manila Bulletin), and *Story Quarterly*. **Prose:** *Siko,* **99. Review:** *Wings of Stone* by Linda Ty-Casper, **248.**

PATTI WARASHINA, Professor of Art at the University of Washington, was born in Spokane (WA) of *Issei* and *Nisei* parents. She is a nationally known ceramic artist whose work has been exhibited at the Whitney Museum of American Art, American Craft Museum, Renwick Gallery of the Smithsonian Institution, the Bronx Museum, and Seattle Arts Museum among others. She has two grown daughters and lives in Seattle (WA). **Art:** *Manning the Shroud,* **134,** *A Procession,* **135.**

JULIA WATSON is an Associate Professor of Humanities at the University of Montana (Missoula) and writes on women's autobiography. Her essay on women's autobiography will appear in *Studies in Autobiography* (Editor James Olney, Oxford University Press, 1988). **Review:** *This Bridge Called My Back: Writings by Radical Women of Color* edited by Cherríe Moraga, Gloria Anzaldua, **253.**

NELLIE WONG is home-grown in Oakland's Chinatown and is active in the Freedom Socialist Party and Radical Women. Her work has appeared in many journals and anthologies including: *This Bridge Called My Back, Conditions, 13th Moon, Bridge, Asian American Perspectives, Ikon 4, Artists Against Apartheid,* and *Working Classics.* She is featured with Mitsuye Yamada in the film "Mitsuye and Nellie, Asian American Poets." **Poetry:** *For An Asian Woman Who Says . . .,* **86.**

ROBERTA MAY WONG received her B.A. in Art from Portland State University (OR) and is an Administrative Assistant with the Interstate Firehouse Cultural Center (Portland, OR). She organized and is director of Asian Artists of Oregon and is active in the Japanese American Citizens League. In 1986 she was the coordinator of the Portland exhibition "Chinese Women of America, 1834-1982." **Art:** *All Orientals Look Alike,* **74, 75,** *The Last Supper,* **76.**

MERLE WOO is a socialist-feminist-lesbian writer/educator, and a member of Radical Women and the Freedom Socialist Party. She is currently fighting the second round of a six-year free speech and multi-discrimination battle against the University of California, Berkeley. **Poetry:** untitled, **131,** *Whenever You're Cornered, The Only Way Out Is to Fight,* **132.**

MITSUYE YAMADA was born in Japan and was growing up in Seattle (WA) when her family was relocated to a concentration camp in Idaho. Her book, *Camp Notes* (Shameless Hussy Press, 1976), recounts her experience. Her second book of poetry, *Desert Run, Poems and Stories,* was published in 1988 by Kitchen Table Press. She teaches Creative Writing at Cypress College in southern California, is a founder of the Multicultural Women Writers of Orange County, and was elected to the Board of Directors of Amnesty International in 1988. **Poetry:** *The Club,* **84.**

MARIAN YEE is Chinese American. She is a student in the Graduate English Program at Rutgers University (New Brunswick, NJ). **Poetry:** *The Handbook of Sex of the Plain Girl,* **78,** *Wintermelons,* **80. Reviews:** *In the City of Contradictions* by Fay Chiang, *Dreams* *in Harrison Railroad Park* by Nellie Wong, *Camp Notes and Other Poems* by Mitsuye Yamada, **243.**

MICHELLE YOKOYAMA is Japanese American and has been writing since she was four years old. Currently she is eleven years old and in the sixth grade. Her stories and poems have been published in *Faces, Gifted Children's Monthly,* and *The Young Entomologists Society Journal.* She is a junior tennis player and the winner of three Pacific Northwest tournaments. **Review:** *Angel Island Prisoner 1922* by Helen Chetin, **263.**

ELAINE S. YONEOKA was born and raised in New York City by an immigrant father and second-generation mother from whom she developed a Japanese aesthetic and attitude toward life. She graduated from Oberlin College (OH) in 1976. Her artwork is principally self taught and has been exhibited in Boston, New York, Los Angeles, the Southwest, and England. She teaches at Mass Bay Community College (Boston, MA). **Art:** *Ring of Forgotten Knowledge,* **141.**

EDITORS NOTES

SHIRLEY GEOK-LIN LIM (see Contributor Notes above)

MAYUMI TSUTAKAWA is a third-generation Japanese American writer and editor. She earned her Bachelor's degree in East Asian History and a Master's degree in Communications from the University of Washington (Seattle). She was the first Asian American female reporting for a major daily newspaper in the Pacific Northwest and spent six years with the Seattle Times. She is currently Assistant Director of the King County Arts Commission (Seattle, WA). She coedited *Gathering Ground: New Writing and Art by Northwest Women of Color* (Seal Press, 1984) and *Turning Shadows into Light: Art and Culture by the Northwest's Early Asian/Pacific Community* (Young Pine Press, 1982).

MARGARITA DONNELLY is the Managing Editor and a founding editor of Calyx Inc. and Calyx Books. She was born and raised bilingually in Venezuela. In 1985 she was awarded the CCLM Editors Grant for excellence which cited Calyx's commitment to publication of work by women of color. She is active in the struggle for peace and justice in the world and in her spare time shepherds a flock of Hampshire sheep who teach her patience.

A BIBLIOGRAPHY OF WORK BY ASIAN AMERICAN WOMEN

This bibliography has been compiled from a wide range of sources. We extend special thanks to Dr. Amy Ling, Dr. Shirley Lim, Alison Kim, Professor Gail Tremblay, and Librarian Susan Searing (with Lyn Christensen, Linda Shult, and Christina Wagner of the University of Wisconsin Women's Studies Library) for use of their bibliographies. We also thank *Calyx* student interns Sara Davis and Teresa Vazquez from Oberlin College, and Librarian Lyn Christopher for their assistance in checking the sources and putting the citations into the database. And last, but not least, thank you to Karen Thieling for the computer program that transfered the bibliography into typeset.

ANTHOLOGIES

Ancheta, Shirley, Jaime Jacinto, and Jeff Tagami, eds. *Without Names: A Collection of Poems [by] Bay Area Pilipino American Writers*. San Francisco: Kearny Street Workshop Press, 1985.

Asian Women. Berkeley: Asian Women's Journal Workshop, 1971.

Bankier, Joanna, and Deirdre Lashgari, eds. *Women Poets of the World*. NY: Macmillan, 1983.

Blicksilver, Edith. *The Ethnic American Woman: Problems, Protests, Lifestyle*. Dubuque, IA: Kendall Hunt Publishing Co., 1978.

Bruchac, Carol, Linda Hogan, and Judith McDaniel, eds. *The Stories We Hold Secret: Tales of Women's Spiritual Development*. Greenfield Ctr., NY: Greenfield Review Press, 1986.

Bruchac, Joseph, ed. *Breaking Silence: An Anthology of Asian American Poetry*. Greenfield Ctr., NY: Greenfield Review Press, 1983.

Bruchac, Joseph, ed. *The Next World: Poems by Thirty-two Third World Americans*. Freedom, CA: Crossing Press, 1978.

Bulkin, Elly, and Joan Larkin, eds. *Lesbian Poetry, An Anthology*. Watertown, MA: Persephone Press, 1981.

Cachapero, Emily, et al., eds. *Liwanag: Literary and Graphic Expressions of Filipinos in America*. San Francisco: Liwanag Publications, 1975.

Chiang, Fay, et al., eds. *American Born and Foreign: An Anthology of Asian American Poetry*. NY: Sunbury Press Books, 1979.

Chin, Frank, et al., eds. *AIIIEEEEE! An Anthology of Asian-American Writers*. Washington D.C.: Howard University Press, 1974 and 1983.

Chinn, Kathy, et al., eds. *Home Grown: Asian American Experiences from the Pacific Northwest*. Seattle, WA: University of Washington Press, 1980.

Chock, Eric, et al., eds. *Talk Story: An Anthology of Hawaii's Local Writers*. Honolulu, HI: Petronium Press/Talk Story, 1978.

Chung, Connie, Alison Kim, and A.K. Lemeshewsky, eds. *Between the Lines: An Anthology by Pacific/Asian Lesbians.* Santa Cruz, CA: Dancing Bird Press, 1987.

Cochran, Jo, J.T. Stewart, and Mayumi Tsutakawa, eds. *Gathering Ground: New Writing and Art By Northwest Women of Color.* Seattle, WA: Seal Press, 1984.

Faderman, Lillian, and Barbara Bradshaw, eds. *Speaking for Ourselves: American Ethnic Writing.* Glenview, IL: Scott, Foreman & Co., 1969 and 1975.

Fisher, Dexter. *The Third Woman: Minority Women Writers of the United States.* Boston: Houghton Mifflin, 1980.

Gee, Emma, et al., eds. *Counterpoint: Perspectives on Asian America.* Los Angeles: Asian American Studies Center, UCLA, 1976.

Gill, Stephen, ed. *Green Snow: Anthology of Canadian Poets of Asian Origin.* Ontario, Canada: Vesta Publications, 1976.

Hahn, Kimiko, Gale Jackson, and Susan Sherman. *We Stand Our Ground: Three Women, Their Vision, Their Poems.* NY: Ikon, Inc., 1988.

Harris, Catherine E., and Barbara B. Robinson, eds. *Sandwich Isles U.S.A.: A Collection, Fifty Views of Hawaii by Forty-Five Authors and Four Artists.* Honolulu: Menehune Pubs., 1973.

Harvey, Nick, ed. *Ting! The Caldron. Chinese Art and Identity in San Francisco.* San Francisco Glide Urban Center, 1970.

Haslam, Gerald W., ed. *Forgotten Pages of American Literature.* Boston: Houghton Mifflin, 1970.

Higa, Lori, et al., eds. *Rising Waters.* Santa Cruz, CA: University of California, Asian American Studies, 1975.

Hsu, Kai-yu, and Helen Palubinskas, eds. *Asian-American Authors.* NY: Houghton Mifflin, 1972.

Lai, Him Mark, Genny Lim, and Judy Yung. *Island: Poetry and History of Chinese Immigrants on Angel Island 1910-1940.* San Francisco: HOC DOI Project, 1980.

Lourie, Dick, ed. *Come to Power.* Trumansburg, NY: The Crossing Press, 1974.

Mirikitani, Janice, ed. *Ayumi: The Japanese American Anthology.* San Francisco: Japanese American Anthology Committee (dist. by Glide Publications), 1980.

Mirikitani, Janice, ed. *Third World Women.* San Francisco: Third World Communications Press, 1972.

Mirikitani, Janice, et al., eds. *Time to Greez! Incantations From the Third World.* San Francisco: Glide Publications/Third World Communications, 1975.

Moraga, Cherríe, and Gloria Anzaldua, eds. *This Bridge Called My Back: Writings By Radical Women of Color.* Latham, NY: Kitchen Table/Women of Color Press, 1983.

Navarro, Jovina, comp. *Diwang Pilipino: Philipine Consciousness.* Davis, CA: Asian American Studies, University of California, 1974.

Planas, Alvin, and Diana Chau, eds. *Hanai: An Anthology of Asian American Writings.* Berkeley: University of California, 1980.

Reed, Ishmael, and Al Young, eds. *Yardbird Lives.* NY: Garden Grove, 1978.

Reese, Lyn, et al., eds. *I'm on My Way Running: Women Speak on Coming of Age.* NY: Avon,

1983.

Saiki, Patsy Sumie, ed. *Ganbarel: An Example of Japanese Spirit. Oral History.* Honolulu: Kisaku, Inc., 1982.

Sheridan, Mary, and Janet W. Salaf, eds. *Lives: Chinese Working Women.* Bloomington, IN: Indiana University Press, 1984.

Simone, Carol A., ed. *Networks: An Anthology of San Francisco Bay Area Women Poets.* Palo Alto, CA: Vortex Editions, 1979.

Sue, Stanley, and Nathaniel N. Wagner, eds. *Asian Americans: Psychological Perspectives.* Palo Alto: Science and Behavior Books, 1973.

Sunoo, Brenda Paik, ed. *Korean American Writings.* NY: Insight, 1975.

Tachiki, Amy, et al., eds. *Roots! An Asian American Reader.* Los Angeles: Asian American Studies Center, UCLA, 1971.

Third World Women. San Francisco: Third World Communications, 1972.

Tsutakawa, Mayumi, and Alan Chong Lau, eds. *Turning Shadows Into Light: Art and Culture of the Northwest's Early Asian/Pacific Community.* Seattle: Young Pine, 1982.

Unbound Feet (A Chinese American Women Writer's Collective). *Unbound Feet: A Collective of Chinese American Women Writers.* San Francisco: Isthmus Press, 1981.

Wand, David Hsin-Fu, ed. *Asian-American Heritage: An Anthology of Prose and Poetry.* NY: Washington Square Press, 1974.

Wilson, Barbara, Rachel daSilva, and Hylah Jaques, eds. *Backbone 2: New Fiction by Northwest Women.* Seattle, WA: Seal Press, 1980.

Woo, Merle. *Balancing. Hanai—An Anthology of Asian American Writings.* Berkeley: Asian American Studies, Dept. of Ethnic Studies, University of California, n.d.

Yellow Peril. NY: Basement Workshop, 1972.

FICTION

Chang, Diana. *Eye to Eye.* NY: Harper and Row, 1974.

Chang, Diana. *The Frontiers of Love.* NY: Random House, 1974.

Chang, Diana. *The Only Game in Town.* NY: New American Library, 1963.

Chang, Diana. *A Passion for Life.* NY: Random House, 1961.

Chang, Diana. *A Perfect Love.* NY: Jove Books, 1978.

Chang, Diana. *A Woman of Thirty.* NY: Random House, 1959.

Chuang, Hua. *Crossings.* NY: The Dial Press, 1968.

Eaton, Edith (a.k.a. Sui, Sin Far). *Mrs. Spring Fragrance.* Chicago: AC McClure, 1912.

Eaton, Winnifred. *Cattle.* London: Hutchinson & Co., 1923.

Eaton, Winnifred. *Daughters of Nijo.* NY: Macmillan Co., 1903.

Eaton, Winnifred. *The Diary of Delia: Being a Voracious Chronicle of the Kitchen, with Some Side-Lights on the Parlour.* NY: Page & Co., 1907.

Eaton, Winnifred. *The Heart of Hyacinth.* NY: Harper & Bros., 1903.

Eaton, Winnifred. *His Royal Nibs.* NY: WJ Watt & Co., 1925.

Eaton, Winnifred. *The Honorable Miss Moonlight.* NY: Harper & Bros., 1912.

Eaton, Winnifred. *A Japanese Blossom.* NY: Harper & Bros., 1906.

Eaton, Winnifred. *A Japanese Nightingale.* NY: Harper & Bros., 1901.

Eaton, Winnifred. *The Love of Azalea.* NY: Dodd, Mead & Co, 1904.

Eaton, Winnifred. *Miss Nume of Japan: a Japanese-American Romance.* Chicago: Rand Mc-Nally & Co., 1899.

Eaton, Winnifred. *Sunny-san.* NY: George H. Doran & Co., 1922.

Eaton, Winnifred. *Tama.* NY: Harper & Bros., 1910.

Eaton, Winnifred. *The Wooing of Wisteria.* NY: Harper & Bros., 1902.

Hagedorn, Jessica. *Dangerous Music: The Poetry and Prose of Jessica Hagedorn.* San Francisco: Momo's Press, 1975.

Jelsma, Clara Mitsuko. *Teapot Tales and Other Stories.* Honolulu, HI: Bamboo Ridge Press, 1981.

Kim, Willyce. *Dancer Dawkins and the California Kid.* Boston: Alyson, 1984.

Kim, Willyce. *Under the Rolling Sky.* n.p. Maude Gonne Press, 1976.

Kin, Hazel Ai Chun. *The Physicians.* NY: John Day, 1951.

Kingston, Maxine Hong. *China Men.* NY: Knopf, 1980.

Kingston, Maxine Hong. *The Woman Warrior.* NY: Knopf, 1975.

Kogawa, Joy. *Obasan.* Boston: David Godine, 1982.

Kuo, Helena. *Peach Path.* London: Methuen, 1940.

Kuo, Helena, trans. by Lau Shaw. *The Quest for Love of Lao Lee.* NY: Reynal & Hitchcock, 1948.

Kuo, Helena. *Westward to Chungking.* NY: D. Appleton-Century, 1944.

Law-yone, Wendy. *The Coffin Tree.* NY: Knopf, 1983.

Lee, Chin-yang. *Flower Drum Song.* NY: Farrar, 1957.

Lee, Chin-yang. *Lover's Point.* NY: Stratford, 1958.

Lee, Virginia. *The House That Tai Ming Built.* NY: Macmillan Co., 1963.

Li Ju-chen, trans. by Tai-yi Lin (Anor Lin). *Flowers in the Mirror.* Berkeley and Los Angeles: University of California Press, 1965.

Lim, Genevieve, trans. by Lew Gordon. *Wings For Lai Ho.* San Francisco: East/West Publishing, 1982.

Lim, Genny. *Paper Angels.* San Francisco: Performed by Asian American Theatre Company, n.d.

Lim, Janet. *Sold For Silver.* Cleveland, OH: World, 1958.

Lim, Shirley. *Another Country.* Singapore: Times Books International, 1982.

Lin, Hazel Ai Chun. *House of Orchids.* NY: Citadel Press, 1960.

Lin, Hazel Ai Chun. *The Moon Vow.* NY: Pageant, 1958.

Lin, Hazel Ai Chun. *The Physicians.* NY: Day, 1951.

Lin, Hazel Ai Chun. *Rachel Weeping for Her Children.* Boston: Branden, 1976.

Lin, Tai-yi (Anor Lin). *The Eavesdropper.* Cleveland, OH: World Publ. Co., 1959.

Lin, Tai-yi (Anor Lin), trans. *Flowers in the Mirror* (by Li Ju-chen). Berkeley: University of California Press, 1965.

Lin, Tai-yi (Anor Lin). *The Golden Coin.* NY: John Day Co., 1946.

Lin, Tai-yi (Anor Lin). *Kampoon Street*. Cleveland, OH: World Publ. Co., 1964.
Lin, Tai-yi (Anor Lin). *The Lilacs Overgrow*. Cleveland, OH: World Publ. Co., 1960.
Lin, Tai-yi (Anor Lin). *War Tide*. NY: Day, 1943.
Lord, Betty Bao. *Spring Moon*. NY: Harper & Row, 1981.
McCunn, Ruthanne. *Sole Survivor*. San Francisco: Design Enterprises, 1985.
McCunn, Ruthanne. *Thousand Pieces of Gold*. San Francisco: Design Enterprises, 1981.
Mirikitani, Janice. *Awake in the River*. San Francisco: Isthmus Press, 1978.
Namjoshi, Suniti. *Feminist Fables*. Exeter, NH: A. Wheeler & Co., Ltd., 1984.
Ota, Shelley Ayame Nishimurs. *Upon Their Shoulders*. NY: Exposition Press, 1951.
Ronyoung, Kim. *Clay Walls*. Sag Harbor, NY: Permanent Press, 1986.
Saiki, Jessica. *Once a Lotus Garden and Other Stories*. St. Paul, MN: New Rivers Press, 1987.
Sugimoto, Etsu Inagaki. *A Daughter of the Narikin*. NY: Doubleday, 1932.
Sugimoto, Etsu Inagaki. *A Daughter of the Nohfu*. NY: Doubleday, 1935.
Sugimoto, Etsu Inagaki. *Grandmother O Kyo*. NY: Doubleday, 1940.
Sze, Mai-mai. *China*. Cleveland, OH: Western Reserve University Press, 1944.
Sze, Mai-mai. *Echo of a Cry. A Story Which Began in China*. NY: Harcourt Brace, 1945.
Sze, Mai-mai. *Silent Children*. NY: Harcourt Brace, 1943.
Telemapue, Eleanor Wong. *It's Crazy to Stay Chinese in Minnesota*. NY: Nelson, 1978.
Ty-Casper, Linda. *Wings of Stone*. London: Readers International, 1986.
Yamada, Mitsuye. *Desert Run Poems and Stories*. Latham, NY: Kitchen Table/Women of Color Press, 1988.
Yamamoto, Hisaye. *Seventeen Syllables and Other Stories*. Latham, NY: Kitchen Table/Women of Color Press, 1988.
Yun, Tan (Adet Lin). *Flame From the Rock*. NY: John Day Co., 1943.
Yun, Tan (Adet Lin). *The Milky Way and Other Chinese Folk Tales*. NY: Harcourt Brace, 1961.

POETRY

Ai. *Cruelty*. Boston: Houghton Mifflin, 1973.
Ai. *Cruelty/Killing Floor*. NY: Thunder's Mouth Press, 1987.
Ai. *Killing Floor*. Boston: Houghton Mifflin, 1979.
Ai. *Sin*. NY: Houghton Mifflin Company, 1986.
Berssenbrugge, Mei-mei. *Fish Souls*. NY: Greenwood, 1971.
Berssenbrugge, Mei-mei. *The Heat Bird*. Providence, RI: Burning Deck, 1983.
Berssenbrugge, Mei-mei. *Packrat Sieve*. Bowling Green, NY: Contact II, 1983.
Berssenbrugge, Mei-mei. *Random Possession*. NY: I. Reed Books, 1979.
Berssenbrugge, Mei-mei. *Summits Move With the Tide*. Greenfield, NY: Greenfield Review Press, 1974.
Bhatt, Sujata. *Brunizem*. London: Carcanet Press, 1988.
Cha, Theresa Hak Kyung. *Dictee*. NY: Tanam Press, 1982.
Chang, Diana. *The Horizon Is Definitely Speaking*. Port Jefferson, NY: Backstreet Editions, 1982.

Chang, Diana. *What Matisse Is After.* NY: Contact 11, 1984.

Chiang, Fay, Helen and Huei Wong et al. *American Born and Foreign.* NY: Sunbury Press, 1979.

Chiang, Fay. *In the City of Contradictions.* NY: Sunbury Press, 1979.

Chiang, Fay. *Miwa's Song.* NY: Sunbury Press, 1982.

Chin, Marilyn. *Dwarf Bamboo.* NY: The Greenfield Review Press, 1987.

Fujita, June. *Poems in Exile.* Chicago: Covic Co., 1923.

Fukaya, Michiyo Cornwell. *Lesbian Lyrics.* NY: Self-published c/o A.L.O.E.C., 1981.

Hagedorn, Jessica. *Dangerous Music: The Poetry and Prose of Jessica Hagedorn.* San Francisco: Momo's Press, 1975.

Hagedorn, Jessica. *Petfood and Tropical Apparitions.* San Francisco: Momo's Press, 1981.

Ikeda, Patricia. *House of Wood, House of Salt.* Cleveland, OH: Cleveland State University Poetry Center, 1978.

Itani, Frances. *No Other Lodgings.* New Brunswick, Canada: Fiddlehead, 1978.

Kim, Alison. *Mirror Mirror (Woman Woman).* Santa Cruz, CA: Dancing Bird Press, 1986.

Kim, Chungmi. *Selected Poems.* Anaheim, CA: Korean Pioneer Press, 1982.

Kim, Willyce. *Eating Artichokes.* Oakland, CA: The Women's Press Collective, 1972.

Kim, Willyce. *Under the Rolling Sky.* n.p.: Maude Gonne Press, 1976.

Kogawa, Joy. *A Choice of Dreams.* Toronto, Canada: McLelland & Stewart, 1974.

Kogawa, Joy. *Jericho Road.* Toronto, Canada: McLelland & Stewart, 1977.

Kogawa, Joy. *The Splintered Moon.* NB, Canada: Fiddlehead, 1969.

Kogawa, Joy. *Woman in the Woods.* Ontario, Canada: Mosaic Press, 1985.

Kudaka, Geraldine. *Numerous Avalanches at the Point of Intersection.* Greenfield, NY: Greenfield Review Press, 1979.

Lee, Mary. *The Guest of Tyn-y-Coed Cae: Poems and Drawings.* Santa Monica, CA: Hightree Books, 1973.

Lee, Mary Wong. *Through My Windows.* Stockton, CA: Roxene Lee Publishing, 1970.

Lem, Carol. *Don't Ask Why.* Los Angeles: Peddler, 1982.

Lem, Carol. *Grassroots.* South Gate, CA: Peddler, 1975.

Lim, Genny. *Winter Place.* San Francisco: Kearny Street Workshop Press, 1988.

Lim, Shirley. *Crossing the Peninsula and Other Poems.* Singapore/Hong Kong: Heinemann Educational Books, 1980.

Lim, Shirley. *Modern Secrets.* London: Dangaroo Press, 1988.

Lim, Shirley. *No Man's Grove.* Singapore: University of Singapore, English Dept., 1985.

Ling, Amy. *Chinamerican Reflections.* Lewiston, ME: Great Raven, 1984.

Mar, Laureen. *Living Furniture.* San Francisco: Nolo Press, 1982.

Matsueda, Pat. *The Fish Catcher.* Honolulu: Petronium Press, 1985.

Mirikitani, Janice. *Awake in the River.* San Francisco: Isthmus, 1978.

Mirikitani, Janice. *Shedding Silence.* Berkeley: Celestial Arts Publications, 1987.

Noda, Barbara, drawings by Wendy Yoshimura. *Strawberries.* Berkeley: Shameless Hussy Press, 1979.

Noguchi, Yone. *From the Eastern Sea.* NY: Kennerley, 1910.

Noguchi, Yone. *The Ganges Calls Me: Book of Poems.* Tokyo: Kyofunkwan, 1938.

Peña-Reyes, Myrna. *The River Singing Stone.* Oregon: Pacific House, 1983.

Sabasu, Irare. *Poems in Unmasked.* Brooklyn: Fordham University, 1980.

Song, Cathy. *Picture Bride.* New Haven, CT: Yale University Press, 1983.

Tsuda, Margaret. *Cry Love Aloud.* NY: Poetica Press, 1972.

Tsuda, Margaret. *Urban River.* Newark, NJ: Discovery Books, 1976.

Tsui, Kitty. *The Words of a Woman Who Breathes Fire.* San Francisco: Spinsters Ink, 1983.

Wong, May. *A Bad Girl's Book of Animals.* NY: Harcourt Brace, 1969.

Wong, May. *Reports.* NY: Harcourt Brace, 1972.

Wong, May. *Superstitions.* NY: Harcourt Brace, 1978.

Wong, Nellie. *The Death of Long Steam Lady.* Los Angeles: West End Press, 1986.

Wong, Nellie. *Dreams in Harrison Railroad Park.* Berkeley: Kelsey St. Press, 1977.

Woo, Merle. *Yellow Woman Speaks.* San Francisco: Radical Women Publications.

Yamada, Mitsuye. *Camp Notes and Other Poems.* San Francisco: Shameless Hussy Press, 1976.

Yamada, Mitsuye. *Desert Run: Poems and Stories.* Latham, NY: Kitchen Table/Women of Color Press, 1988.

Yup, Paula. *Love Poems.* East Talmouth, MA: Peka Boo Press, 1984.

AUTOBIOGRAPHIES/BIOGRAPHIES

Chao, Buwei Yang. *Autobiography of a Chinese Woman.* Westport, CT: Greenwood Press, 1970.

Chennault, Anna. *The Education of Anna.* NY: Times Books, 1980.

Chennault, Anna. *A Thousand Springs: The Biography of a Marriage.* NY: Paul S. Eriksson, 1962.

Chou, Cynthia L. *My Life in the United States.* North Quincy, MA: The Christopher Publishing House, 1970.

Eaton, Winnifred. *Me, A Book of Remembrance.* NY: Century Co., 1915.

Eaton, Winnifred. *Marion, The Story of an Artist's Model by Herself and the Author of Me.* NY: W.J. Watt & Co., 1916.

Houston, Jeanne Wakatsuki. *Beyond Manzanar: Views of Asian American Womanhood.* Santa Barbara: Capra Press, 1985.

Houston, Jeanne Wakatsuki, and James D. Houston. *Farewell to Manzanar.* San Francisco: Houghton, 1973.

Hsieh, Ping-ying. *Autobiography of a Chinese Girl.* Boston: Pandora Press, 1986.

Joe, Jeanne. *Ying-Ying: Pieces Of A Childhood.* San Francisco: East/West Publishing, Inc., 1982.

Kikumura, Akemi. *Through Harsh Winters: The Life of a Japanese Immigrant Woman.* Novato, CA: Chandler and Sharp, 1981.

Kim, Elaine H., and Janice Otani. *With Silk Wings: Asian American Women At Work.* Oakland: Asian Women United of California, 1983.

Kingston, Maxine Hong. *The Woman Warrior: Memoirs of A Girlhood Among Ghosts*. NY: Knopf, 1976.

Koo, Hui-lan (Madam Wellington Koo). As told to Mary Wan Rensselaer Tahyer. *Hui-lan Koo*. NY: Dial, 1943.

Kuo, Helena. *I've Come a Long Way*. NY: D. Appleton-Century Co., 1942.

Martin, Mildred Crowl. *Chinatown's Angry Angel: The Story of Donaldina Cameron*. Palo Alto: Pacific Books, 1986.

Noguchi, Yone. *The American Diary of a Japanese Girl (Miss Morning Glory)*. NY: Frederick A. Stokes Co., 1902.

Noguchi, Yone. *The Story of Yone Noguchi Told by Herself*. London: Chatto, 1914.

Ohara, Tomie. *A Woman Called En*. NY: Pandora Press, Routledge, Kegan and Paul, 1986.

Okubo, Miné. *Citizen 13660*. Seattle: University of Washington Press, 1983.

Soong, Irma Tam. *Chinese-American Refugee: A World War II Memoir*. Honolulu: Hawaii Chinese History Center, 1984.

Sugimoto, Etsu Inagaki. *A Daughter of the Samurai*. NY: Doubleday, 1925.

Sugimoto, Etsu Inagaki. *A Daughter of the Narikin*. NY: Doubleday, 1932.

Tamagawa, Kathleen. *Hoy Prayers in a Horse's Ear*. NY: Long & Smith, 1932.

Uchida, Yoshiko. *Desert Exile: The Uprooting of a Japanese American Family*. Seattle: University of Washington Press, 1984.

Uchida, Yoshiko. *Journey to Topaz: A Story of the Japanese-American Evacuation*. Berkeley: Berkeley Creative Arts Book Company, 1985.

Uchida, Yoshiko. *Picture Bride*. NY: Simon and Schuster, 1987.

Wong, Jade Snow. *Fifth Chinese Daughter*. NY: Harper and Row, 1945.

Wong, Jade Snow. *No Chinese Stranger*. NY: Harper and Row, 1975.

Wong, Su-ling, and Earl Herbert Cressy. *Daughter of Confucius*. NY: Farrar Strauss, 1952.

Yamazaki, Tomoko. *The Story of Yamada Waka: From Prostitute to Feminist Pioneer*. Tokyo, Japan: Kodansha Int'l. (Distr. Harper & Row, NY), 1985.

Yun, Tan (Adet Lin), and Anor Lin, trans. *Girl Rebel.The Autobiography of Hsieh Pingying with Extracts from her New War Diaries*. NY: John Day Co., 1940.

Yun, Tan (Adet Lin), Meimei Lin, and Anor Lin. *Dawn Over Chungking*. NY: John Day Co., 1941.

Yun, Tan (Adet Lin). *Our Family*. NY: John Day Co., 1939.

REVIEWS/LITERARY CRITICISM

Chai, Alice Yun. "Towards a Holistic Paradigm for Asian American Women's Studies: A Synthesis of Feminist Scholarship and Women of Color's Feminist Politics." *Women Studies International Forum* 8.1 (1985): pp. 59-66.

Demetrakopoulus. "The Metaphysics of Matrilinealism in Women's Autobiography: Studies of Mead's *Blackberry Winter*, Hellman's *Pentimento*, Angelou's *I Know Why the Caged Bird Sings*, and Kingston's *The Woman Warrior*." *Women's Autobiography: Essays in Criticism*, ed. Estelle C. Jelinek, Bloomington, IN: Indiana University Press, 1980:

pp. 180-205.

Douglas, Carol Anne. "Lives: Chinese Working Women." *Off Our Backs* 16, no. 3 (March 1986): p. 28.

Douglas, Carol Anne. "A Passion For Friends: Toward A Philosophy of Female Affection. By Janice Raymond." *Off Our Backs* 16, no. 4 (April 1986): pp.20-21.

Hill, Patricia Liggins. "The Third Woman Minority Women Writers of the United States." *MELUS* 7:3 (1980): pp.87-89.

Holaday, Woon-Ping Chin. "From Ezra Pound and Maxine Hong Kingston: Expressions of Chinese Thought." *MELUS* 5, (1978): pp. 15-24.

Homsher, Deborah. *"The Woman Warrior,* by Maxine Hong Kingston: A Bridging of Autobiography and Fiction." *Iowa Review* 10, (1979): pp. 93-98.

Iwataki, Miya. "Asian American Art and Culture: A Melody of Resistance." *East Wind* 4.1 (1985): pp. 31-33.

Juhasz, Suzanne. "Towards a Theory of Form in Feminist Autobiography: Kate Millet's *Flying* and *Sita*; Maxine Hong Kingston's *The Woman Warrior.*" *International Journal of Women's Studies* 2 (1979): pp. 62-75.

Juhasz, Suzanne. "Maxine Hong Kingston: Narrative Technique and Female Identity." *Contemporary Women Writers*, ed. C. Rainwater and W.J. Soheik. Lexington, KY: University Press of Kentucky, 1985: pp.173-189.

Kim, Elaine. *Asian American Literature: An Introduction to the Writings and Their Social Context.* Philadelphia: Temple University Press, 1982.

Kim, Elaine. "Asian American Literature and the Importance of Social Context." *ADE Bulletin* 80 (1985): pp. 34-41.

Lau, Alan Chong, and Laureen Mar, eds. "Asian American: North and South." *Contact II* 7.38-40 (1986): p.1.

Lim, Genny. "On Weaning in America." *Bridge* 7 no. 1 (Spring-Summer 1979): pp. 28-29.

Lim, Shirley. "Twelve Asian American Writers in Search of Self-Definition." *MELUS* 13.1 & 2 (1986).

Lim, Shirley. *"Picture Bride,* Cathy Song, Yale Younger Poet Series." *MELUS* 10:3 (1983): pp. 95-99.

Lim, Shirley. *"Breaking Silence, An Anthology of Asian American Poetry,* edited by Joseph Bruchac, Greenfield Review." *MELUS* 11:2 (1984): pp. 85-90.

Lim, Shirley. "Exotics and Existentials: The Course of Asian American Writing." *Homegrown* 11 Winter 1984: pp. 26-31.

Lim, Shirley. "Recontructing Asian American Poetry: A Case for Ethnopoetics." Forthcoming, *MELUS* (1988).

Ling, Amy. "Embroidering New Skin: A Review of *Dreams in Harrison Railroad Park.*" *MELUS* 6:1 (1979): pp. 91-93.

Ling, Amy. "I'm Here: An Asian American Woman's Response." *New Literary History*, 19.1 (1987): pp. 151-160.

Newman, Katharine. "An Ethnic Literary Scholar Views American Literature." *MELUS* 7.1 (1980): pp. 3-19.

Noda, Barbara. "Asian American Women: Two Special Issues of *Bridge*: An Asian American Perspective." *Conditions* 6 (1980): pp. 203-211.

Sledge, Linda Ching. "Teaching Asian American Literature." *ADE Bulletin* 80 (1985): pp. 42-45.

Yamada, Mitsuye. "Asian American Women and Feminism." *This Bridge Called My Back: Writings by Radical Women of Color.* Ed. Cherríe Moraga and Gloria Anzaldua. Latham, NY: Kitchen Table/Women of Color Press, 1982: pp. 71-75.

INTERVIEWS/LETTERS

Anno, Kim, et al. "Unbound Feet: A Response." *Coming Up* (Nov. 1981): p. 8.

Bagley, Peter. "Stepping Out: A Look at the Local Asian Gay Scene." *Sampan* 11 (Sept. 1985): pp. 1-2.

Brownmiller, Susan. "Interview with Maxine Hong Kingston." *Mademoiselle* (March, 1977): p. 210.

Burning Cloud. "Open Letter from Filipina/Indian Lesbian." *Lesbians of Color Caucus Quarterly* 1, no. 1(1979): p. 12.

Chow, Christopher, and Russell Leong. "Pioneer Chinatown Teacher: An Interview with Alice Fong Yu." *Amerasia Journal* 5, no. 1 (1978): pp. 75-86.

Hahn, Kimiko. "A Talk with the Woman Who Breathes Fire." *Bridge* 8, no. 3 (Summer 1983): pp. 14-15.

Interview with Jeanne Wakatsuki Houston. "Farewell to Manzanar: How a Young Woman's Experience Became a Book." *Rafu Shimpo* 19 Dec. 1973: p. 4.

Islas, Arturo. Interview with Maxine Hong Kingston. *Women Writers of the West Coast Speaking Their Lives and Careers.* Ed. Marilyn Yalon. Santa Barbara, CA: Capra Press, 1983: pp. 11-19.

Lee, Teri. "An Interview With Janice Mirikitani." *Asian American Review* (1976): pp.34-44.

Lenhart, Maria. "Combining American Know How with a Chinese Legacy: Jade Snow Wong Blends Two Diverse Cultures as Author, Potter, Mother." *Christian Science Monitor* 31 March 1981: p.23.

Mahon, Denise. Profile of Ruthanne Lum McCunn. "Amerasian Author Draws on Both Cultures in Producing Her Books." *East/West* 7 March 1984: p. 9.

Nakao, Annie. Profile of Yoshiko Uchida. "Nisei Author's Gift to Children." *San Francisco Examiner* 29 Sept. 1985.

Nemy, Enid. Interview with Bette Bao Lord. "It's Nice to Be Rich and Famous." *San Francisco Sunday Examiner and Chronicle* review section, 3 January 1982: p. 5.

Noda, Barbara, Kitty Tsui, and Z. Wong. "Coming Out. We Are Here in the Asian Community. A Dialogue with Three Asian Women." *Bridge* 7, no. 1 (Spring 1979): pp. 22-24.

Noda, Barbara. "Letter to Editors." *Conditions* 7 (1981): p. 185.

Nomaguchi, Debbie Murakatani. "Cathy Song: 'I'm a Poet Who Happens to Be Asian American.'" *International Examiner* 2 May 1984: p. 9.

Profile of Joy Kogawa. "Face to Face." *Asianadian* 2.1 (1979): pp. 22-25.

Rieko, Nancy, et al. "Letter to Editors re: Lesbians of Color Conference in Malibu, CA." *Lesbians of Color* (Sept. 8-11, 1983): p. 4.

Wakayama, Mary. "A Talk with Joy Kogawa." *Literary Arts Hawaii* 76-77 (Spring 1985): pp. 6-7.

Wong, Eddie. "An Interview with Genny Lim." *East Wind* 1.2 (1982): pp. 48-50.

Wong, Diane Yen-Mei. "Dear Diane: Letters from Our Daughters." Asian Women United, Oakland: 1983.

Woo, Merle. "Letter to Ma." *This Bridge Called My Back: Writings by Radical Women of Color.* Eds. Cherríe Moraga and Gloria Anzaldua. Kitchen Table/Women of Color Press, Latham, NY: 1983: pp. 140-147.

ARTICLES

Aquino, Belinda. "The History of Filipino Women in Hawaii." *Bridge* 7, no. 1 (Spring 1979): pp. 17-21.

"Asian Women: Cross Cultural Exchange: Asian Lesbians of the East Coast." *Off Our Backs* (June 1985): pp. 5, 24.

Bagley, Peter. "Stepping Out: Groups Affirm Identity of Asian Gays, Lesbians." *Sampan* 25 (Sept. 1985): pp. 1-3.

Bickner, Mei Liang. "The Forgotten Minority: Asian American Women." *Amerasia Journal* 11 (Spring 1974): pp. 1-17.

Blasing, Anne. "The Lavender Kimono." *Connexions* 3 (Winter 1982): pp. 21.

Blicksilver, Edith. "The Japanese-American Woman, the Second World War, and the Relocation Camp Experience." *Women's Studies International Forum* 5, nos. 3 and 4 (1982): pp. 351-353.

Boyd, Christine. "Double Isolation for Minority Gays." *Daily Californian* (Apr. 29, 1983): pp. 1, 18.

"Bury Us Together." Compiled from *The World of Homosexuals*, Shakuntala Devi, Bell Press, 1978 (India): *Gay Scene* no. 2 (Nov./Dec. 1980): and *Manushi* no. 5. p. 7.

Calhoun, Mary Atchity. "The Vietnamese Woman: Health/Illness Attitudes and Behaviors." *Health Care for Women Int'l.* 6, nos. 1-3 (1985): pp. 61-72.

Chai, Alice Yun. "Toward a Holistic Paradigm for Asian American Women's Studies: A Synthesis of Feminist Scholarship and Women of Color's Feminist Politics." *Women's Studies Int'l. Forum* 8, no. 1 (1985): pp. 59-66.

Chen, Amy. "Women Directors at the Forefront." *Bridge* 9, nos. 3-4 (1984): pp. 14-18.

Chen, May. "Teaching a Course on Asian American Women." *Counterpoint: Perspectives on Asian America.* Ed. Emma Gee. UCLA Asian American Studies Publications, 1976: pp. 234-239.

Cheng, Lucie. "Asian American Women and Feminism." *Sojourner* 10, no. 2 (Oct. 1984): pp. 11-12.

Chu, Judy. "Asian American Women's Studies Courses: A Look Back at Our Beginnings at San Francisco State University, UC Berkeley, and UCLA." *Frontiers* 8, no. 3 (1986):

pp. 96-101.

Chu, Judy. "A Thousand Years Of Life." *Bridge* 8 (Summer 1983): pp. 9-13.

Chua, Chen Lok. "Two Chinese Versions of the American Dream: The Golden Mountain in Lin Yutang and Maxine Hong Kingston." *MELUS* 8.4 (Winter 1981): pp. 61-70.

Davidson, Sue. "Aki Kato Kurose: Portrait of an Activist." *Frontiers* 7, no. 1 (1983): pp. 91-97.

Di Leonardo, Micaela. "Warrior Virgins and Boston Marriages: Spinsterhood in History and Culture." *Feminist Issues* 5, no. 2 (Fall 1985): pp. 53-55.

Ding, Barbara. "Researching Chinese American Women: Difficult But Needed." *East/West* (Nov. 18, 1981): pp. 4-5.

Douglas, Carol Anne. "Asian American Women's Studies." *Off Our Backs* 13, no. 8 (Aug./Sept. 1983): p. 7.

Hall, Katherine Ekau Amoy. "Asian Lesbians of the East Coast: Breathing Fire of Resistance." *Between Our Selves: Women of Color Newspaper* 1, no. 1 (Winter 1985): p. 6.

Hart, Gail. "No Susie Wongs Here." *Women of Power* 4 (Fall 1986): pp. 32-34.

Hirata, Lucie. "Free, Indentured, Enslaved: Chinese Prostitutes in Nineteenth-Century America." *Signs* 5, no. 1 (Autumn 1979): pp. 3-29.

Ichioka, Yuji. "America Nadeshiko: Japanese Immigrant Women in the United States, 1900-1924." *Pacific Historical Review* 49, no. 2 (May 1980): pp. 339-357.

Ichioka, Yuji. "Ameyuki-san: Japanese Prostitutes in Nineteenth-Century America." *Amerasia Journal* 4, no. 1 (1977): pp. 1-21.

Ikeda-Spiegel, Motoko. "Concentration Camps in the U. S." *Heresies* 8 (1979): pp. 90-97.

Ikkyu, trans. Miyuki Tanemura. "Japanese Lesbian Reports." *Out and About* (March 1980): p. 18.

"Japanese Lesbians." *Lesbians of Color Caucus Quarterly* 1, no. 1 (Sept. 1979): p. 4.

Kim, Willyce. "Look, I Am Huddled on Your Door Step." *Amazon Quarterly* 1, no. 3 (May 1973): p. 45.

Krich, John. "Here Come the Brides: The Blossoming Business of Imported Love." *Mother Jones* 11, no., 2 (Feb./Mar. 1987): pp. 34-37, 43-46.

Kunitsuga, Patty. "Needs of Third World Dykes." *Out and About* (Oct. 1977): p. 21.

Kunitsuga, Patty, and Consuel Sison. "Open Letter to the Womyn's Community." *Out and About* (Aug. 1977): p. 9.

Lemeshewsky, Kaweah Asano. "Stranger in Her Own Land." *Matrix* (Nov. 1984): pp. 1, 5.

"Lesbian Poets." Trans. and excerpted from an interview in *Clit 007* June 1983. *Connexions* (Fall 1983): p. 18.

Leslie, S. "Thoughts on Racism." *Lesbians of Color Caucus Quarterly* 1, no. 1. (Sept. 1979): p. 2.

"Linking Our Lives: Chinese American Women of Los Angeles." A Joint Project of Asian American Studies Center, UCLA, and Chinese Historical Society of Southern CA. Los Angeles: The Society, 1984.

"Mainichi Daiku: Statement of Purpose." *Lesbians of Color Caucus Quarterly* 1, no. 1 (Sept.

1979): p. 5.

Matsumoto, Valerie. "Japanese American Women During World War II." *Frontiers* 8, no. 1 (1984): pp. 6-14.

Namjoshi, Suniti. "Tales Tell Tales." *Manushi* no. 5 (May/June 1980): pp. 47-49.

Patton, Cindy. "Up from the Invisible." *Gay Community News* 27 (February 1982): pp. 7-10.

Ratliff, Bascomb, et al. "Inter-Cultural Marriage: The Korean-American Experience." *Social Casework* 59 (April 1978): pp. 221-226.

Sawada, Noriko. "Memoir of a Japanese Daughter." *Ms.* 8 (April 1980): pp. 68-70.

Serita, Toko. "Sexual Exploitation of Asian Women." *Bridge: An Asian American Perspective* 9, no. 2 (1984): pp. 39-41.

Sunoo, Sonia. "Korean Women Pioneers of the Pacific Northwest." *Oregon Historical Quarterly* 79 (1978): pp. 51-63.

Tanemura, Miyuki, ed. "Raicho and Kokichi: The Hidden Past of Japanese Lesbians." *Out and About* (May 1980): p. 31.

Tsutakawa, Mayumi. "The Asian Women's Movement: Superficial Rebellion?" *Asian Resources* (1974): pp. 55-64.

Uyehara, Grayce. "Asian Women: Our Responsibility for Outreach in Sisterhood." *Bridge* 7 (Spring 1979): pp. 36-38.

Wakatsuki, Jeanne. "Beyond Manzanar: A Personal View of Asian American Womanhood." *Asian Americans: Social and Psychological Perspectives*, Volume II. Ed. R. Endo, et al. Palo Alto, CA: Science and Behavior Books Inc., 1980: pp. 17-26.

Wilkinson, Willy. "Asian Lesbianism as a Political Identity." *Sojourner* (Aug. 1984): pp. 8, 28.

Wong, Linda. "The Esther Lau Trial: A Case Study of Oppression and Sexism." *Amerasia Journal* (Summer 1975): pp. 16-26.

Woo, Merle. "Recovering." *Bridge: An Asian American Perspective* 6, no. 4 (1978-79): pp. 43-45.

Woo, Merle, Nellie Wong, and Mitsuye Yamada. "Three Asian American Writers Speak Out on Feminism." San Francisco: Radical Women Publications.

Yamada, Mitsuye. "Invisibility Is an Unnatural Disaster: Reflections of an Asian American Women." *This Bridge Called My Back: Writings by Radical Women of Color.* Eds. Cherríe Moraga, and Gloria Anzaldua. Latham, NY: Kitchen Table/Women of Color Press, 1982: pp. 35-40.

Yamasaki, Emily Woo. "Breaking Racist Barriers: Lesbians of Color Conference." *Womanews* (Nov. 1983): p. 4.

Yung, Judy. "A Bowlful of Tears: Chinese Women Immigrants on Angel Island." *Frontiers* (Summer, 1977): pp. 52-55.

RESEARCH

Asian American Studies Center. *Asian Women.* Berkeley: Asian American Studies Center, Univ. of Calif., 1971.

Chih, Ginger. *The History of Chinese Immigrant Women 1850-1940.* North Bergen, NJ: G.

Chih, 1977.

Chipp, S. A., and J.J. Green. *Asian Women in Transition.* University Park, PA: Pennsylvania State University Press, 1980.

Chun-hoon, Lowell. "Jade Snow Wong and the Fate of Chinese-American Identity." *Asian Americans: Psychological Perspectives.* Ed. Stanley Sue and Nathaniel N. Wagner. Palo Alto: Science and Behavior Books, 1973: pp. 125-135.

Fujitomi, Irene, and A. Nieto-Gomez. "New Asian American Woman." *Female Psychology: The Emerging Self.* Ed. Sue Cox. Chicago: Science Research Associates, 1976: pp. 236-248.

Fujitomi, Irene, and Diane Wong. "The New Asian-American Woman." *Asian Americans: Psychological Perspectives.* Ed. Stanley Sue and Nathaniel N. Wagner. Palo Alto: Science and Behavior Books, 1973: pp. 252-263.

Hymowitz, Carol, and Michaele Weissman. *A History of Women in America.* NY: Bantam Books, 1978.

Kim, Elaine H. "Asian Americans and College English." *Education and Urban Society* 10, no. 3 (May 1, 1978): pp. 321-336.

Kim, Elaine H. "The Myth of Asian American Success." *Asian American Review* 2, no. 1 (1975): pp. 123-149.

Kumagai, Gloria Li. "The Asian Woman in America." *Explorations in Ethnic Studies* 1, no. 2 (July 1978): pp. 27-39.

Maruyama, Magoro. "Yellow Youth's Psychological Struggle." *Mental Hygiene* 55, no. 3 (July 1971): pp. 382-390.

Melendy, H. Brett. *Asians in America.* Boston: Twayne Publishers, 1977.

Miyasaki, Gai. *Montage: An Ethnic History of Women in Hawaii.* Honolulu: University of Hawaii Press, 1977.

Odo, Franklin Sochiro. *Movement: A Pictorial History of Asian America.* Los Angeles: Visual Communications/Asian American Studies Central, 1977.

Osako, M.M. "Aging and Family Among Japanese Americans: The Role of Ethnic Tradition in the Adjustment to Old Age." *Gerontologist* 19 (Oct 1979).

Raymond, Janice. *A Passion for Friends: Toward a Philosophy of Female Affection.* Boston: Beacon Press, 1986.

Rojo, Trinidad A. "Social Maladjustments Among Filipinos in the United States." *Sociology and Social Research* 21 (May-June 1937): pp. 447-457.

Saiki, Patsy Sumie. *Japanese Women in Hawaii: The First 100 Years.* Honolulu: Kisaku, 1985.

Sommers, Vita S. "Identity Conflict and Acculturation Problems in Oriental-Americans." *American Journal of Orthopsychiatry* 30, no. 3 (July 1960): pp. 637-644.

Sue, Gerald Wing. "Ethnic Identity: The Impact of Two Cultures on the Psychological Development of Asians in America." *Asian Americans: Psychological Perspectives.* Ed. Stanley Sue and Nathaniel Wagner. Palo Alto: Science and Behavior Books, 1973: pp. 140-149.

Sue, Gerald Wing, and Stanley Sue. "Chinese American Personality and Mental Health." *Roots: An Asian American Reader.* Ed. Amy Tachiki et al. Los Angeles: UCLA

Asian American Studies Center, 1971: pp 72-82.

Sue, Stanley, and Nathaniel Wagner, eds. *Asian Americans: Psychological Perspectives*. Palo Alto: Science and Behavior Books, 1973.

Sunwandra, Batya. *The Political Creation of a Lesbian*. NY: Radical Women in the Woods Press, 1981-82.

Tsuchida, Nobuya, ed. *Asian and Pacific American Experiences: Women's Perspectives*. Minneapolis, MN: University of Minnesota, 1982.

Ueda, Reed. "The Americanization and Education of Japanese Americans: A Psychological and Dramaturgical Perspective." *Cultural Pluralism*. Ed. Edgar G. Epps. Berkeley: McCuthan Publishing Corp., 1974.

Yung, Judy. *Chinese Women of America: A Pictorial History*. Seattle: University of Washington/Chinese Cultural Education Center, 1986.

NONPRINT/FILMS/VIDEOS/SLIDE TAPE/PHOTOGRAPHS

Agbayani, Amy, dir. *Immigrant Women and Employment in Hawaii*. Video. Operation Manong. 1980.

Asian American Women Vs. the Women's Movement. Cassette tape. Pacifica Tape Library, 33 min. 1979.

Asian Women in the U.S. Photo boards. Visual Communications. n.d.

Cho, Renee, dir. *Jazz Is My Native Language: A Portrait of Tishiko Akiyoshi*. Filmstrip. Renee Cho, 59 min., 16 mm., color. 1983.

Cho, Renee, dir. *The New Wife*. Filmstrip. Asian Cine-vision, 30 min., 16 mm., color. 1978.

Choy, Christine, dir. *Fei Ten*. Filmstrip. Asian Cine-vision, 20 min., 16 mm., color. 1983.

Choy, Christine, dir. *Mississippi Triangle*. Filmstrip. Third World Newsreel, 110 min., 16 mm., color. 1983.

Choy, Christine, dir. *Permanent Wave*. Filmstrip. Third World Newsreel, 20 min., 16 mm., color. 1986.

Ding, Loni, dir. *With Silk Wings*. Video in four parts. Asian Women United, 30 min. ea., color. 1982.

Dong, Arthur, dir. *Sewing Woman*. Filmstrip. Third World Newsreel, 14 min., 16 mm., B/W. 1983.

Finley, Ron, dir. *Jade Snow Wong*. Filmstrip. Films Incorporated, 27 min., 16 mm., color. 1976.

Freyer, Ellen, dir. *Marathon Woman*. Filmstrip. Asian Cine-vision, 30 min., 16 mm., color. n.d.

Frieda, Lee Mock, and Terry Sanders, dirs. *Jung Sai: Chinese American*. Filmstrip. Audio Brandon Films Inc., 29 min., 16 mm., color. 1976.

Gold Mountain Heroes. Video. BBC Writers and Places Series, 35 min. 1982.

Half of Heaven. Video. KQED TV, San Francisco. Film Makers' Cooperative, 29 min., color. n.d.

Hashii, Virginia, dir. *Jenny.* Filmstrip. Asian Cine-vision, 19 min., 16 mm., color. 1976.

Hsia, Lisa, dir. *Made in China.* Filmstrip. Filmmakers Library, 30 min., 16 mm., color. 1986.

Jokel, Lana Pih, dir. *Chiang Ching: A Dance Journey.* Filmstrip. Asian Cine-vision, 30 min., 16 mm., color. 1982.

LaDoux, Rita, dir. *Great Branches, New Roots: The Hmong Family.* Video. Hmong Film Project, 42 min., 16 mm., color. 1983.

The Life History of a Hawaiian-Chinese Woman in Hawaii, The Life History of a Picture Bride in Hawaii, and *The Life History of a Pioneer Filipina in Hawaii.* Filmstrips. Women's Studies Program, University of Hawaii at Manong, 60 min. ea. 1976.

Light, Allie, and Irving Saraf, dirs. *Mitsuye and Nellie.* Filmstrip. Light-Saraf Films, 58 min., 16 mm., color. 1981.

Lowe, Felicia, dir. *China: Land of My Father.* Filmstrip. Asian Cine-vision, 28 min., 16 mm., color. 1981.

Lum, Jon Wing, dir. *Ourselves.* Filmstrip. Asian Cine-vision, 60 min., 16 mm., color. 1979.

Miyamoto, Robert, dir. *Gaman.* Filmstrip. Asian Cine-vision, 6 min., 16 mm., color. 1983.

Okazaki, Stephen, dir. *The Only Language She Knows.* Filmstrip. Mouchette Films, 19 min., 16 mm., color. 1983.

Okazaki, Stephen, dir. *Survivors.* Filmstrip. Mouchette Films, 58 min., 16 mm., B/W. 1982.

Omori, Emiko, dir. *The Departure.* Filmstrip. Asian Cine-vision, 13 min. 1983.

Oshana, Maryann, dir. *Women of Color: A Filmography of Minority and Third World Women.* Filmstrip. Garland, 1985.

Pearls. Video in five parts. Educational Film Center, 30 min. ea. 1979.

Portrait of Three Chinese American Women. Asian American Theatre Workshop. Video. Asian Cine-vision, 28 min., B/W. n.d.

Shaffer, Beverly, dir. *My Name is Susan Yee.* Filmstrip. Media Guild, 12 min., 16 mm., color. 1976.

Takagi, J.T., dir. *Community Plot.* Video. Third World Newsreel, 20 min., 16 mm., color. 1983.

Taketa, Victoria, dir. *Japanese American Women in America.* Slide show/tape. Victoria Taketa, 1980.

Uno, Michael Oshiyuki, dir. *Emi.* Filmstrip. Asian Cine-vision, 28 min., 16 mm., color. 1978.

Vidor, King, dir. *Japanese War Bride.*Filmstrip. Twentieth Century Fox, 91 min., 16 mm., color. 1952.

We Are Asian Women. Video. KQED TV, San Francisco, 30 min., color. n.d.

Yonemoto, Bruce and Norman, dirs. *Green Card: An American Romance.* Video. Asian Cine-vision, 80 min. 1982.

DISTRIBUTOR ADDRESSES

Asian Cine-Vision, 32 E. Broadway, NY, NY 10002.
Asian Women United, 3538 Telegraph Ave., Oakland, CA 94609.
Audio Brandon Films, 6420 W. Lake St., Minneapolis, MN 55426.
Cinelight, 2051 Third St., San Francisco, CA 94107.
Educational Film Center, 5401 Port Royal Rd., Box 1444, Springfield, VA 22151.
Film Makers' Cooperative, 175 Lexington Ave., NY, NY 10016.
Filmmakers Library, 133 East 58th St., NY, NY 10022.
Films Incorporated, 440 Park Ave. S., NY, NY 10016.
Hmong Film Project, 2258 Commonwealth Ave., St. Paul, MN 55108.
Light-Saraf Films, 264 Arbor St., San Francisco, CA 94131.
Marlene Shigekawa, 2250 Greenwich St. #4, San Francisco, CA 94123.
Media Guild, Box 881, Solano Beach, CA 92075.
Mouchette Films, 548 5th, San Francisco, CA 94107.
Operation Manong, East West Center Rd. #4, Honolulu, HI 96822.
Organization of Asian Women, PO Box M-71, Hoboken, NJ 07030.
Pacifica Tape Library, Dept. W 801, 5316 Venice Blvd., Los Angeles, CA 90019.
Renee Cho, 315 Riverside Dr., NY, NY 10025.
Third World Newsreel, 335 W. 38th St., NY, NY 10018.
Victoria Taketa, 98 S. 13th St. #B, San Jose, CA 95112.
Visual Communications, 313 South San Pedro St., Los Angeles, CA 90013.
Women's Studies Program, Crawford 201B, 2550 Campus Rd., University of Hawaii at
    Manong, Honolulu, HI 96822.

BIBLIOGRAPHIES

Cheung, King-Kok. Stan Yogi, eds. *Asian American Literature, An Annotated Bibliography.*
    NY: The Modern Language Association, 1988.
Ethnic Display Status in Higher Education: State of the Arts and Bibliography. American Asso-
    ciation of State Colleges and Universities, n.p., 1972.
Fong, Elaine, and Stephanie Yoo. "Bibliography in Women's Resource Guide." *Bridge* 8:3
    (1983): pp. 29-31.
Hiura, Arnold T., and Stephen H. Sumida. *Asian American Literature of Hawaii: An Anno-
    tated Bibliography.* Honolulu: Hawaii Ethnic Resource Center, Talk Story, 1979.
Ichioka, Yuji et al. *A Buried Past: An Annotated Bibliography of the Japanese-American Research
    Project Collection.* Berkeley: University of California Press, 1974.
Kim, Elaine H. "Asian American Writers: A Bibliographical Review." *American Studies
    International* 22.2 (1984): pp. 41-78.
Kim, Elaine H. "Bibliography." *Asian American Literature: An Introduction to the Writings
    and Their Social Context.* Philadelphia: Temple University Press, 1982: pp. 321-353.
Ling, Amy. "Asian American Literature: A Brief Introduction and Selected Bibliography."

Association of Departments of English Bulletin 80 (1985): pp. 29-33.

Ling, Amy. "Chinamerican Literature: A Partly Annotated Bibliography." *NAIES Newsletter* 7.1 (1982): pp. 34-48.

Ling, Amy. *Selected Bibliography of Asian American Literature. Redefining American Literary History*. NY: MLA Press, forthcoming.

Searing, Susan. *Women, Race and Ethnicity: A Bibliography in Progress*. Compiled by the Office of the University of Wisconsin System Women's Studies Librarian. Madison, WI: June, 1988.

Sumi, Pat, et al. "Asian Women's Panel." *Proceedings of the National Asian American Studies Conference*. Eds. George Kagidawa, Joyce Sakai, & Gus Lee. Davis, CA: University of California, 1973.

Women's Educational Equity Communications Network. *Asian Pacific Women in America*. San Francisco: Far West Laboratory for Educational Research and Development, 1980.

Woo, Merle, and Nellie Wong. "Bibliography of Asian American Women Writers." *Three Asian American Writers Speak Out on Feminism*. San Francisco: Karen Brodine, SF Radical Women, 1980.

Yoshitomi, Joan, et al. *Asians in the Northwest: An Annotated Bibliography*. Seattle: Asian American Studies Program, University of Washington, 1978.

Yung, Judy, et al. "Asian American Women: A Bibliography." *Bridge* 6.4 (1978-79): pp. 49-53.

PERIODICALS

Akemai Sister. Honolulu: Hawaii Women's Liberation.

The Amerasia Journal. Los Angeles: Asian American Studies Center, University of California. (Each Fall issue contains a selected bibliography on women. Special Issue, Spring, 1977, 4 no. 1, "Women and Koreans.")

Asian American Review. Berkeley: Asian American Studies, Department of Ethnic Studies, University of California.

Asianadian. Toronto, Canada: Asianadian Resource Workshop.

Asian Women. Berkeley: Asian American Studies Center, University of California.

Bamboo Ridge: The Hawaii Writers' Quarterly. Honolulu: Bamboo Ridge Press and the Hawaiian Ethnic Resource Center, Talk Story.

Bridge: Asian American Perspectives. NY: Basement Workshop/Asian Cinevision. (Winter 1978/79, 6.4; Spring 1979, 7.1; Summer 1983, 8.3; all special issues on Asian American Women.)

Bulletin of Concerned Asian Scholars. Berthoud, CO: Committee of Concerned Asian Scholars.

Contact/II. NY: Contact II Publications. (Special Issue, Winter/Spring 1986, "Asian American: North and South.")

East/West: The Chinese American Journal. San Francisco: East/West Chinese-American Journal.

East Wind: Politics and Culture of Asians in the U.S. San Francisco: Getting Together Publications. (Spring/Summer 1983, 2.1, "Focus: Asian Women.")

Echoes. Formerly *Echoes from Gold Mountain.* Long Beach: California State University.

The Greenfield Review: A Magazine of Contemporary Poetry. Greenfield Center, NY: The Greenfield Review Press/Ithaca House. (Special Issue, 6.1-2, 1977, "Asian American Writers.")

Insights. NY: Insights.

The Journal of Ethnic Studies. Bellingham, WA: Western Washington State College. (Special Issue on the Asian experience in America, 4.1, 1976.)

Just Us: Young Asian Females and the Juvenile Justice System. Washington D.C.: Pan Asia.

Mana: South Pacific Journal of Language and Literature. Formerly *Mana Annual of Creative Writing.* Fiji: South Pacific Creative Arts Society, Mana Publications.

MELUS: The Journal of the Society for the Study of the Multi-Ethnic Literature of the United States. Irregular place of publication.

OCAW Speaks. Arlington, VA: Organization of Chinese American Women.

Pan Asia News. Washington D.C.: Organization of Pan American Women.

The Paper. Honolulu: Petronium Press. Independent publication. Ed. Pat Matsueda. Includes a bimonthly literary magazine.

Quilt. Berkeley.

The Vietnam Forum: A Review of Vietnamese Culture. New Haven: Yale Southeast Asia Studies.

Yardbird Reader. Berkeley: Yardbird Publishing. (Special Asian American Issue, 3, 1974.)